Glimpses of Evenlode

The story of a Cotswold village

To Margaret and Barry
With best wishes

Michael

Michael Banks

Published by MTHB

ISBN 978-0-9559897-0-4

Recommended retail price: £14.99

Photo: Jenny Hill Exhibition

The Parish Church of
Saint Edward, King and Martyr

Contents

Preface

Perfect Evenlode

In his poem, *The Perfect Evenlode,* Hilaire Belloc describes how the little River Evenlode "lingers in the hills" around Moreton-in-Marsh, then meanders through a "hundred little towns of stone" before it flows into the River Thames. The first of the "hundred little towns of stone" the river passes by is the village that gives it its name, the village of Evenlode. Belloc thought these villages "forgotten in the western wolds" but in this book the story of one of them, Evenlode, may be read.

The meandering little river still forms the western boundary of Evenlode today, as it did in Saxon times when the village was established. Now, as then, the eastern boundary lies towards Chastleton and Adlestrop Hill. Here and there little copses are reminders of ancient wildwood that once crept down to the rich river meadows. Cattle graze the fields where luscious grass still grows greenly in the damp, fertile soil.

The people of Evenlode live in fine sixteenth century houses of Cotswold stone, pretty, mellow stone cottages and traditional brick and slate homes. The village clusters in gentle informality round the village green and along the leaf-strewn lanes. Amidst the trees lie the old Manor Farm and near it, an old stone cottage. Next to them the ancient Church of Saint Edward, King and Martyr, seated in its holy garden, looks over the village and its people like a protective mother.

The disastrous flooding of Moreton-in-Marsh on 20 July 2007 brought my wife and me to Evenlode to live for a short while. Very quickly we both developed affection for the people, the village and its church. So I have written this book in gratitude. It tells the story of this quiet Cotswold village as I have discovered it. I have called it "Glimpses of Evenlode " for glimpses are all there are of events and "lives that have been lived", during the long years of its existence.

Michael Banks
Christmas 2008

Acknowledgements

My thanks are extended to the people of Evenlode who have enquired with interest and regularity about the progress of this book, and have contributed much to it in anecdotes and legends, sources of information and historic documents. I have welcomed their interest and moral support.

In particular I want to thank those who have gone before me on this path.

Guy Stapleton, Chairman of Moreton-in-Marsh and District Local History Society, who prepared material for a history. This is contained in Elizabeth Bell's collection. I am grateful for her permission to use this.

The late Stanley Harris for his memoirs of Evenlode first presented in the published papers of the Moreton-in-Marsh and District Local History Society. Likewise I thank Kerry Johnson, Andrew S Jackson and others who also have written informative papers published by the Society.

I thank Jenny Hill, who prepared the Evenlode Millennium Exhibition and pursued many of the areas I have since explored, for allowing me to use her collection.

I am grateful to Virginia Henderson for permission to use her collection. This includes items about the church not otherwise available.

Special thanks is extended to a number of people who have given me access to collections of documents relating to their properties: John and Margaret Aird, David and Claire Armfield, Paul and Faith Ayshford Sanford, Ian and Susan Medhurst, Colin and Cathy Methven, Tim and Judy Proger, George Wightman and Michael and Betty Woolliams. I owe them my deepest gratitude because this resource support has been essential.

I have numbered the collections and use this identification in the text. Where I have quoted directly from these primary sources or paraphrased them, I have usually acknowledged the source in the text. There are many other places where information from these sources has formed my judgement, but to avoid repetition I have not usually acknowledged this. The book that has emerged could not have been written without these documents.

I want also to thank those who have allowed me to use their photographs: Paul Ayshford Sandford, Susan Medhurst and Colin and Cathy Methven. My thanks also to Jenny Hill for use of photographs displayed in the Millennium Exhibition, and also to the Bob Sharpe Collection for the use of photographs. Villagers are familiar with a set of old photographs of Evenlode, some of which I have re-used. I believe these orginated with a set of photographic plates that were in the possession of Margaret Aird and I thank her for freedom to use them. If another owns them I can only plead ignorance and offer apology for not seeking permission. I have called these the Evenlode Photographs.

Finally I want to thank Andrew and Tracey Blakeman for reading the book critically as I wrote it and for giving generous encouragement. Their comments and questions changed the slant I was taking in a number of places and more than once persuaded me to re-draft whole sections. They have also very kindly proofread the book for me.

I have tried to write a flowing book that is as accurate as I can judge, yet is a good "read". Some knowledge of the general history of the times has helped me to put the story into context. However, on a number of occasions crafting the narrative proved to be a little like making sense of a jigsaw puzzle where more than half the pieces are missing. This has been a challenge.

The meaning of some of the sources I have used is obscure. These documents have required interpretation. Interpretation is often a matter of personal judgement and readers must judge my success in interpreting what I have gleaned from such sources. Of course any mistakes are entirely mine.

Photo: Jenny Hill Exhibition

Eowla the Angle gives the River and the Village his name

Chapter 1

An Angle settles in Roman Britain (AD 500)

Ancient places and ancient tracks

Evenlode's story begins in the dawn of history. Peering through the mists of time, try to catch a glimpse of it several millennia ago. The glacier of the last Ice Age that crept as far south as Moreton-in-Marsh is melting. The lake it created is filling the valley. When it drains away it will leave rich fertile land, soon to be populated with trees and plants and animals. In due time hunter-gatherers come and make their camps and build their shelters.

It is generally assumed that because the valleys were filled with beech trees and dense undergrowth, these hunter-gatherers kept to the tops of the hills. Here the land was easier to clear, and it also gave opportunity to have lookout places for security. Here they built their barrows. Nearby there is a fine example of a long barrow of the Neolithic period at Belas Knap near Winchcombe. This barrow is 178 feet long, 60 feet wide and 18 feet high. It was a well-made structure to house the dead of these people. Barrows were still being built in the Iron Age. Barrows exist locally at Condicote and Chastleton.

The Ordnance Survey map shows no barrows in the parish of Evenlode and so a superficial conclusion could be that in those very early times nobody was here. However, in a late Saxon Survey, a copy of which is in Collection Three of the Evenlode Documents, the boundary of the parish is described in a revealing manner. Even if one has no Anglo-Saxon, it seems to make sense, "...than on Gild (Ild) beorh and lang Sealt Straete...to Lafercan beorh...than hit cymth to than Ealden Slo...to than Lytlan Beorhe..."

"Beorh" or "beorhe" has been translated as "barrow". If this is correct then there used to be three barrows on the boundary of Evenlode though no remains now exist: "gild (ild)" barrow, "lafercan" (lark) barrow and "lytlan" (little) barrow.

Elsewhere the survey also notes an "Old Way." Tracks of this nature are considered by historians to be exceedingly ancient, and this "Old Way" could conceivably belong to the era of the barrows. This is particularly possible as it was evidently a lane from a place the Anglo-Saxons called the "gild (ild) beorh" (at Four Shire Stone) to Chastleton. Parts of this lane still exist as a pleasant bridleway.

So tantalisingly vague as the information is, it does seem possible that in those long distant ages there were those who walked the ways, hunted the deer and buried their dead in Evenlode, but identification of it as a place with a name in recorded history begins much later. In fact it begins millennia later in those times when Anglo-Saxon England grew out of the remains of Roman Britain.

An Anglo-Saxon comes to Evenlode

The Angles, Saxons and Jutes were a rough lot. They came here first in AD 449 as mercenary soldiers to fight the marauding Picts and Scots from the North. Eventually they brought their goods and families with them and built houses and cleared land, or seized farms without recompense from British owners who had fled in fear from them. The story of Evenlode emerges with these settlers from the tribes of the Angles, and with a man called Eowla. He gave his name to the place. Information can be gleaned from his name and he can be placed in a general historical setting. From this there is a glimpse of what life was like at the beginning in Evenlode.

Several interpretations of the meaning of "Evenlode" have been given. It seems wise to accept the scholarly work of the English Place Name Society. The root name of Evenlode consists of two parts. There is a proper name of a man. This is "Eowla" or "Eowa". There is also the Anglo-Saxon word "gelade". This is a word describing a point in a river where someone has constructed a way to cross, "river crossing" is the meaning usually given. By adding "n" to a name, the Anglo-Saxon language creates the possessive tense. So "Eowlan" means "of Eowla". In this way one arrives at "Eowlan gelade," which means "Eowla's river crossing".

Eowla was an Angle. His name is Germanic in origin. These parts were settled by Angles of the Hwicci tribe and its associated tribes. The fact that he settled and gave his name to a place indicates that he was probably not one of the original mercenary soldiers hired by the Romano-British leader Vortigern, to fight the Picts and Scots. His forebears (perhaps he himself) were settlers. They came from the mainland of Europe to settle in what returning mercenaries said was a good place to live.

The Angles came in boats with their wives and families and possessions. It must have been both exciting and fearful to leave the security of their homeland to seek a new home across the stormy sea. Having arrived at the coast, they sailed up the rivers of the east coast of Britain from the River Trent in the north to the River Thames in the south. The Jutes sailed at the same time to Kent. The Saxons sailed both to the north of Britain and also to the south coast.

By AD 500, the Angles had occupied the middle of Britain from the East Coast to the border with Wales in the west and as far as the Humber to the north and the Thames to the south. This land was soon recognisable as the Kingdom of Mercia.

The Hwicci association of tribes (to which Eowla belonged) seem to have sailed up the Thames to where Oxford now is, and then decided to explore the tributary heading northwest rather continuing along the Thames. The prevalence of the name "Wychwood" indicates this. Soon they established villages along this tributary of the Thames. They named the tributary the River Bladon. The river is presumably named after the settlement of Bladon. "Bla" or "Blad" may have been a chief who built his camp there (Bla's "ton").

In those days the river valley was substantially wildwood, but someone explored the river to its source. Perhaps it was Eowla, or maybe he followed others. Whenever it was that he came, Eowla reached a place where he discovered cultivated land with a fine highway, the Fosse Way. Here he settled beside a river crossing to which his name became attached.

Other Angles came and some built new villages for more and more members of their tribe the Hwicci. We know this from the place names that include "Wych". Others took over land abandoned by those of the inhabitants who fled from them. Eventually the Hwicci and their associates occupied what we now call Oxfordshire, Gloucestershire, Warwickshire and Worcestershire.

Eowla must have liked this particular spot on the east bank of the River Bladon where he found (or built) a good river crossing. Presumably here he made his home. From our point of view and much more importantly he gave the place his name, in the Anglo-Saxon tongue Eowlangelade: Eowla's River Crossing.

Eowla's neighbours, the Romano-British

The first glimpse of Evenlode in history is thus its name. Eowla gave his name to a settlement that can be placed in the sixth century. He settled at a time of conflict, as his fellow Angles created Mercia amidst the remnants of a Romano-British Province. The Mercian Angles could not but be aware that they were conquering the land of (and in some cases accepting as neighbours and more often seizing as slaves) a people who were civilised and cultured. They may have known that they were settling in a land that the residents thought of as a Province of the Roman Empire, and that it had a noble history.

When the Roman Empire expanded and absorbed Britain, its soldiers and administrators found a Celtic tribe called the Dobunni occupying these parts. The Dobunni fought hard against the legions in those days, but when the Roman legions left four hundred years later the British Celts had merged into a Romano-British population. Alongside the British Celts, Roman soldiers from all parts of the Empire had been given land in Britain on which to retire. This had been customary for four hundred years. The retired men brought wives and children, slaves and servants from all over Europe and Asia. Locals and newcomers inter-married and created this new population.

The old royal families of the Celts remained, became wealthy and were held in esteem. They lived alongside equally wealthy and long-settled Roman families. These families were often indistinguishable through inter-marriage. The richer people spoke Latin as their first language though most could use the British Celtic tongue of the peasants and tradesmen. Those who worked on the land or plied a trade had enough Latin to get by. They needed it for commerce, for the Law and later at Church, but kept the Celtic for normal use.

Roman soldiers and administrators had ensured the construction of a great network of well-built roads. There was plenty of trading and travelling and making money. These parts were in the northern half of the Province of *Brittania Secunda* and the artery north to south was the Fosse Way. It was built in sections over many years but eventually it linked *Isca Dumnoniorum* (Exeter), *Corinium* (Cirencester), *Ratae Corieltauvorum* (Leicester) and *Lindum Colonia* (Lincoln).

Along these roads there were centres for hospitality and trading. Dorn was one such place in this area. Dorn is a British-Celtic name that has survived through the Anglo-Saxon years. Another hint of survival from those years is Hinchwick. The current farm at Hinchwick is nineteenth century with additions in 1937, but there are older barns nearby, and the Ordnance Survey map shows an ancient mound. If this name has lingered from Roman British times the "wick" indicates a "vicus". "Vicus" was originally the Latin word for a farmhouse and land. Later it was used to describe a small settlement. Hinchwick is well placed for a Villa being (like Chedworth) in a secluded valley with easy access to the Roman road network. Wyck Hill near Stow-on-the-Wold may also point to a similar origin.

The woods on either side of Roman roads were originally cleared for security purposes, but after four hundred years the clearance of wood stretched miles from the road, usually by clearing wood along new minor roads normally built at right angles to the main road. The land to the east of the Fosse Way, in the vicinity of what was to be Eowlangelade, was cleared too in these Romano-British times, probably to the little river to the east that we now know as the Evenlode, though Eowla knew it as the Bladon.

In this land between the Fosse Way and the river, Eowla would have spied neat British farms with their tiny fields. He would have been delighted to see this rich land after walking through mile after mile of forest and fen, following the course of the river. (Although he would recognise his need for the wildwood. The wildwood was the source of firewood and provided timber for buildings. It was home to wild deer and other game and a place to gather forest fruits.)

To what extent Eowla was aware of the effect of his people's invasion on this civilised Romano-British nation can only be a matter for speculation. Mercia was emerging, but to the southwest stiff resistance was being encountered. Romano-British leaders like Ambrosius Aurelius and the legendary half-Welsh Uther Pendragon (King Arthur) led this resistance. Gloucester, Cirencester and Bath fell to Mercia in AD 577 and the Romano-British drew further back into Somerset and the West or fled to Wales.

The Romano-British had gradually left the old gods. By the fourth century they were turning to Christianity and the early Christians of the Romano-British Church suffered martyrdom under the Emperor Diocletian, as Christians did in the rest of the Empire. The story of the martyrdom of Saint Alban at Verulamium in AD 305 is well known. Other Christians were martyred elsewhere in Roman Britain. The names of Aaron and Julian are revered at Chester.

Bede, writing much later, in the Anglo-Saxon kingdom of Northumbria, knew of the martyrdom of Romano-British Christians in these periodic persecutions initiated in Rome. He recorded that when the time of persecution had ceased, the faithful Christians, who during the time of danger had hidden themselves, re-appeared in public and rebuilt their churches.

Helen (a daughter of the Romano-British King Coel of Colchester) married a Roman Officer Constantius whilst he was stationed in the area. Her first son was Constantine. He became a Roman Officer and rose to command the legions in Britain. Constantine led all the British legions to Rome and became Emperor after a great battle. He made his troops paint their shields with the Christian "Xp" (chi rho) symbol. According to the story, before the battle he saw a huge cross in the sky and a voice came to him saying, "In this Cross you will conquer". Although clearly attracted to Christianity it was only after this battle that Helen became a Christian. Her son Constantine probably became a Christian at that time too.

Constantine built Constantinople as the new Rome for the eastern half of his Empire. His mother accompanied him as Empress. Helen travelled extensively and found, in Jerusalem, Jesus's Cross. After her death she was revered as a Saint. The Romano-British Christians built many churches in her honour such as Saint Helen's Church, Worcester, probably the oldest church in the area.

To what extent Christianity spread from the towns into the countryside is not known. So we do not know whether or not Eowla met up with Christians as he settled on the banks of the river and founded the river crossing that still bears his name.

It used to be said that all the Romano-British fled to Wales, Cornwall or Brittany when the Anglo-Saxons came, but it is now believed that there was considerable assimilation into Anglo-Saxon society. There is also evidence that the Anglo-Saxons learned much from the Romano-British in turn. Eowla would have shared in this process.

Hereabouts Christianity survived in Worcester and elsewhere and it seems (from hints in Bede's *Ecclesiastical History*) that Romano-British priests and bishops may have continued to minister to the remnants of their fellow citizens whilst the Anglo-Saxon kingdom of Mercia emerged. The fact that Dorn (and perhaps other places) kept their names, indicate a continuing Romano-British presence in the immediate area. There is no evidence though to link Dorn with a Christian presence.

Interestingly, the Hwicci tribe of Angles who settled here already had Christians amongst them, though most were pagan. This is no help of course in understanding Eowla. There is no way we could conclude he was a Christian unless some very early Christian artefact were to be discovered in Evenlode. It is believed that Evenlode would be likely to give up rich archaeological findings in the event of a "dig".

Inevitably, however, the arrival of the Anglo-Saxons brought considerable changes, even if they were not as dramatic as was once supposed. Such changes as there were were not rapid. It took one hundred and fifty years before government by Anglo-Saxon kings was recognised as irreversible, and even then parts of Roman Britain held out. Cornwall remained a distinct British kingdom. The legends of King Arthur witness to this, though the tales are fictional and originate in much later times.

The conversion of Eowla's people

The British bishops seemed to have been more concerned about the state of the Church than bothered about newcomers like Eowla settling in the countryside. They felt that the Romano-British Christians needed some discipline in their ideas and devotions. They sent to Gaul to seek the help of Saint Germanus. Christianity in Gaul had been revived by the work of Saint Martin of Tours who died in AD 397. It is believed that it was in his monastery that the Romano-British missionary Patricius, known as Saint Patrick, Apostle of Ireland, learned his version of Christianity. Likewise the Romano-British Saint Ninian, who is known as the Apostle of Galloway.

Martin of Tours adapted for Gaul, much that he had learned about asceticism from the writings of the Desert Fathers (who lived in Greek-speaking Roman Egypt), and from the many scholars of Alexandria, (then a great centre of Christian learning). Martin's monks followed his strict teaching. It was this revived Christianity that Saint Germanus brought to the Romano-British Church.

Today this brand of Christianity is known as "Celtic Christianity" and it is associated with Ireland and Scotland, yet it originated in Gaul, prospered in Roman Britain, and spread to Wales, Scotland and Ireland. The Romano-British Saint Patrick took it to Ireland in AD 430.

Celtic Christians from Iona converted the Anglo-Saxon kingdom of Northumbria in the sixth century. The story is told that Columba in Ireland copied a book that he proposed to keep. He was taken before the elders and the verdict given was that as to every cow belongs its calf, so to every book belongs its bookling. Columba handed the book back and left Ireland in a coracle. He landed on Iona and was joined by companions and formed a monastery. From Iona, there began a great missionary sweep by the monks into north Scotland and down into Northumbria and then into Mercia.

The mission of Saint Augustine from Rome converted the Anglo-Saxon kingdom of Kent and the south of Britain to the Roman form of Christianity. Pope Gregory sent Saint Augustine in AD 597 with a number of companions. At one point in his ministry he met with Romano-British Bishops on the southern boundary of the Hwicci, but because he was converting Jutes and Saxons they would have nothing to do with him. Their hatred was intense for those who were their conquerors. Augustine chided them for their failure to convert the invaders.

The story about how Augustine brought Christianity to the Anglo-Saxons is well known. It is said that Pope Gregory was walking through the slave market in Rome when he saw a group of blonde haired children offered for sale.

"Who are they?" he asked.

"Angles" was the reply.

"Not Angles but angels," he quipped.

This prompted the Pope to send Augustine to convert the English.

The two traditions (Roman and Celtic) clashed but harmony was achieved at the Synod of Whitby in AD 663. Shortly after this in AD 669 the Pope appointed as Archbishop of Canterbury a man who was neither Roman nor Celt but a Greek. His name was Theodore. Theodore found that it had become the custom for an Anglo-Saxon kingdom to have one Bishop. As they were regularly at war with each other the kingdoms expanded and contracted and so therefore did the bishopric. Theodore changed this and re-introduced the old Romano-British idea of geographical dioceses. Moreover he divided up the kingdoms into several dioceses.

In Mercia in AD 680, Theodore established a bishop in Leicester for the East Angles in the land to the sea. A bishop remained in Lichfield for the northern part of the Kingdom. He appointed a bishop at Worcester for the southern part.

The diocese of Worcester covered the area settled by the Hwicci, which we now call Worcestershire, Warwickshire, Oxfordshire and Gloucestershire. There was also a sub-kingdom, based on Winchcombe. The first Mercian Bishop of Worcester was Bosel. He established a monastery-Cathedral dedicated to Saint Peter in Worcester. Bishop Egwin, the third bishop, founded the monastery at Evesham. Eanulf founded a monastery at Bredon. Land was given to support the monks.

Bede tells a delightful tale about Saint Chad who was Bishop of Lichfield at this time. Theodore was horrified to discover that the elderly Chad still walked everywhere on missionary journeys. Bede relates:

> Seeing that it was the custom of Chad to go about the work of the Gospel to several places rather on foot than on horseback, Theodore commanded him to ride whenever he had a long journey to undertake. And finding Chad very unwilling to omit his former pious labour, he himself, with his own hands, lifted him on the horse. (1)

From the monasteries (called "minsters") monks had become accustomed to travel on long missionary journeys in the way Bede describes the journeying of Saint Chad. They would visit settlements and farms near and far away. All their journeys were on foot. It was from travelling monks that Eowla's successors living at Eowlangelade would have heard about Christianity.

A wandering monk would arrive, preach a sermon and if he had the voice would teach some religious songs. The monk would say Mass and baptise the babies. He would bless any new graves and bless any new marriages. He would minister from a Cross shaped from wood or stone permanently fixed in the ground. If there were no Cross he would place one in the ground. It was a reminder to the villagers of what he had said and what he had done. Afterwards he would share a meal and accept the corner of a barn for a night's rest, then move on to the next place.

However, Archbishop Theodore at the Council of Hertford in AD 673 ordered monks to stay in their monasteries, so this practice gradually ceased.

By the eighth century villagers would have built a simple church and in Evenlode's case, the Bishop of Worcester would have appointed a resident priest as the Rector.

Note
(1) Bede *Ecclesiastical History of the English Church and Nation* Book 4, Chapter 3.

Photo: Susan Medhurst

Manor Farm

The probable site of Ridda's Saxon Hall and subsequent Manors

Chapter 2

Ridda, Thegn of Evenlode (AD 775)

In the kingdoms of seventh century Anglo-Saxon Britain, the king held all the land. Mercia was no exception. Evenlode was within this feudal system.

Land was devolved from the king in what we might today think of as a system of leasing and renting. In this way, land was passed to sub-kings (such as the sub-king at Winchcombe for the Hwicci association of tribes) and to a very few powerful thegns. These owed loyalty, men and services, produce and money to the king in return for their land. They then devolved the land to those they wished to hold it. These in turn paid them in kind or service. Such were expected to respond to a call to engage in a military campaign and bring men with them to fight too.

The word "thegn" began to be used more freely to include the king's ministers and eventually anyone who held land would be termed a thegn. Later as land became identified by boundaries into manors the thegn who held a manor was called the "Lord of the Manor". Manors and their lords eventually became the backbone of the administrative system of the country.

The thegn had servants (sometimes slaves) and used local people to give service. The amount of service owed varied according to their status. This pattern was emerging in the eighth century and reached its final form in the tenth century.

Increasingly the king devolved land to the Church. This was usually to bishops and to monasteries. Often a bishop was closely linked with a monastery so the grant was to a bishop and his monastery.

Monasteries were usually of male monks only but some dual gender monasteries existed (the men and women being separated for all things but worship). Many monks would not be priests but having received the tonsure, were termed "clerics".

In the seventh and early eighth centuries monasteries that were sending priests to serve the villages round about as missionaries acquired the title of "Minster." Some minsters did not have monks but priests who were called "Canons" because they lived under a rule. ("Canon" is the Latin word for a rule.)

The land given to the church was usually called "bookland" because it was land allocated by a "charter". Most of the lands given to the church are recorded in the Anglo-Saxon charters. These charters were legal documents written in Latin by educated secular clerics (thus clerks) who worked for the king. It is unlikely that an eighth century king would know enough Latin to compose these charters in the correct manner, so he relied on the clerks to fill out the details.

The charters are sometimes very detailed in describing boundaries and also listing what produce had to be given in return. Such a charter might order the holder to send yearly to the king, beer, cheeses, grain, milled grain, cattle and sheep. They might number how many armed men had to be supplied should the king decide on an "expedition". The charters often detailed duties to be undertaken such as the maintenance and repair of bridges.

Ridda and his family at Euulangelade

The first recorded mention we have of Evenlode is in a charter of King Offa of Mercia dated AD 775, giving the land to a man called Ridda. However according to Thomas of Marlborough, King Offa of Mercia donated land at Evenlode to the Abbey of Saint Mary, Mother of God, at Evesham, in AD 772 (three years earlier). How is this resolved?

Historians have considerable scepticism about Anglo-Saxon charters. They believe that many are not authentic. The reason for this is that a simple method to provide "proof" of ownership (if there was no document available) was to get your clerk to invent, write and backdate a charter. Such charters are termed spurious, but a spurious charter does not imply that the claim to hold the land is necessarily untrue. Modern scholars place the charter of AD 772 (claiming Evenlode for Evesham Abbey) in the spurious category.

Unusually, scholars judge the charter of AD 775 leasing land to Ridda to be probably authentic. So the first authentic recorded mention we have of Evenlode is in this charter of AD 775. This records the donation by King Offa of eight hides of land at "Euulangelade" to a faithful minister called Ridda.

In this charter there is the first indication of Evenlode as a place with a thegn and with recognised boundaries. In effect we can discern the origin of a manor at Evenlode and a lord of the manor.

The names in this charter are the names of real people living at the place named after the long dead Eowla. The clerks at this time spelt "Eowlangelade" as "Euulangelade" and the charter reveals that there are eight hides of land in use. These eight hides of land were donated to these named individuals for their three lives, Ridda, his wife Bucga and his daughter Heaburg.

Ridda whose name means, "Counsel" is called a "minister" in the Latin of the charter. This was not an ecclesiastical title. It indicates that Ridda was an administrator for the king. His personal name reinforces this. (In those days men took a name that they believed revealed their qualities.) It may be that the land in this charter is reward for his work.

The charter gives four points to outline a boundary for the land that Ridda has been given. First there is the river to the west of the land. The boundary extends north up the river to a tributary and then to a place that is named "Cenepe's marsh". (This lies just to the west of Heath End Farm where the footpath crosses this same little tributary over a bridge.) The boundary continues north and slightly west along this tributary to a place called "Alfhere's pool" near "Cetta's tree". (This is near the Four Shire Stone.) It then turns south and slightly east to follow an ancient track to just east of Horn Farm. (This green lane only remains in existence for a couple of miles.) The boundary then swings up the ridge above Horn Farm to a place identified as "Harts' spring" and "Mules' mound or hill" and then southwest back to the river.

Eight hides of land is a huge acreage. Originally a hide was the measure of land needed by a family to live on. The acreage varied from place to place depending on the nature and goodness of the land. In one place it could be as little as sixty acres. In another it could be over one hundred acres. The arable land in Evenlode is said (in the charter) to lie on the east side of the river. This indicates that the remains of ridge and furrow farming observable in the island formed by the present road system of the village are the oldest in the parish. The hides would also include the open meadows on the banks of the river.

The farmed land would not extend far beyond the village for as Della Hooke remarks in her book *The Anglo-Saxon Landscape* (in a quotation in Collection Three of the Evenlode Papers) there was to the east of the village then sufficient woodland to provide shelter for wild deer, giving rise to a "Harts' spring". This indicates that pushing into the wildwood to create arable land was still in the future in the time of Ridda.

Some parts of the eight hides may have been neither arable nor meadow. Farms need woodland. Woodland provides fuel for fires, split logs for buildings and a rich source of berries and wild fruits. It gives a place for pigs to root and space for deers to forage. Hunting game was a major source of food.

Ridda would have employed a number of people on his land. These, and their ancestors, may have long been resident. Indeed parts of his eight hides may already have been sub-let to peasants. Some names are recorded in place names in the charter. "Alfhere" was linked with a pool and "Cenepe" (which means "moustache" and as others have observed it sounds like a nickname) was linked with a marsh. "Cetta" had something to do with a tree. The man called "Mules" was associated with an "hlawe". The translators of Mercian Anglo-Saxon say this means "mound or tumulus". In Northumbrian Anglo-Saxon it may mean a "steep hill-side". It is possible that the latter translation is correct and this could indicate that Mules was a shepherd.

It seems to be generally accepted that sheep were reared here in these times, but it is hard to find any evidence to prove it. (It is said in local histories that in the eighth century, Saint Peter's Abbey Gloucester had a large flock of sheep at Evenlode. There are no charters to support the claims of Gloucester. Nevertheless it should be noted that later, Saint Peter's Abbey at Gloucester built the first church on the site of the present Saint Nicholas Church at Oddington. This does indicate a link between Gloucester Abbey and the local area.)

Men such as Alfhere, Cetta, Cenepe and Mules, having given their names to places, may even have lived at the time of Eowla. Their families, by Ridda's time, would have been long resident.

Ridda would have found men at Evenlode who had their own duties in the community and worked a little land. Each would have had a hut for their families to live in and a common place to keep a cow and a pig. Under the feudal system, they would discover that they owed Ridda service and loyalty, but in those times such men gladly accepted this in return for security, and access to justice from a thegn who had the right to approach the king.

Such an important man as Ridda would have a hall. It is not too fanciful to imagine this on higher land overlooking the open meadow down to the river, on the site known as Manor Farm. Local history constantly points to continuity of usage when dealing with churches and manors.

Ridda may of course have found his hall already built, or he may have had one built. The typical manorial hall in the eighth century would have been a timber frame and a certain amount of timber walling (using split logs felled in the woodland) filled in with wattle and daub. The floor would have been beaten earth strewn with reeds from the river. There would have been a central hearthstone and benches around. The roof would have been of thatch with a hole for smoke to escape. A platform may have created an upper floor, giving sleeping quarters for Ridda and his wife and daughter. Later the kitchen would be relegated to an extension like a small hall and the thegn's family bedrooms to another extension.

Around would be huts and barns for the storage of food, not only for Ridda and his family and his household, but also to pay his dues to the king. The servants would curl up where they could at night, though those married would have a hut.

Ridda managed the farm with his men. Bucga (and perhaps her daughter Heaburg) would manage the hall with slaves and servants. The work was considerable and included cooking, weaving, sewing, preserving and mending.

A golden era for the Church

The eighth century was a golden era for the Anglo-Saxon Church. The minsters flourished with monks and canons. Also convents were established for nuns. Women often chose the life of a nun as a better alternative to marriage as they observed it.

Bede became known as "The Father of Church History". Benedict Biscop had enormous influence on the design of churches. He introduced art into church buildings by importing icons from Byzantium. Aldhem of Malmesbury presided over a school where Latin, Hebrew and Greek were taught. Alcuin from York travelled to

Paris where he was acclaimed as the founder of University education. Willibrord from York went as a missionary to Germany and became first Archbishop of Mainz. Boniface from Crediton travelled to Frisia and became Archbishop of Utrecht.

In this golden era, kings regularly gave land to support the minsters as has been noted and these donations are recorded in the charters. Such charters record the spiritual point of such giving. They regularly begin with a phrase such as: "I give this land for the eternal salvation of my soul." The idea being that this "good work" indicates to God the faith of the donor and so helps to ensure he is welcomed by Saint Peter at the gates of heaven on his death. The charter granting land to Ridda is a good example of this.

Reversion of the land at Evenlode

King Offa's charter of AD 775 granting land to Ridda was for "three lives". This meant that the tenancy stayed with Ridda and Bucga and Heaburg until the death of the final one of these three. The charter also stated that after this the land was to revert to the church at Bredon. This indicates that the King was giving overlordship of the land to the Church, but appointing the lord of the manor. The Bishop of Worcester had overlordship over Bredon monastery, so in effect Evenlode's overlord was the Bishop of Worcester.

However, King Offa and Evenlode are linked with another charter in AD 777 that says: "I have, of my own free will, donated for the redemption of my soul and the souls of my predecessors departed, to the Church of Saint Mary at Evesham and the monks serving God there, land from the other side of the river called Bladon, at...Evenlode..."

Nineteenth century historians of Evenlode seem to have believed this charter, but like the Evesham charter of AD 772 this is now considered spurious too. The charter is almost certainly a later forgery made by Evesham Abbey.

There is a further charter. This also links Evesham Abbey with Evenlode. This is dated AD 784. It is considered to be spurious too. It grants three hides of land at Evenlode to a man-at-arms called Esme and his male heirs with reversion to Evesham Abbey if the line failed.

The Evesham monks certainly wanted it to be known that their belief was that Evenlode was Evesham's and not Worcester's. This controversy fed continuous disagreement for centuries between the Abbey of Evesham and the Bishop of Worcester.

Why should Evesham Abbey want Evenlode Manor?

Saint Egwin had founded Evesham Abbey in about AD 701. The popular story is that Evesham gets its name from a herdsman called Eoves. Eoves had stumbled across an old chapel (from Romano-British times). There he had a vision of our Lady. Word of this spread rapidly and Egwin came quickly to the place too. He also had a vision of our Lady and realised that this old chapel was a holy place. As a result he founded a monastery there. This rapidly grew into the Abbey of Saint Mary, Mother of God, at Eovesham. With this heavenly patronage, and in this golden era of Christian piety, monks soon came to Evesham, and in a short time a full complement of about forty learned monks lived there doing God's work. It needed produce from many manors. The overlordship of Evenlode was sought to obtain dues paid in food for the monks' larder.

Why should Worcester want Evenlode?

Worcester with its Bishop and Abbey was a thriving Christian centre. Two more churches had been built in AD 721. These were Saint Alban's and Saint Margaret's. The Church of Worcester was playing a major role in developing the town. It held land and so employed people. It owned six salt furnaces in Droitwich and so was involved commercially in the selling and distribution of salt. This was a vital commodity in those times, for preserving food over the winter. The income from manors enabled this to develop. The Bishop and monastery at Worcester needed as much income as they could get. So they wanted the overlordship of Evenlode to obtain more income.

Ridda, the thegn, and his family would continue to hold the tenancy of Evenlode during their lifetimes but it must have been difficult coping with the conflict between Evesham and Worcester of which they must have been aware and so must the people of Evenlode.

It must have been harder for the next thegn because after the death of the last of the three the tenancy would have passed to someone else who may not have been so aware of the arguments being used.

Was there a Saxon Church at Euulangelade?

The building of churches and the appointing of parish priests in a village happened in a haphazard way. Usually, whoever held the place took upon himself the task of finding a priest and building a church. One would expect Ridda to have taken on this task at Evenlode if no church had been built at Evenlode by then. The Bishop and Prior of Worcester would have sent a priest. The appointment would have been of a secular priest, but there is no record to indicate whether Evenlode had a priest or not in the eighth century. It is likely, as it was the custom elsewhere.

In AD 793 the Danes invaded the country for the first time. By AD 828 Mercia was succumbing to the Danes though King Egbert of Wessex ruled as King of England. In AD 866 the Danish Kings launched a ferocious invasion and by AD 870 ruled the north, the midlands and the southeast.

When Alfred became King of England in AD 871 it was the worst of times. He held only the country south of Sherborne. The Danes ruled the rest of the country as a colony. Thus Evenlode had fallen into Danish hands. We do not know anything about what happened. If the Danes behaved as they had elsewhere the story (if it were ever discovered) could be grim.

Photo: Susan Medhurst

Two Stones Cottage

Two Stones Cottage is the surmised site of
The Priest's House that preceded the Rectory

Chapter 3

The Hundred of Oswaldslaw (AD 964)

Establishing the Manor of Evenlode: conflict and order

Alfred the Great of the West Saxons became King of England in AD 871. He gradually recovered and incorporated into the kingdom the former Danish occupied territories of Kent, Essex and West Mercia and also Dumnonia (the British kingdom of Devon and Cornwall). So by AD 878 Evenlode was back under English rule. It had been in the hands of the Danes for at least a decade and possibly longer. There is no evidence of Danish settlement nearby so life may have continued as before, but the Danes did have a habit of burning places they came across. Perhaps little Evenlode lay low and survived.

King Alfred the Great made peace with the Danish leader Guthrun. They agreed a border along Watling Street. The Danes occupied the land to the north and east of this. This did not end invasions and armed conflicts. After King Alfred died in AD 899 his son, Edward the Elder, spent his reign subduing the Danes south of the Humber. Athelstan succeeded his father, Edward the Elder, in AD 924 and by the time of his death in AD 939 exercised control over all the English and was accepted as overlord by the Scottish kings and the Welsh princes. However the Danish kingdom of York was not brought to an end until AD 954 when Athelstan's brother drove out Eric Bloodaxe.

After the death of King Athelstan there was much family feuding and fighting but eventually Edgar wrested control of all England (as we know it today) and ruled from AD 959. Danish invasions continued intermittently throughout his reign but the emphasis began to shift from seizing land to gathering treasure in order to fund life in Denmark and Scandinavia.

Ecclesiastical conflict continued too over the Manor of Evenlode. From the time when Ridda was thegn of Evenlode there was dispute between Evesham Abbey and the Bishop and Prior of Worcester over who was the overlord. The conflict involved Evenlode and also a number of other manors, but the real reason for the conflict lay in the areas of authority and power. Worcester sought to have control over Evesham Abbey and Evesham Abbey fought furiously for independence. Disagreement over the overlordship of the manor of Evenlode gave opportunity to argue over these deeper issues.

The continuing story of Evesham Abbey and the Manor of Evenlode can be picked up in AD 941. In that year the Danes ravaged the Abbey and the majority of the monks was dispersed. King Edmund (a grandson of King Alfred) drove the Danes out. He gave the almost deserted Evesham Abbey to Aldhem in return for his support in driving the Danes out. Aldhem received the overlordship, therefore, of all the manors belonging to the Abbey. He evicted the few remaining monks and installed some Canons to keep the Church open but no more than that. He kept the profits from the Manors for himself. Aldhem died in AD 946 and the Abbey and its manors were then stolen! Wulfric and Oswulf (who was Bishop of Ramsey) simply seized them.

In AD 960 Dunstan restored Evesham Abbey to the monks. He searched out a few of the remaining monks and attracted new ones to enter the Abbey. He re-introduced the Rule of Saint Benedict and the Abbey began to re-discover something of its past, but it was too weak to argue for its supposed right to the Manor of Evenlode.

Order in the Hundred of Oswaldslaw

This tale of arguments between Evesham Abbey and the Bishop and Prior of Worcester over the Manor of Evenlode (and the others) is typical of the times across the country. Despite these disputes over land and power and despite the constant threat and intermittent reality of invasions by the Danes (and despite conflict among members of the royal family) a governed and administered land began to emerge under the rule of King Edgar. The next glimpse we have of Evenlode is in his reign.

In AD 964, King Edgar established by charter a system of local government that proved to be so efficient that William the Conqueror adopted it after the Norman Conquest. It is the basis of local government even in our own time.

Edgar advocated, confirmed and instituted where necessary a structure of administration in England involving "shires" and "hundreds" and "vills". The shires evolved into the counties, with their specific role in local government. The hundreds were units of administration for groups of manors with (between them) one hundred hides of land. The vills were the towns and fortified boroughs that had their own administrative system. All were under one king in one nation called England.

According to this same charter of AD 964, the Bishop of Worcester and the Prior of Worcester Abbey held, in the Shire of Worcester, manors that amounted to 300 hides of land. Among these was the Manor of Evenlode.

The original three hundreds for these groups of manors were Cuthbergelaw (the manors around Worcester), Wulhereslaw (the manors around Deerhurst) and Winburgetrowe (the manors around Blockley). The Manors of Evenlode, Daylesford and Icomb together with the Manors of Dorn, Shipston on Stour and Blackwell were linked with the Manors of Blockley and Tredington in the Hundred of Winburgetrowe.

It was normal for a hundred to consist of an area with 100 hides of land and these groups of manors fulfilled this. Unusually King Edgar decided that these three distinct hundreds of the Bishop and Prior of Worcester could more conveniently be managed as a single "hundred". There are other hundreds with 300 hides. It is believed that this meant the King could demand a warship for his navy from a grouping this size. This was certainly the case later when the demand was known as "shipsoke". A ship was very important to engage the Danes at sea.

The new hundred of 300 hides was called Oswaldslaw, as Oswald was the then Bishop of Worcester. He was Bishop from AD 961 to AD 992. However within the 300 hides of the Bishop of Worcester and the Prior of Worcester in the Hundred of Oswaldslaw were two groups of 50 hides. The Prior of Worcester Abbey took the profits of these for the support of the Worcester monks. One group of 50 hides was at Copthorne. The other group of 50 hides was the Manors of Evenlode, Daylesford and Icomb together with the Manors of Dorn, Shipston on Stour and Blackwell. The remaining 200 hides with their manors belonged to the Bishop of Worcester for his ministry and work.

The Manor of Evenlode was thus one of the larders for the sustenance of the monks of Worcester Abbey.

Taxes and Justice

The hundred was the unit for (among other things) administering the law and collecting taxes. The beadle was the legal officer and summoned the people to the Hundred Courts. The people had to attend to bring their "pledges". In fact three beadles were appointed (100 hides each) in Oswaldslaw Hundred. The bailiff collected the taxes but there was only one bailiff to collect taxes in Oswaldslaw Hundred. Among the taxes collected were fines for ecclesiastical offences and a number of taxes with (to our ears) quaint names, such as the "over-seunesse" tax and the "gylt-wit" tax. King Edgar began the practice of paying the Danish fleets not to invade. The money for this came from the tax known as "Danegeld". In Oswaldslaw Hundred the Bishop of Worcester had to transfer this money to King Edgar, call up men for military service when the king or his representative demanded an army, and (apparently) supply a warship.

Each manor in a hundred had a thegn. By now, he was known as the lord of the manor. He held the tenancy of his manor from the overlord and paid rent in money or kind or both. In Evenlode's case, as recorded above, the overlord was the Bishop of Worcester and the Prior of Worcester (though, as explained above) goods from the Evenlode Manor would go to the Prior for the monks. The bishop (as overlord) had the authority to appoint thegns to the tenancy (lordship) of the manor.

There is no record of who the thegns of Evenlode had been since Ridda. In AD 969 Bishop Oswald of Worcester in a charter gave the Lordship of the Manor of Evenlode to someone named Ealhstan. This is recorded in a printout in Collection Three of Evenlode Documents. The Bishop described Ealhstan as one who was faithful to him. The charter also says that the tenancy of the manor reverts to the bishop on the death of Ealhstan.

"Faithful" Ealhstan had been heavily involved in Bishop Oswald's work and particularly in his main pre-occupation of building the first Worcester Cathedral. (Until this time, the Abbey had also served as the Cathedral.) Ealhstan was rewarded with enjoyment of life as Lord of the Manor of Evenlode for his remaining days. The feudal system is clearly illustrated in this appointment, for Bishop Oswald notes that it has been made by permission of King Edgar. King Edgar is the ultimate owner of all the land.

After the death of Ealhstan the bishop donated the tenancy of the Manor of Evenlode to Athelstan, of whom no more than his name is known.

Evenlode was linked firmly with Worcestershire both ecclesiastically and politically. Through Worcester it paid its fines and taxes to the king. It paid dues to the Bishop of Worcester as overlord. It was linked to Blockley for Hundred Court purposes (though over the centuries, the courts have been held in different places). It remained in Worcestershire until 1931.

Boundaries of Evenlode

The beginning of organisation in the country by King Edgar's charter of AD 964 covered a number of matters, which required accuracy of boundaries. It is a matter of considerable surprise that the boundaries of Evenlode in the tenth century are substantially the same as they are today.

The charter of AD 775 had given Ridda four landmarks in order to identify his land and these were described above. In the tenth century these landmarks were further defined.

The two Saxon surveys (AD 775 and AD 964) are recorded in Collection Three of the Evenlode Papers. The later one gives greater detail but one or two landmarks in the earlier are not repeated. It is relatively easy to put these both together and give a fascinating description of the boundary as it was then. This can be compared with what the land is like today.

The description of the boundary starts at the point in the River Evenlode where the boundary of Donnington Parish touches it. This is due west of Manor Farm. It extends north past the mill along the river. (This mill had ceased to exist at the time of Domesday though it was rebuilt in the seventeenth century. It no longer exists, though the field name "Mill Pound" or "Mill Holme" and a number of features in the land continue the memory.)

The boundary continues along the river to the tributary that bears to the northeast and follows that to a field now called Bog Meadow but in Saxon days called "Cenepe's swampy ground". It was noted earlier that "cenepe" (moustache) could be someone's nickname.

(In this field the present footpath from Evenlode to Moreton-in-Marsh crosses the tributary on a bridge. Later maps seem to imply that this footpath to Moreton-in-Marsh is the original road from Evenlode to Moreton-in-Marsh, predating the current road.)

The boundary continues along the tributary passing over the current road to Moreton beyond Bluebell Wood to the point where the footpath from Moreton to Wells Folly crosses it. The Saxon Charters now mention two pools, one on either side of the stream. These are noted as "bird pools" so presumably they were recognised as places for fowling. They no longer exist.

The little brook continues to the A44 opposite the Four Shire Stone. This point is carefully described as being at "Gild or Ild barrow" beside "Alfhere's pool" and "Cetta's Tree".

Here there were four separate stones. One was for Evenlode (Worcestershire). Another was for Great Wolford (Warwickshire). Another was for Long Compton (Gloucestershire). Another was for Chastleton (Oxfordshire). They were placed along the road only a few yards from each other. The Anglo-Saxon is quite precise and its meaning can be made out: "andlang Sealt Straete to than Stane, to than otheran Stane, than awa to than thirddan Stane, to than feorthan Stane".

(The present Four Shire Stone is relatively new. It marks where, in the eighteenth century, the point of contact between Worcestershire, Gloucestershire, Oxfordshire and Warwickshire was.)

The A44 is described as the "Salt Street". Mickleton (as well as Worcester) had rights to mine salt in Cheshire and a regular route for distribution from Mickleton followed this part of the A44.

The Saxon boundary continued along Salt Street past these four stones and then moved south and west. It is possible that the boundary (which is the current county boundary too) follows an old way to Chastleton even though it no longer exists at this point. Following the boundary southwest the charters refer to "Lark Barrow" (which can no longer be identified), then the boundary reaches the beginning of the present bridleway. This bridleway is the pleasant green lane to Chastleton much used by walkers.

The lane continues to Chastleton, but further along, the Saxon Evenlode boundary turns south, to east of Horn Farm. In the survey the place is called the "old slough", which may be where the lane still floods badly.

The boundary line continues south to a jink in the fields where the "Little Barrow" was and then onto Horn Lane just east of Horn Farm. The boundary then passes up the hillside (heading south) to the spring level where there was a spring known as "Harts Spring" and a Stone known as "Hwetta's Stone". The boundary then follows the "headland" (which is the contour line) to an obvious turning point. This is called "Mules mound or tumulus", or as suggested above, "Mules hillside".

The charters then simply say that the boundary follows "the furrow" (the edge of Adlestrop's ploughland) to the River Evenlode and then along the river to where it began.

Church and Priest at Evenlode

Very few tenth century village churches have survived, for they were made from split logs. Either the Danes burnt them or the weather destroyed them. In the vast majority of cases a stone church replaced them, almost always on the same site. It is sensible to assume that this is what happened at Evenlode.

Given that Ealhstan (Lord of the Manor in AD 969) was "faithful" to the Bishop of Worcester, it seems very reasonable to assume he would have built a church, if there was not one already. Nevertheless it would have been a wooden church. If the task was not taken up or completed by Ealhstan, then Athelstan (also the Bishop's servant) would have done this.

There would have been a priest. A good deal is known about the priests of those days. The priest was often known as the altar thegn. To refer to a priest as an altar thegn put him on a par with the local thegn in dealing with village affairs.

Most parish priests in the tenth century were secular priests. They were usually married. Celibacy was not enforced rigorously (though urged) until the twelfth century. They and their family would see that the glebe was farmed for their subsistence. The parish clergy did not receive parochial fees at this stage. The payment of fees to the parish clergy for duties carried out dates from the Council of Westminster in AD 1200.

The priest ensured that all the people attended Evensong on Saturday (Evensong at dusk on Saturday was considered the First Evensong of Sunday), and Mass on Sunday morning. Some would attend Nocturnes (Matins) at dawn on Sunday, returning for Mass sometime later.

He had to preach sermons and provide literature for the people to read, which indicates a literate population. Each day he recited in the church the seven daily services: Uhtsong, Primesong, Undernsong, Middaysong, Noonsong, Evensong, Nightsong. Often villagers would attend and join in the psalms, particularly at Evensong, for the Evensong bell marked dusk and the end of work in the fields. Ordinary people learned a number of psalms (in Latin). Some psalms were linked with particular occasions, like the psalm "De profundis" (Out of the deep), recited after someone had died.

In addition the parish priest had to teach the children to understand and recite by heart the Lord's Prayer and the Creed. John Moorman records in his book *A History of the Church in England* that Bishop Theodulf (AD 994) instructed that priests ought always to have a school of learners in their houses, and "if any good man will commit his little ones to be taught they ought gladly to accept them, and to teach them at free-cost".

The Church building consisted of two Saxon halls. One hall was the nave in which the people stood for worship. (Benches along the walls were for the elderly.) The other smaller hall was the chancel in which the priest said Mass. There was an open doorway from the nave to the chancel.

Evenlode's patron saint

Each Saxon Church was dedicated to a patron saint. In feudal times it was essential to know someone in authority who would speak well of you to a higher authority. You could not speak to such a higher authority yourself because you were too low in the social scale. The same thought applied in spiritual matters. Every manor and church sought a saint in heaven to speak well of it before God and protect all the villagers. The patron saint of a place (church and village together) interceded for the families and for the manor, sought good weather for the crops, cure for sickness and escape from plague. The patron saint heeded all the many problems of life.

Politically, a patron saint was necessary. After the death of King Edgar and the brief reign of his eldest son, King Edward the Martyr, the land slipped into Civil War. When Ethelred the Unready was king, the Danes led by Olaf Tryggvason of Norway and Swein Forkbeard of Denmark, constantly raided. A real low point was the defeat of the English at the Battle of Maldon in AD 991. A patron saint became essential for any village. He or she fought on your side.

Evenlode today acknowledges Saint Edward as its patron saint. In recent times it has been assumed that this is King Edward the Confessor. However it is more probable that the patron saint is Saint Edward, King and Martyr.

The compelling argument in favour of this Saint is that he died and was declared a Saint in AD 981, which is exactly when the faithful servants of the Bishop of Worcester, Ealhstan and then Athelstan, were Lords of the Manor of Evenlode, and were likely to have been either buiding or re-building the church.

It is also obvious to conclude that Saint Edward, King and Martyr, is Evenlode's patron saint from the history of the time. In the struggle between the English and the Danes it was essential for the English Kings to convince the people of their spiritual supremacy over the Danish Kings. One way to do this was to show the spiritual worth of the English royal family. As a consequence a very large number of "royals" of the tenth century were proclaimed Saints. Therefore for tenth century Evenlode to have a member of the Royal Family as its patron saint made sense, and was politically wise, and it was fashionable.

There may just possibly be a local reason too. Relics from the body of Saint Edward, King and Martyr, were taken to a place called Edwardstow to be enshrined there. That is the old name for Stow-on-the-Wold.

Saint Edward King and Martyr

Edward was the eldest son of King Edgar. There is dispute concerning his mother. One recorded piece of malicious gossip is that

Edward was the product of Edgar's seduction of a nun. Later it is recorded that Ethelfled was his mother. His stepmother, Queen Elfrida, believed this, so it is likely to be true. Ethelfled was Edgar's first wife and died before he became King.

Malicious gossip described Edward as an unruly young man and rather naïve. He is said to have had a temper and even resorted to violence to make his point. From which it may be concluded that Edward was a frustrated and mixed-up teenager. He was only thirteen years old when his father died. However his entry in Butler's *Lives of the Saints* relates that he followed in all things the counsels of Saint Dunstan. The same source remarks on his modesty, clemency, prudence, charity and compassion to the poor.

Edward became king after the death of his father in AD 975 amidst a dispute initiated by Queen Elfrida. She was King Edgar's third wife. She desperately desired that her son Ethelred be king. (He was to be nicknamed "The Unready".) He was only seven when his father died. The reason she gave for her opposition to Edward was that his mother was never crowned queen. Having died before her husband became king, how could she have been?

The truth seems to be that Elfrida saw herself potentially in a position of power with her little boy as king. She also saw that Edward (unmarried yet expected to marry) was a real threat to her ambition for her son and his (therefore, her) descendants. Despite the opposition, Saint Dunstan, Archbishop of Canterbury, crowned Edward on 8 July AD 976.

A couple of years later Edward was hunting in Dorset and called on his stepmother and stepbrother at Corfe Castle on the site of the present ruined Norman Castle. Elfrida invited her stepson to have refreshment with her and her son Ethelred. It looked as if relationships were being mended. It was 18 March AD 978. The seventeen-year-old Edward was murdered.

Different stories were spread abroad. One story tells that Elfrida stabbed him. Another, that she put him off his guard by lulling him with wine and sweet talk and then her attendant stabbed him. Others relate that his stepmother stabbed him and he tried to escape on his horse, clutching the wound in his belly, but quickly died. What is true is that on her orders, her men took the body and threw it into a swamp.

The scandal delayed the coronation of the child Ethelred for it was argued that King Edward should first receive a proper burial. This argument was supported by apparently miraculous events. Months afterwards a column of fire was seen by locals to be burning over the spot in the swamp where his body had been thrust. Digging there, local people exhumed his body and gave it a Christian burial in the churchyard of the Church of Our Lady of Wareham. This was on 13 February AD 979.

Soon it was observed that a spring bubbled up near the grave. It was said that blind people who bathed their eyes in the water gained their sight. The Church authorities realised that this was the beginning of a popular pilgrimage so they exhumed the body and took it to the nuns at Shaftesbury Abbey. During the journey as the body passed through the villages, cripples said that they recovered the use of their limbs.

The body of King Edward was re-buried in the churchyard whilst a shrine was created in the Abbey. In AD 981 (two years after his death) Edward's remains were again exhumed and enshrined in the Abbey. His stepbrother King Ethelred proclaimed him a Saint.

The knife that killed him was kept for many years in the Church at Faversham. With an attitude to human remains different to ours, it is said that part of his body was kept at Wareham and that his lungs were taken to a place called Edwardstow. It would explain the dedications to Saint Edward both at Stow-on-the-Wold as well as at Evenlode, if "Edwardstow" in this story were Stow-on-the-Wold (known originally as Edwardstow).

Queen Elfrida later built two convents and retired to one where she is said to have lived a life of penance.

The *Anglo-Saxon Chronicle* describes poetically how people felt towards Edward, King and Martyr:

"No worse deed for the English was ever done than this was,
since first they came to the land of Britain.
Men murdered him, but God exalted him;
In life he was an earthly King,
but after death he is now a heavenly Saint.

His earthly kinsmen would not avenge him
yet his heavenly Father has amply avenged him.
Those earthly destroyers
would have destroyed his memory on earth,
but the celestial Avenger has spread his fame abroad.

In the heavens and on earth,
those who before would not bend in reverence to his living body
they now humbly bend the knee to his dead bones.

Now can we perceive that the wisdom of men,
their deliberations and plots,
are as naught against God's purpose". (1)

The feast day of Saint Edward King and Martyr in the Roman Martyrology is 18 March. Pilgrims continued to come to the Shrine of Edward King and Martyr at Shaftesbury Abbey until the fourteenth century; after that the numbers began to fall.

Shaftesbury Abbey was dissolved in the time of King Henry VIII but what remains of it is now preserved, and there is a garden and a museum. Recently, interest has been renewed in Saint Edward. Bones have been found in circumstances that some speculate might indicate that they are those of Saint Edward. A pilgrimage was held on 22 June 2008.

Note
(1) The Laud Chronicle (E) 978 (979)

Photo: Paul Ayshford Sanford

Four Shire Stone Farm

In the vicinity is the pre-historic barrow that the Saxons named
Gild or Ild Barrow, beside Alfhere's pool and Cetta's tree.
Here were the four stones of the Saxon boundaries.
Here King Edmund Ironside fought King Canute; and
here, Odo of Bayeux met the knights to hear their grievances.

41

Chapter 4

Danes and Doomsday (AD 1000)

One Sunday morning in 1009 the people of every town and village in England assembled in church for the Sunday Mass and to listen to a letter from King Ethelred and Wulfstan, Bishop of Worcester and Archbishop of the Northern Province of the English Church. (This was not Saint Wulfstan of Worcester. He was born in 1009.) Evenlode was not excluded. All the people of the village listened to it being read out.

Life had been horrendous for several years because of Danish (Viking) invasions, warfare and famine. The King and the Bishop addressed the whole nation and called for a spiritual revival. They blamed the horror of all that had happened on the sins of the nation from king to the lowest commoner.

The letter ordered sacrificial almsgiving to make up for sin. Great demand was made on all. Every thegn had to give in alms one tenth of all he possessed. The ordinary farmers of the Evenlode found they were required to contribute one penny for every ploughland that they held.

Michaelmas Day (29 September) fell that year on a Thursday and everyone was instructed to fast on the Monday, Tuesday and Wednesday prior to Saint Michael's day. Fasting involved abstention from meat and alcohol so all they could eat was bread and vegetables and all they could drink was water. Moreover, whereas they could take a crust in the morning, the amount of food was restricted to one meal of modest proportion each day.

For three days nobody was allowed to wear shoes so all had to be barefoot for the whole period. Every man, woman and child (old enough to understand) had to reflect on their life and make a general confession to God of all the sins they had ever committed in the presence of the priest in order to receive priestly absolution.

The priests were instructed to say Mass daily "against the heathen" for thirty days.

What had brought this about?

Wulfstan, who signed all his letters simply as "The Wolf", was originally a monk. He had been made Bishop of London in 996. He was then transfered to the stronghold of Worcester as bishop in about 1002. He was elected Archbishop of the Northern Province in 1003. The old Roman city of Eboricum and the land between the Tyne and the Humber had become the Danish kingdom of Jorvic. The name stuck (York) though the Danish kingdom was defeated. From his arrival at Worcester fighting between the Danes and the English was escalating. Archbishop Wulfstan was unfortunate in that the King was the badly counselled Ethelred.

The escalation of hostilities began after the massacre of Saint Brice's Day, 13 November 1002. On this day King Ethelred engaged in ethnic cleansing. He had arranged a truce so that the Danes were off their guard and then ordered the murder of every Danish immigrant in the land. The event is described in the *Anglo-Saxon Chronicle:*

> In this year (1002) the king and his councillors decided to pay tribute to the (Danish) fleet and to make peace on condition they ceased from their evil deeds. The king sent Alderman Leofsige to the fleet and he, at the command of the king and his councillors, arranged a truce with them and that they should receive maintenance and tribute. This was accepted and they were paid twenty four thousand pounds. Then the king gave orders for all the Danish people who were in England to be slain on Saint Brice's Day, because the king had been told that they wished to deprive him of his life by treachery. (1)

As a response to this massacre, Danish pirates attacked from their Irish bases, and a furious King Swein embarked with his army and attacked and occupied England as far as Norwich. The Danes only left when 1005 turned out to be a very bad year for the harvest and people died of starvation.

In what seems a strange decision King Ethelred sacked his generals and the leadership of the English forces was handed to the Earl of Mercia.

The Earl paid the Danish fleet off in 1007 to buy time. By 1008 he had raised a huge army. For the first time each shire had to produce its full quota. Those who together farmed eight hides had to supply a helmet and a coat of mail for (unlike the Danes) the English soldiers had never possessed armour. Every hundred of 300 hides had to supply a warship.

In 1009, ready to repel invaders, a new threat emerged. Thorkell had raised a private army of bloodthirsty murderers from all over Denmark, Sweden and Norway. They sailed up the Thames stealing everything on the way. One branch of this horde continued to Cambridge and sacked it, another branch sacked Oxford and then Bedford. They burnt everything they could not steal.

Whatever Archbishop Wulfstan thought of the King's policies he agreed with the king that something dramatic needed to be done.

So it was at this point that the terrified population (and amongst them the inhabitants of Evenlode) gathered in church to hear the letter from King Ethelred and Bishop Wulfstan read to them. The letter demanded penance for sin because sin was the reason why they were suffering the horrors of burning and looting and murder, and also the failed harvest of 1005 from which so many had died of starvation. At least that is what the letter said.

Despite the penance Thorkell continued unabated. His men captured the Archbishop of Canterbury and in drunken frenzy killed him. By 1011 Thorkell had occupied Kent, Sussex, Surrey, Berkshire, Hampshire and Wiltshire. In the east he had occupied East Anglia, Essex, Middlesex, Oxfordshire, Cambridgeshire, Hertfordshire, Buckinghamshire, Bedfordshire and parts of Huntingdonshire and Northamptonshire. Eventually Thorkell was bought off and he withdrew with his booty.

Then incredibly King Ethelred tried to hire him with his private fleet and army to defend England against King Swein. Even more incredibly Thorkell actually prepared to do this. Calling Thorkell a traitor to his nation King Swein responded by invading England. The Earl of Mercia withdrew but remained defiant.

Evenlode was in a horrible geographical situation. Evenlode people were living on the border facing the Danes.

The early English word "unready" has the meaning "badly counselled" rather than unready. Certainly things like ordering ethnic cleansing, attempting to hire your enemies to defend you and sacking all your leaders in battle seem at the least, unwise. Wisely however in 1002 he married Emma and a parallel story emerges.

Emma was the sister of Richard the Good, Duke of Normandy. Ethelred was suspicious that the Normans were giving shelter to the Danish fleet so this was a political marriage, normal for the time. Both the king and the future queen understood this. However Queen Emma came to England on a mission. She saw England as an uncivilised place with an uncouth language so her mission was to introduce Norman culture, Norman attitudes to nobility and Norman French as the normal language of the Court. In this she paved the way for William the Conqueror some sixty years later. She was the mother of two princes fathered by King Ethelred, one of whom would be King Edward the Confessor. She was to prove a most able woman and on one occasion successfully organised defence against the siege of London by the Danes.

When King Swein heard of the strange attempt of Ethelred to hire Thorkell, he returned to England, but to the north where there were generations of Danish settlers. He successfully attempted to re-establish Danish supremacy from York with the north as a firm base. The north submitted to King Swein and after a show of force in Oxford so did the whole of the West Country. This led to the submission of London and so in desperation the Witan invited Swein to become King of England. Queen Emma had fled and after a while so did King Ethelred. Emma's relatives in Normandy provided a home for them.

Meanwhile King Swein died on the Feast of Candlemas (2 February) 1014. Canute was elected King but had to return to Denmark to re-build his army and fleet. So King Ethelred was called back by the Witan. The other duly crowned King of England, Canute, returned in 1015. War again ensued, this time between two crowned Kings of England.

King Ethelred was ill by this time and the burden of fighting the Danes fell on his nephew Edmund Ironside.

This is the period to which the Evenlode tale of the "Battle of Four Shire Stone" is dated.

To fight King Canute, Edmund Ironside raised troops in Mercia and no doubt a weary and fearful Evenlode saw another young man departing to war. During 1016 Edmund Ironside and King Canute fought six major battles and chased each other around the country.

On Saint George's Day (23 April) Ethelred died. Edmund Ironside was crowned King in his stead. King Edmund and King Canute met and fought. They engaged in battle in Wiltshire and in London.

King Canute withdrew to his stronghold in Jorvic (York), and King Edmund followed but was heavily defeated. Chased by the army of King Canute he fell back into Gloucestershire. It seems the route he took was along the road from Oxford heading towards Worcester and thus passing by the four shire stones (as they were then).

There was indeed another major battle between the two kings. This may or may not have taken place at the Four Shire Stone for the site is disputed. However there is a strong Evenlode tradition that this was indeed the site. If it was not the last major battle between the two Kings, at least it was the site of a skirmish as King Canute advanced and King Edmund fought a stout rearguard action. Whatever it was, battle or skirmish, Evenlode folk would bury the dead where they fell, and the Evenlode priest would say a Requiem Mass for the dead soldiers.

After this the two Kings decided that it was time to make peace. They met on what was then an island in the River Severn and came to terms. King Edmund was to be King of Wessex (everything south of the Thames) and King Canute was to be King of the rest of England. The arrangement was that whoever died first would be succeeded by the other. King Edmund Ironside died on 30 November in the same year and so King Canute became sole King of England.

Queen Emma, the widow of King Ethelred then married King Canute. It was a good healing move. Moreover the country soon realised that King Canute was not a bloodthirsty murderous pirate but a wise, honourable and sincere Christian who spent much of his time in England. The raids stopped and the fighting stopped. The country settled down to a time of calm, and Queen Emma continued to use her influence to make it Norman.

Reflections on the Four Shire Stone

The present Four Shire Stone is the successor of the four shire stones of Evenlode's Saxon boundaries. The four stones (as observed above) were landmarks for the four parishes in the four shires.

Brigadier General A C Painter CMG wrote these notes, a copy of which is in Collection One of the Evenlode Papers.

On the northeastern side of the County, at the point where the four counties of Gloucester, Warwick, Oxford and Worcester meet is Four Shire Stone. When Saxton made his survey (1577) there were four such stones, of which he shows two pictorially with the name "The four shire stones" against them. Hole's map (1607 – derived from Saxton) shows three of them, with the name "The shire stones". Lea (1690 – derived from Saxton) had to modify Saxton's plate at this point so as to show an important road, which he could hardly have done without ocular evidence, and he re-engraved the stones, showing four of them, and left Saxon's original wording. The maps of Group B (Speed 1610, Jansson 1646, Blaeu 1648, Blome 1673) show four stones pictorially without mentioning the number. Morden (1695) does the same, specifying also the number 4 in the name; but Bowen (1760), while still showing four stones pictorially, partially obliterated the last "s" of "stones", the result being "Four Shire Stone". "The plate having been thus altered deliberately, it is reasonable to infer that Bowen found in 1760 that there was only one stone at the junction of the counties and that its name was "Four Shire Stone" as at the present day. This is borne out by Taylor's map of 1777, and appears to show that the four stones were replaced by one single one at some time between 1690 and 1760. The fact that other maps refer uniformly to "stones" is no evidence as they merely copied each other. It is interesting to know that as far back as AD 969 four stones existed at this spot. Ref: English Place-names Society, vol iv, Worcestershire, p 124). (2)

The Four Shire Stone we see today is a square eighteenth century monument with a sundial. The four sides of the monument have carved on them: Gloucestershire on the west side Warwickshire on the north side Oxfordshire on the east side, and Worcestershire on the south side. It does not record the Four Shire Stone battle nor does it record the purpose of the original four shire stones.

The end of Saxon rule

The marriage of Queen Emma and King Canute brought peace at last to the Saxon kingdom of England. At the Manor of Evenlode it is unlikely that Athelstan (who succeeded Ealhstan as Lord of the Manor earlier in the tenth century) was still lord in 1016 when King Edmund Ironside fought King Canute at Four Shire Stone, nor a little later when the marriage of Emma and Canute took place. In fact the next glimpse there is of Evenlode is to note that Lyfing Bishop of Worcester gave, in 1038, the tenancy of the manor to a person whose name is indecipherable. However after Ealhstan and Athelstan it can at least be surmised that Bishop Lyfing's appointment would have been another Saxon thegn.

Meanwhile Evesham Abbey had been restored and in 1044 Abbot Manny and a monk called Aethelwig from Evesham set about taking Manors they believed rightfully belonged to Evesham Abbey. They persuaded the new King Edward the Confessor to give the Lordship of the Manor of Evenlode to Evesham Abbey. Presumably Bishop Lyfing's appointee to the Lordship had died. The overlordship of Evenlode remained with the Bishop of Worcester and dues were paid to him. However Evesham Abbey took the tenancy and appointed a steward. The steward ensured that all that would have gone to the Lord of the Manor went to the Abbot of Evesham instead.

After the Conquest William the Conqueror set about "Normanising" his new realm, and did this by building on the achievements of his great aunt Queen Emma.

In 1077 William the Conqueror sent a Norman cleric named Walter (who had been chaplain to Lanfranc the Norman Archbishop of Canterbury) to be the Abbot of Evesham. Walter was young and high-handed and upset a number of local people. Some of these were already resentful because (as related above) Abbot Manny, some thirty years earlier, had acquired for Evesham Abbey the tenancies of the manors that had been held by their families. Evenlode was one.

These Saxon thegns nursed their anger and sought opportunities to win the manors back for their families. Domesday provided an opportunity.

The Domesday Book

William the Conqueror spent Christmas Day 1085 at Saint Peter's Abbey at Gloucester. He presided at the Christmas Feast in the Chapter House. He wore his crown and was dressed in robes of state. It was there that he announced that he wanted a survey made of all the lands and their values in England.

There are three versions for Evenlode in different copies of the Domesday Book. The first reads: "Hereward held 5 hides in Evenlode. 2 ploughs. 9 villagers with 3 ploughs; 1 slave. A Mill at 32 pence. Value is and was £3".

The second reads: "Hereward holds 5 hides in Evenlode. The Abbot of Evesham holds these lands from the Bishop of Worcester. The Bishop of Bayeux received them from the Abbey. The lands which Odo of Bayeux violently took away (were) from the Church of Saint Mary, holy mother of God at Evesham".

The third reads: "7 hides of lordship land; now a man of arms called Brian has them".

It seems that these three versions are the result of different copies of the Domesday Book being "upgraded" as circumstances changed. This gives three pictures of Evenlode at a tumultuous time.

The first version relates that "Hereward" holds the manor. This version must refer to the period when Evesham Abbey held the tenancy of the Manor of Evenlode. Presumably Hereward was Evesham Abbey's steward. So this story is about what the inspectors believed to be the situation when they visited Evenlode to record what they found in the Domesday Book.

The second version reveals a fascinating tale of what happened shortly after the inspectors visited as related above. The Saxon thegns had been nursing their anger over the taking of the manors from their fathers by Abbot Manny of Evesham Abbey, and the high-handedness of Abbot Walter. They contacted Odo of Bayeux claiming that Evesham Abbey had forcefully taken these manors.

Odo, Bishop of Bayeux, was a half-brother of King William. William had made Odo, Earl of Kent. In the absence of the King in Normandy, Odo was Regent of England. Odo was busy collecting English manors. Among these was the Manor of Deddington in Oxfordshire. It is said that at the height of his power Odo possessed one third of England.

Odo was the son of a daughter of a tanner of Falaise. Her name was Herleve. She had (when aged seventeen) given birth to Robert, Duke of Normandy's son, the future William the Conqueror. Later the Duke married her off to Herluin, Vicomte of Conteville, by whom she had Odo. Odo was made Bishop of Bayeux about 1050 (when he was only nineteen years old). The re-building of Bayeux Cathedral and the making of the Bayeux Tapestry are attributed to his leadership.

Odo was heavily involved with his brother in planning the invasion of England. He is depicted on the Bayeux Tapestry at the Battle of Hastings holding a mace and rallying the Norman soldiers. By the time of the Domesday Book he was the largest landholder in England.

To return to the story, Odo agreed to meet the complainants. The meeting place was Ildeburg in the parish of Evenlode. "Ildeburg" is the place described in the Saxon surveys as the Gild or Ild barrow near Alfhere's pool and Cetta's tree along from the four shire stones (at Four Shire Stone Farm).

What happened to the Saxon thegns when they met Odo is unrecorded but the outcome for the Manor of Evenlode was that Odo simply seized the Lordship for himself. As this version of the Domesday Book states, the Abbot of Evesham held Evenlode of the Bishop of Worcester until the Bishop of Bayeux received it ("violently took it away") from the Abbey and appropriated it for the sustenance of his monks.

The third version of the Domesday Book entry relates that the Manor of Evenlode was in the hands of a man at arms called Brian. This probably refers to the time when Odo held it and one of his knights was resident on his behalf.

With three versons, who was Lord of Evenlode in those years is unclear.

Evenlode as described in Domesday

The setting of Evenlode in the Domesday Book is significant. It is in a group headed by Blockley and so is clearly still within the Hundred of Oswaldslaw. The whole Blockley group is within the general heading of land owned by the Bishop of Worcester. This confirms that local government continued as set up by the Saxon King Edgar.

Examining the three entries together, the manor seems to have been reduced since Ridda's day. In his day it was eight hides but in the Domesday Book it is variously said to be five or seven hides. This may only mean that the understanding of the size of a hide had changed. Included within this (or additional to it) were two ploughs. This implies ploughed land for which two ploughs were needed.

There are nine "villagers", (Domesday does not record wives, children nor dependent elderly relatives). These villagers were likely to be holders of land for fruit trees, vegetables and herbs, and would have had cows and sheep on common land. Domesday says they shared between them three ploughs of arable land to grow corn. They would additionally have had the duty of giving time to the manor lands. Some of them may have had communal jobs such as being the smith. One of the villagers may have devoted time to the mill. It seems likely that this was an occasional activity for a small place like Evenlode.

The picture that emerges is typical. Evenlode is a small manor with a lord and his family and staff (normally). There are nine farmers with families and servants who also owe time to the manor. There is pasture and arable land. The whole is worth £3. There is a mill worth 32 pence. There is no mention of a priest (although there are priests at nearby Daylesford and Broadwell).

Knowledge of the times tells us that these people had very hard lives often suffering from illnesses and in the winter from hunger and cold. Life was short. People grew old quickly. The infant mortality rate was high. They lived their lives beholden to the whim of a lord of the manor and, at the time of Domesday, completely at the mercy of a greedy decision made by a Norman baron.

The eleventh century was a horrible century for most people in England and so it was for Evenlode too.

Note
(1) The Laud Chronicle (E) 1002
(2) Transactions of the Bristol and Gloucestershire Archaeological Society, *Notes on some old Gloucestershire Maps,* Brig. Gen. AC Painter CMG (Collection One of the Evenlode Papers)

*From an unattributed sketch in
Collection One of the Evenlode Papers*

*The stone church was built by the end of the 12th century. The Deyville
family members were lords of the manor. Later Deyvilles added the
tower and the Lady Chapel, in the fourteenth century.*

Chapter 5

The Deyville dynasty 1182–1485

The end of overlordship of Evenlode

How long Odo of Bayeux held the Manor of Evenlode is unknown. Nor is anything further known of the knight Brian. No further claims of Evesham Abbey to the Lordship are recorded.

The overlordship remained with the Bishop and Prior of Worcester, as had been agreed in the days of King Edgar, in the tenth century. The overlord had the right of presentation to a lordship of a manor, and John of Pagham (who was Bishop of Worcester from 1151 to 1158) gave the tenancy and Lordship of the Manor to Hugh Poer (pronounced Power) upon Hugh's marriage to his (the bishop's) niece.

The Poer family were a Norman family. They carved out great estates in Ireland where "Power" remains a common Irish surname. They had estates locally as the name Guiting Power recalls but they also had land in Worcestershire. It seems probable that Hugh belonged to either the Worcestershire or Gloucestershire branch of the family. It is unlikely that Hugh Poer and his bride resided at Evenlode. A steward would have handled daily business.

Meanwhile the concept of the overlord was becoming less significant. A contributory factor may have been that it became the custom of the kings to reward friends with the "tenancies" (the lordships) of manors but in order to enhance the gift the rent to the overlord was set at an extremely low rate. This attitude seems to have spread. In fact as far as Evenlode was concerned, dues still had to be paid to the Hundred Court in terms of a quantity of oats, but it is recorded in Collection Three of the Evenlode Papers that Godfrey Giffard, who was Bishop of Worcester from 1268 to 1302, commuted this to a lump sum of forty shillings.

Other rights of an overlord may have lingered, for John Carpenter (who was Bishop of Worcester from 1444 to 1476), in correspondence during 1455 with the Prior of Worcester, enquired who was the overlord of Evenlode, the bishop or the prior? The occasion for this enquiry was because a minor had inherited the Manor of Evenlode. Presumably the bishop was wondering if he had any rights in this matter. There is no further mention of the rights of overlordship of the Bishop of Worcester or the Prior concerning Evenlode.

However, ecclesiastical links remained with the Bishop of Worcester as records exist of ordinations and appointments of clergy. Some of these have been edited in papers of the *Worcestershire Historical Society*, copies of entries being in Collection Three of the Evenlode Papers.

The Deyvilles (from before 1182 – 1485)

Some time before 1182 the tenancy and lordship of the Manor of Evenlode passed from the Poers to Matthew Deyville. The Deyvilles mark a change from a feudal system in which the overlord appoints a lord of the manor (explicitly and later implicitly, with the king's permission), to a system whereby the lordship of a manor is inherited.

The Deyvilles were a Norman family. Norman families came to England with or after William the Conqueror. The Poer family was one such. The de Ville family was another.

The surname "de Ville" simply means "from the town" and is found in a variety of forms all over France. The French stems from the Latin word "villa" which originally meant an estate or large house. Over the centuries it was applied to a settlement ("le village") and then to a small town ("la ville"). It comes in a variety of forms in English. The most significant family name originating from "de Ville" in English history is the Villiers family.

The Deyvilles frequently described themselves as being "of Evenlode". Sometimes they added this after using their surname. For example, Richard Deyville described himself as "Richard Deyville of Evenlode". They regularly refer to themselves as Lord of the Manor of Evenlode. These are clear indicators that the first generations of the Deyvilles certainly resided at Evenlode.

The names of the Deyville lords of the manor are recorded in the *Victoria County History for Worcestershire*.

Before 1182, Matthew of Evenlode
Nicholas of Evenlode (Matthew's son)
About 1288, Richard Deyville of Evenlode
Before 1327, William Deyville (Richard's son)
1348 Piers (Peter) Deyville (William's son)

Piers (Peter) Deyville died in 1398 and after that the line of the lords of the manor becomes complicated. His heirs were John Petyt and his wife Philippa. It may be assumed that Philippa was the daughter of Piers or possibly a niece.

Piers left a widow called Amice. After his death, Amice married a second time. Her second husband was William Lisle. Later it is noted in the *Victoria County History for Worcestershire* that the Petyts held land at Knowle in Warwickshire (although the manor was held by the Grevilles) and it seems sensible to surmise that in fact it was at Knowle that John and Philippa Petyt lived rather than at Evenlode.

This would make sense of a transfer of land at Evenlode from John and Philippa Petyt to Amice and William Lisle in 1415, after which William Lisle assumed the title of lord of the Manor of Evenlode. If the surmise is correct that Philippa and John Petyt lived at Knowle, then Amice continued to live in her old home, the Manor House of Evenlode.

However this was not a transfer in perpetuity but only for their lifetimes. In fact William Lisle died in 1421 and Amice married a third time, to Richard Eton. John and Philippa Petyt continued the arrangement and Richard Eton became Lord of the Manor. There is no further mention of Amice. Richard Eton died in 1431.

In 1441 John and Philippa settled the Manor of Evenlode on the "heirs of the body of Philippa" or if for some reason there were no direct heirs upon her rightful heirs. However sometime after 1451 they gave arable land and fourteen acres of meadow to William Haynes. The Haynes family farmed this land at least until 1765 when Thomas Haines died, by then it was called Horn Farm.

After the death of Philippa, John lived alone until his own death in 1455. The Manor of Evenlode then came into the hands of Philippa's grandson Thomas Petyt. He was a minor and his inheritance prompted the enquiry mentioned above by the Bishop of Worcester to the Prior of Worcester as to who was the overlord? In fact the guardianship of Thomas Petyt was given to John Gloucester. Thomas died at a young age and William Petyt succeeded him as Lord of the

Manor. William Petyt is assumed to be his brother. He was Lord by 1473.

William Petyt was a supporter of the Yorkist cause in the Wars of the Roses and seems to have been held in some favour by King Edward IV. It is not known whether or not he fought with King Richard III at the Battle of Bosworth in 1485. All that is known is that after the accession of Henry Tudor, William Petyt lost the Manor of Evenlode.

Houses during the Deyville dynasty

At the time of the Deyvilles it is almost certain that the Manor House was on the site of the present Manor Farm but even the oldest part of this house is only dated to the sixteenth century. The early Deyvilles' Manor House was probably a wooden hall.

Where the ordinary people lived in these days is unclear. Most of them would have been villeins farming their own strips for their own subsistence, but also working without wages for the lord of the manor. The positions of the Manor House, St Edward's Church and the mill indicate the likely general area of their dwellings.

A track exists to the east of the Church and continues to Moreton. Another track would have led to the mill where the present drive to Two Stones Cottage is. Cottages may have fronted onto one or other or both of these. The blocked doorway in the north wall of the church may simply have given access to the churchyard but possibly indicates that people once lived to the north of the church.

However, the existence of a reliable spring of clean water may indicate an early settlement where the present Poplars Farm is.

The cottages were no more than small wooden huts with a thatched roof and a hole in the roof for smoke to escape. Toilet facilities were against the back wall. The well provided water for cooking, brewing beer and washing.

Life for a villein working on the land and for his wife working in the home and the garden was hard, frequently miserable in winter, and often short.

Paying tithes

Taxes were constantly collected upon order of the king and during these years the system of tithing was perfected for the national Church. At Evenlode the tithes were paid to the Rector and according to church law he split the money in four ways. A quarter went to the upkeep of the Rector and the assistant clergy of Evenlode (who also had the glebe to farm although how much land this involved at this time is not known). A quarter went to the Bishop of Worcester for his maintenance and to maintain the diocese. A quarter was put to one side for the poor. The final quarter was used for the upkeep of the nave of the church (the Rector maintained the chancel out of his income).

The tithing was of corn, hay, vegetables, milk, eggs, butter, cheese, honey, wax, fallen timber and animals born. If tithing was difficult (for example if only one foal per year was born on a farm) the farmer had to pay in cash one tenth of the value of the foal. Tradesmen had to pay one tenth of their profits.

In addition from the year 1200, fees were payable to the Rector for weddings and funerals and for saying Mass at a person's request.

Fowls had to be given to the clergy as a Christmas offering. Eggs were given as an Easter offering, and cheese as a Whitsunday offering.

The whole system was resented. Lord and peasant alike hated it. By contrast in these years of the high Middle Ages the people were religious. They said their prayers and attended their parish church.

Evenlode Church in the twelfth century

The core of the stone church that exists today is dated to the twelfth century. This is the period in which Matthew Deyville of Evenlode was Lord and resident in the Manor House. The construction of the original stone church perhaps should be attributed to him. However little remains of the twelfth century church except for the chancel arch and the stones of the walls.

Inside the church the priest's sedilium from the original stone church remains. It is commonly called the "sanctuary chair" and is currently in the south aisle. Despite speculation in the recent past that this chair was used to give "sanctuary" from the law the chair is called the sanctuary chair because it was originally in the sanctuary. The sanctuary is that part of the chancel divided from the rest by the communion rail and in which stands the altar. It was the seat ("sedilium" in Latin) on which the Priest sat as he presided at the first part of the Mass, the Ante Communion or Liturgy of the Word.

This unsigned document of 1916 is contained in Collection One of the Evenlode Papers:

The only distinguishable survival of the Church of the transitional Norman period, late in the twelfth century, is the chancel arch, a magnificent though small example. The round mouldings of the arch, or "relic" are Norman, but the pointed form introduced what afterwards became the Gothic style – hence the name "transitional." The three-quarter "shaft" or small column each side, with its scallop pattern capital, and the form of the base (reminiscent of the Greek Ionic base as imitated in the British Museum front) are Norman in style and delightful. It will be noticed that the shape of the arch on the left (north) of the point is flatter, showing settlement of the wall above (one reason for introducing the pointed arch in this country was to avoid this). The arch on the chancel side is plainer.

Parts of the walls of the nave and chancel, particularly the quoins (corners), are probably of this time; the Church may not have extended beyond these.

In the north wall outside are the remains of a doorway at low level, now blocked, which was probably of this early date.

A mason's mark can be seen on the Chancel Arch. From the thirteenth century, a lancet window in the north wall remains. A fragment of stained glass from this period also remains in the windows of the south aisle.

The document continues:

The end of the thirteenth and the beginning of the fourteenth century...called the Early Decorated...style, saw the full development of tracery which had arisen from single windows grouped together with holes pierced above and between them. The south window of the nave (west of the south aisle) is of the long-lobed kind of tracery of this time - and a rather uncouth example, perhaps late twelfth century, of a more elegant kind. Perhaps about 1300 are the two remaining north nave windows and perhaps the east window, if the modern restoration (has) followed the original pattern…

As noted above the church has two rooms, a larger room for the nave, and a smaller room for the chancel. The nave is where the people gathered for worship but it was also used for public meetings. It would be used on any occasion when some official needed to inform the villagers about something. Most villages also recognised unofficial spokesmen who would call meetings. Often these were called in order to protest about something.

The churchyard was not quite the hallowed spot it is now. Animals grazed on it and it was a playground for children. The church walls were ideal to throw or kick a ball at. The ball was made out of an air-filled pig's bladder. In fact in these games are the origins of squash and many wall games.

King Edward II and William Deyville,

There is a glimpse of Evenlode in national history during the lordship of William Deyville (Lord of the Manor before 1327). This is in the reign of King Edward II. King Edward II was sandwiched between two fierce kings, his father and his son. He preferred working in the garden to politics. He enjoyed learning rural crafts such as thatching. He delighted in peasants' rustic pleasures after work was done. He also liked lots of money. He showered this on his friends and studiously refused to listen to advisers at Court. He had grown up with a Gascon of his own age called Piers Gaveston. The two were inseparable and even his father thought there was a homosexual relationship. Twice his father exiled Gaveston but Edward always got his friend back.

When his father died in 1307 he had left his son with the political problem of subduing Scotland. With those barons who supported him, King Edward II half-heartedly engaged the Scots in battle at

Bannockburn. England was soundly thrashed leaving Robert the Bruce to settle the kingdom and harass the North of England at his leisure.

Edward refused to allow the barons any power and played off baron against baron, but the barons under the leadership of Thomas of Lancaster forced him to accept reforms. Gaveston was murdered.

Edward began to shower money and land on new friends the Despensers. Hugh Despenser was married to a sister of the Earl of Gloucester and was busy building up an empire in Worcestershire. He also acquired manors in South Wales and aroused the anger of the Marcher Lords especially Roger Mortimer.

Edward had married Isabella of France and they had children including the crown Prince Edward. However conflict arose with the King of France so he sent Isabella to negotiate peace. Roger Mortimer met up with her and they became lovers. They conspired together against Edward and built up an army of mercenaries and landed in Sussex. Everyone turned to the Queen.

King Edward and the Despensers withdrew to the Despenser stronghold in the West. At some point Hugh Despenser came across William Deyville, Lord of the Manor of Evenlode. It seems that Despenser demanded a fine from William for holding the Manor. It was indeed customary to pay a "fine" on inheriting a manor and presumably William had done this. So by what authority Despenser made this further demand is unknown. However it seems that William supported Roger Mortimer so this fine might have been linked to a test of loyalty. William did not pay the fine and it is recorded that later Roger Mortimer cancelled it and left William in peace.

The Despensers were caught and executed. The King was imprisoned in Berkeley Castle. The gaolers were told to kill him but in a way that left no mark on the outside of his body. They tried starvation but he clung to life so they killed him be forcing a redhot poker into his innards through the rear orifice. These were cruel and shocking days and life, even the life of the king, was disposed of at will. The people were glad to forget his reign.

However the coronation of his son, King Edward III, led the country into a new era. There was peace and prosperity for fifty years.

William Deyville (Lord of the Manor of Evenlode before 1327) bought the Manor of Sezincote additionally in 1341. Two sisters had inherited it but they did not live there and wished to sell it. William Deyville bought it and Peter (Piers) Deyville inherited this manor from his father in 1348 along with the Manor of Evenlode. He must have chosen to live at Sezincote because he leased Evenlode Manor House to John Greville (though he retained the Lordship of the Manor).

The later development of St Edward's Church seems to have taken place whilst Piers was Lord of the Manor of Evenlode from 1348 to 1398, and Richard Deyville (presumable a relative) was Rector, from 1335 to 1384. During this time the church was beautified and extended.

The Doom

The arch so lovingly described above connects the chancel and the nave. The chancel arch was seen as a transition place. The nave was the world where people lived but passing through the arch one entered heaven on earth around the altar. In Evenlode Church there was also a colourful painting above the arch. This would presumably be of Judgement Day. The phrase used then was the Day of Doom and such pictures were called "dooms". A sketch was made of this painting before it was covered. This hangs on the south wall of the nave.

The Rood

Within the arch there was a screen dividing the nave from the chancel on the top of which was placed a carved image of Jesus on the Cross. On the screen also were placed carved images of Mary the Mother of God and of John the beloved disciple. These were on each side of Jesus.

The image of Jesus on the Cross was known as the "Rood." The screen was thus called the "Rood Screen." The remains of steps to this screen are clearly visible from the south aisle.

The Rood was not just decoration. On certain occasions such as Good Friday the priest would stand on the screen beside the figures and proclaim in the language of the people the passion story from one or other of the Gospels. On a gloomy day, lit only by candles, this must have been most dramatic. In some places the figures were made in such a way that they could be moved like marionettes. This was even more dramatic. In these uses lie the beginning of religious drama and the Passion Play so regularly performed in churches on Good Friday evening, not all that many years ago.

The addition of the South Aisle

The major structural change of a chapel being added to the south side of the nave is dated to the latter part of the fourteenth century. This coincides with a growth in devotion to Mary the Mother of God. Despite later puritan propaganda, Mary was never worshipped but was seen as the loving mother who would speak to Jesus on behalf of the one praying and obtain graces and favours. The concept of praying to the saints emerged not only from a feudal understanding of intercession but also from a deep understanding of fellowship and a realisation that the Communion of Saints embraced not only the Church in heaven but also the Church on earth. The extension to the church would have been built not because more room was needed, but as a chapel dedicated to Mary, hence its title, the "Lady Chapel".

Particular devotion was paid in this century to our Lady of Walsingham at her Shrine in Norfolk. The image at the shrine was often replicated in parish churches such as Saint Edward's in Evenlode and placed in the Lady Chapel. In many places (long after the fittings of the chapel had been removed) people referred to this part of the church as the Lady Chapel.

The Deyville Lords of the Manor added a Lady Chapel to Saint Edward's Church in the fourteenth century. The architecture inside linking the nave and the south aisle (Lady Chapel) is described in the same document quoted above:

The twin arcade between nave and south aisle is very unusual…The piers, diagonal faced or lozenge shaped on plan, with the arches of steep splay and of two unequal "orders" (rings of stones) are very striking.

The Black Death

The Lady Chapel might have served another purpose too. It was a place to pray for the dead. From 1348–50 the Black Death swept the country and Evenlode would not have been immune. There is no record of a burial place for those who died of the plague but it is likely a pit was dug in the churchyard into which all were placed, old and young, freemen and serfs.

The Black Death created an obssesion with death and the after-life. Praying for the repose of the souls of the dead became a major part of people's spirituality. Offering Mass or paying a priest to offer Mass for the dead was a significant trend. Rich men often employed an additional priest for this purpose and to serve as a curate to the Rector. Frequently he used the Lady Chapel as a "chantry" in which to say Requiem Masses, whilst the Rector used the high altar in the chancel.

The tower

The tower also can be dated to this period when Richard Deyville was Rector of Evenlode. It is recorded that in 1732 the tower had five bells (the tenor of this peal still exists). When these bells were put in the tower is unknown, but during Richard Deyville's tenure, it was customary for at least one bell to be hung. This bell not only called everyone to worship but also was tolled when someone died. It was rung at the consecration of the elements at Mass so that those not attending would know that this was a moment to stop what they were doing for a moment of prayer.

A further addition dated to this time was the installation of the pulpit. The arrival of itinerant friars in England (of several different Orders) had introduced the idea of popular preaching and Evenlode had connections with the Augustinian Canons who encouraged the friars. (This link with the Augustinian Canons will be mentioned later. Martin Luther was an Augustinian Canon.) The friars often preached in the churchyard and everyone gathered around for they gave good entertainment in the course of their preaching. Usually they re-told bible stories and legends of the Saints and everyone likes a story. There was always a final part to such a sermon. This was when the preacher threatened hell and damnation to sinners, and the good folk shivered with delight as they contemplated the end of neighbours from hell.

Another advocate of preaching at this time was John Wyclif. He taught at Oxford and then was dispossessed in favour of a monastic foundation. He heralded the emergence of Protestantism with his views on the sacrament of Holy Communion and his support for the translation of the bible into English. His influence may have been of equal importance to the friars in Evenlode, as the Rector of Evenlode was an Oxford man.

As a consequence of the rise of the importance of preaching, the sermon was re-emphasised as part of the Mass. As the people stood in the Nave for Mass, a pulpit was needed for the preacher in order to be seen. Evenlode has a very fine example of a pulpit dated to about 1400 but likely to be a little earlier given the long period of time in which there was but one Rector and one Lord of the Manor who were relatives. The same document continues:

The pulpit is a rare medieval example in wood. Only three sides of a six-sided plan exist; one has a repeated curvilinear pattern, the others have more vertical lines; it may be northern French or Flemish, judging by the all-over pattern.

Stained glass

Some stained glass would have been placed in the windows but how much cannot be now known. A fragment remains in a south aisle window. Some say it depicts Saint Edward the Confessor but there is no apparent justification for this. Lovely though it is to have it, from the size it seems but a subsidiary figure from a lost main window.

The Clergy

The clergy were central to everyday life for the Christian during the late middle ages. Membership of the Church was taught as a prerequisite to salvation. Pardon for sin was mediated through priestly confession. Failure to attend Mass on Sundays and Holy Days was deemed a serious sin endangering salvation. Babies were christened shortly after birth for a baby dying without baptism would miss the chance of heaven and stay in limbo. The Christian dead were buried in the churchyard awaiting the Day of Doom. Couples were wedded in the church porch after which they entered the church to receive the nuptial blessing at Mass. After the wedding feast the couple retired to bed with good-natured ribaldry, and the priest blessed the bed with them in it.

It is not surprising that many young men saw a priest's life as an attractive life, even though by this time a priest was not supposed to be married. It has been estimated that at this time perhaps one third of all men in the country had received the tonsure and were technically clerics, though only a proportion would have been ordained priest. There was no universal education for future clergy other than attendance at university, but a large number of non-graduates were ordained by way of monastic education. The monasteries had extensive libraries and often the monks acted as teachers. Evenlode had links with the Augustinian Canons (see later).

It is interesting to note that the Rector was not necessarily the only cleric in the parish of Evenlode. The records indicate several clerics from Evenlode receiving a variety of Orders. There may have been other clerics living with him in the Priest's House. Some of these may have been priests with no parish to serve or some may have been clerics in minor Orders aspiring to be priests. They attended church daily, studied, and involved themselves in the life of the village and farmed the glebe. There was a "Priest's Page" who managed the house and its servants for them.

The Rectors of Evenlode during the Deyville dynasty

William de Saltmarsh is the first priest of Evenlode whose name is known (Collection Three of the Evenlode Papers). He was appointed Rector of Evenlode in 1270. Bishop Godfrey Giffard appointed him. Giffard was Bishop of Worcester from 1268 to 1302. This was during the time when Nicholas Deyville of Evenlode was Lord of the Manor. In 1307 the Rector (who was probably not William de Saltmarsh by that time but whose name is unrecorded) received from the bishop notice of his share in a tax imposed by the king. He had to pay eight shillings. Three times the tax was demanded from the Rector of Evenlode. It seems he simply ignored it and never paid.

Later rectors are:

Before 1330, Master Thomas Deyville became Rector of Evenlode either when Richard Deyville was Lord of the Manor or William his son was. His name is recorded in the register of Adam Orleton, Bishop of Worcester from 1327 to 1334.

In 1330, William Reynall was Rector.

In 1335, Master Richard Deyville became Rector. Bishop Simon Montacute ordained him. Montacute was Bishop of Worcester from 1334 to 1337.

In 1384, William Marssh became Rector of Evenlode. This was when Piers (Peter) Deyville was Lord of the Manor. This is recorded in the register of Bishop Henry Wakefield. Wakefield was Bishop of Worcester from 1375 to 1396.

In 1389 Master William Frankelyn became Rector. Piers (Peter) Deyville was still Lord of the Manor. William Frankelyn's appointment is also recorded in the register of Bishop Henry Wakefield.

Although these are the only records available, the presentation of each new Rector of Evenlode was by the Lord of the Manor as Patron. The right to appoint remained with the Lord of the Manor until 1601 when the advowson (right to appoint) was sold to Margaret Farr.

The registers also reveal the names of other clergy appointed to other places who are connected with Evenlode. Sometimes their name is written "of Evenlode"; sometimes it merely indicates that they originate in Evenlode. Perhaps they had been resident in the Priest's House whilst they studied.

These are:

Before 1327, Thomas Frethorne of Evenlode was ordained priest and went to Winchcombe.
Before 1327, Richard of Evenlode was ordained deacon and went to Lechlade.
In 1337 John Jones of Evenlode was ordained Acolyte.
In 1339 John Evenlode was ordained sub-deacon and went to Cold Norton Priory. Robert de Halford, son of John of Evenlode, was consecrated Abbot of Osney.
In 1349 William Jones went to Cold Norton Priory.

The appointment to Osney Abbey at Oxford is very significant as this was one of the major houses of the Augustinian Canons. Later it became a Cathedral for Oxford until the Chapel of Christ's College was designated as such. After the dissolution, the Abbot of Osney became Bishop of Oxford. (Osney Abbey was then closed and became a quarry for good stone. The railway laid tracks and built Oxford Station on the site. A tiny amount of ruined wall from the Abbey is visible near the canal marina.) Cold Norton Priory was also a house of Augustinian Canons.

It is surprising that the son of an Evenlode man became Abbot of Osney Abbey and two other Evenlode men were ordained to be Canons at Cold Norton Priory. There is no evidence as to why there should be a link between Evenlode and the Augustinian Canons but a possibility presents itself. It may be that Evenlode boys aspiring to be clerics who could not obtain entrance to the University (perhaps for financial reasons) were welcomed to study with the Augustinian Canons. It would be unsurprising then if some opted to join the Canons.

In 1473 William Petyt was Lord of the Manor of Evenlode. The Deyville blood flowed through his veins from Matthew of Evenlode (Lord of the Manor before 1182) through Philippa who married John Petyt (who gave William his surname).

As stated earlier in this chapter, William favoured the Yorkist cause and in the Wars of Roses he gained the favour of King Edward IV. After the defeat of King Richard III and the accession of Henry Tudor as king, William lost the Manor. The Manor was awarded to Lawrence Albrighton and William Leicester jointly. William Petyt was living at Knowle in Warwickshire and tried twice to get the Manor of Evenlode back but was denied it. He conveyed his claim to the Manor to Robert Tate.

A branch of the Petyts continued to farm at Evenlode. Robert Tate and Richard Petyt drove cattle between Knowle and Evenlode.

Photo: Colin and Cathy Methven

Evencourt

One of the fine small mansions of Evenlode built by
Sir Henry Compton, Lord of the Manor of Evenlode.
The Fletcher family farmed here for 200 years.

Chapter 6

Sir Henry Compton (1546–89)

The sixteenth century was a century of change. There are glimpses of Evenlode in the life and times of Henry Compton.

The lordship of the Manor of Evenlode had passed into the hands of the Comptons of Compton Winyate, but how this happened is unrecorded. Sir William Compton died in 1528 leaving his estates to his son Peter, who was then a minor. Sir William's widow married again to Sir Philip Hoby. Sir Philip became Lord of the Manor. The Manor came to Peter Compton on his majority. From Peter the Manor passed to his son Henry in 1546-7, when the latter was still a child.

Henry Compton was born on 16 February 1538. He was the son of Peter Compton and his wife Anne who was the daughter of George Talbot, Fourth Earl of Shrewsbury. He inherited the Manor of Evenlode and the lordship in 1546-7, on the death of his father. He was eight years old. He did not live at Evenlode, for the Compton Estates were substantial and the family home was at Compton Winyates in Warwickshire. During the minority his guardian was William Herbert, First Earl of Pembroke.

He grew up towards the end of the life of King Henry VIII and during the short reign of the boy King Edward VI. As he grew into manhood he accepted his responsibilities as (among many other things) Lord of the Manor of Evenlode. He was educated at Grays Inn and so with a legal background he was well able to tread carefully in difficult times. When he reached his majority he entered the House of Commons, but he did not participate in the work of the House. In fact, Henry was much more at home as a courtier in the Court of Queen Elizabeth. She had become Queen after the death of Queen Mary in 1558 and she knighted him in 1567 as a member of the Order of the Bath. He was listed among her "noble men" who received a grant of wine, free of duty.

Henry Compton was considered to be a "person of florid wit and solid judgement". He married twice. The first marriage was to Frances daughter of Francis Hastings, Second Earl of Huntingdon and then to

Anne, the daughter of Sir John Spencer. He was created the First Baron Compton in 1572 when he accompanied Queen Elizabeth on a visit to Warwick.

Baron Henry Compton lived in a time of change. There were changes in the Church of England, changes in the Manorial system, and changes in social class.

Changes in the Church of England

Henry Compton lived through four reigns, King Henry VIII, King Edward VI, Queen Mary and Queen Elizabeth I. He witnessed in the Church of England changes, reversal and changes again. These changes were mirrored in his manors and their churches, including the Manor of Evenlode and the Church of Saint Edward. Throughout this time, William Farr was Rector of Evenlode.

Despite King Henry VIII's break with Rome over the matter of divorce, and his dissolution of the monasteries for financial reasons, he was not attracted to the idea of Protestantism. Therefore whilst Henry was king, the Church of England changed little, though it was separated from the Pope.

However Edward Seymour was Lord Protector during the reign of King Edward VI and a firm supporter of reform, so he ensured that after the death of King Henry, the boy king followed the wishes of the reformers. This meant changes in the Church of England. Thus when Henry Compton was eight years old he witnessed the breaking up of the chantries in the parish churches of his manors (which held before God the memory of his predecessors). When he was nine years old, the vestments, candlesticks, images and stained glass were either vandalised or sold. When he was ten years old Latin was virtually abandoned in the Church of England, and the ancient Latin Mass was replaced with the 1549 Book of Common Prayer compiled in English by Archbishop Cranmer (though mainly from the original Latin).

When Henry Compton was fifteen years old, King Henry VIII's daughter Mary became Queen. Mary was the daughter of King Henry VIII and Queen Catherine. Catherine was Henry's first (and, some would whisper, his only lawful) wife.

Mary was a devout Catholic brought up in the "old Faith" by her mother. She ardently wanted the Church of England to cease from being two "protesting" Provinces of York and Canterbury and for it to be re-connected with the rest of the Catholic Church under the Pope. After her accession she proceeded to bring this about. The Church of England restored images and vestments and in some cases the stained glass was replaced. People could again pray for the dead and light their candles. The priest once again wore vestments and the Latin Mass was once again celebrated.

If Mary had immediately followed her father as Queen the established Church of England would now be Roman Catholic as in France and Spain. As it was she received a cautious welcome from most of the country people and especially the northerners. They did not like the protestant changes. However during the reign of Edward VI many people in London (but not so much in the country) had become committed to the Protestant way of thinking and they immediately opposed her.

In fact Queen Mary made three huge mistakes. These turned people against her. She married King Philip II of Spain, whom the English feared as a foreigner. She deprived bishops who continued to maintain the Protestant view from their posts, and after a trial had them burned at the stake as heretics, together with many others both lowly and powerful. She evicted all the clergy who had taken the opportunity to marry, unless they disowned their wives and children. People disliked her husband, felt abhorrence at the fires of Smithfield and rejected the treatment of their clergy. She was her own worst enemy.

Upon the accession of Elizabeth, things changed again. The jurisdiction of the Pope was again repudiated and Elizabeth became Supreme Governor of the Church of England (not Head, as her father had proclaimed himself). English came back with the re-introduction of the Book of Common Prayer. Elizabeth wanted a compromise that would hold within the Church of England, not only those who were committed to the old Faith, but also the reformers. In pursuing this, she invented (probably without realising it) what came to be known as the "middle way" or in its Latin form the "via media".

One of the consequences of this was that she wanted little outward change in the "ornaments" in a parish church. So she commanded, "such Ornaments of the Church and of the Ministers thereof shall be retained and be in use as was in the Church of England by authority of Parliament in the second year of the reign of King Edward VI". This instruction is still recorded in the Book of Common

Prayer. This date was craftily chosen because by using Edward's name she hoped to be seen to be with the reformers, in order to placate them. However the date was before King Edward ordered the removal of things from the Church, so much that Mary had re-introduced into the churches, Elizabeth expected to continue in use. This she hoped would keep the Catholics in the Church of England.

As far as his religion was concerned it seems that like so many people Henry Compton, Lord of the Manor, was confused. It would not be surprising to discover that the people of Evenlode, and indeed, the Rector, were confused too in those chaotic times.

William Farr, Rector of Evenlode from 1541

William Farr had become Rector of Evenlode in 1541 when Henry Compton was a minor. Sir Philip Hoby was Lord of the Manor of Evenlode during Henry Compton's childhood and he presented William Farr to the living.

Where the Priest's House (later known as the Rectory) was in those days is not definitely known but there is a clue that would place it quite near the Manor House. It begins with the story of Joan Bliss's cottage.

Joan Bliss's cottage is connected with the Manor House in the later sale of the Manor, and linked with the cottage is the land around it. This is almost certainly where the present Two Stones Cottage is. So it may be assumed that the proximity of the Manor House and Joan Bliss's cottage was how things were, when William Farr was Rector.

(The present Manor Farm buildings and Two Stones cottage are generally later that than this period, but there is evidence to indicate that they absorbed parts of older buildings).

The story continues. A woman called Margaret Farr (who it has been suggested became William Farr's wife after the split with the Pope and clergy began to marry) bought land that had been held by Joan Bliss. The land therefore may have been part of the land linked with Joan Bliss's cottage. The argument continues that if Margaret Farr wanted to buy land there, it must mean that that was where she lived too. Therefore it is suggested that Margaret and Joan were neighbours.

This could mean one of two things. There is some evidence in the structure of Two Stones cottage to indicate that it may once have been divided in two. So it is plausible that the "Two Stones Cottage" of that period was in fact two stone cottages. One would have been Joan Bliss's home and one possibly the Priest's House where Margaret Farr lived.

The other possibility is that there was a third separate building between the present Two Stones cottage and the churchyard. Excavations have discovered some large stones. In which case one could have been Joan Bliss's cottage and the other the Priest's House.

It is curious that a few years ago a resident of Two Stones cottage recorded the shadowy appearance of a cowled figure on certain occasions.

Religious changes at Evenlode

What stance William Farr took in the matter of reform is not known, but in any case the furious debate between Catholic bishops and the reformers may have seemed a long way from tiny Evenlode.

In his early days as Rector, William no doubt carried on saying Mass in Latin as he always had done, taught the children the Faith and their prayers, tidied his Priest's House, tended his poultry, cared for his vegetables in his garden and saw to the farming of his glebe. He would not have been married at this early time when the Church of England was still Catholic at heart.

The changes ordered during the reign of King Edward VI must have made Evenlode Church seem extremely bare to the worshippers. The stone altar at the east end was ripped out (though they kept the stone sanctuary chair), the candles and cross and images were taken out and either burned or buried in the graveyard or sold. The vestments were sold too for the material to be re-used. The Lady Chapel was dismantled and abandoned. The stained glass was smashed and replaced with plain except for the little portions Evenlode is so pleased to have today. The whole interior was whitewashed to cover up the colour and the paintings.

William was bound by law to use the new services but like many a rector of those days he may have said the Latin Mass privately and illegally in church, before the hour of the new service, for the one or two who held firmly to the old Faith. Everyone else would have resented the change in Evenlode as they did elsewhere, but they were law-abiding so they would have attended the new services.

Why change the services?

The theory of the new worship was that on Sunday morning the minister first would recite matins and then the litany in English from the Book of Common Prayer. After that he would continue to read the Holy Communion Service until the Sermon (this was termed the Ante-Communion). After the sermon he would continue with the sacrament if at least twelve people stayed on in Church to receive it, otherwise worship ended with the Sermon.

This worship was very long and frequently lasted over two hours and it is no wonder that few if any stayed to receive the sacrament.

It is true that Thomas Cranmer in compiling the Book of Common Prayer was attempting to simplify things and also to introduce English as the language of worship. He wrote in the *Preface to the Book of Common Prayer:*

And moreover, whereas Saint Paul would have such language spoken to the people in the church as they might understand and have profit by hearing the same, the service in this Church of England (these many years) hath been read in Latin to the people, which they understand not. So that they have heard with their ears only: and their hearts, spirit and mind have not been edified thereby.

Moreover, the number and hardness of the rules, the manifold changings of the service, was the cause that to turn the book was so hard and intricate a matter, that many times there was more business to find out what should be read, than to read it when it was found out.

Although it was the common language the words of the new Service required a scholarship far beyond the capacity of most. Probably it was just as incomprehensible to the honest yeomen and their families as the Latin had been. But the Latin Mass was familiar. The people were used to attending Church to light a candle and say their prayers (and pass on news to each other in whispers) whilst the priest muttered the Mass on their behalf in about half an hour. Now they had to listen to very wordy prayers in English. This did not attract the conservative country folk to the changes.

The Mass brought back

When Queen Mary came to the throne she had Cranmer tried for treason (he had opposed offering the crown to Mary) and heresy. He was burnt at the stake in 1556. Despite this, if Evenlode were typical, there would have been great rejoicing when, under Queen Mary, they were told that things could go back to the way they had been.

There is one set of Churchwardens' accounts in another place that reveal how an entrepreneur made a fortune. He bought up everything cheaply from the church when the law demanded everything be taken out and then he stored it. When Mary became Queen and ordered the restoration he made a huge profit selling everything back to the churchwardens at a high price!

William Farr, like so many of his generation, had to implement the changes and then the restoration. What did the priest and people of Evenlode make of it?

Part of the restoration was that Queen Mary deposed all clergy who had taken the opportunity to marry provided by the reforms of King Edward VI. As indicated above, it may be that William Farr had married, for the Margaret Farr who appears in a later Evenlode document could have been his widow. If William had married Margaret, he would have been deprived of the living of Evenlode.

But then Elizabeth became Queen. Was William still alive? Did he and Margaret return joyfully to the ministry of the parish? There is no way of knowing. At the beginning of Elizabeth's reign there was a huge shortage of clergy and there is no record of an appointment to Evenlode after William Farr until 1610. So either William continued (like the Vicar of Bray) or there was no Rector of Evenlode for a long time.

In Collection Two of the Evenlode Papers it is interesting to read that Margaret Farr, after becoming a widow, bought land that carried with it the "advowson". This means the right to present a priest for the living. It does seem that Margaret Farr wanted to ensure that the next

Rector had the same views as William Farr. It is this that gives substance to the supposition that she had become William Farr's wife.

The Elizabethan settlement

Earlier historians emphasised the great good that came to England from the Reformation. Revisionist historians like Eamon Duffy in his book *The Stripping of the Altars* have spelled out the resentment and resistance expressed in the countryside, the consequent breakdown in popular religion and the drift away from church.

During Elizabeth's reign religion was intensely political and belief was not a private matter. She insisted on one Church for England, and that was the Church of which she was Supreme Governor. Thus the Church of England had both Puritans and Catholics within it (pulling different ways to bring the Church in line either with Geneva or with Rome) whilst outside the Church of England there were refusing Catholics and non-conforming Puritans. These did not attend their parish church on Sundays despite the fine of twelve pence for non-attendance. There is no reason to suppose that Evenlode was spared these disagreements.

Henry Compton, Evenlode and Recusancy

Religion was linked to loyalty to the Queen. Henry Compton did not escape the dilemma.

Queen Elizabeth in rejecting the jurisdiction of Rome forced some of the adherents of the old Faith (the Catholics) into a position where they had to refuse to accept her lead. Hence they were called "recusants" from the Latin verb "recusare" meaning "to refuse". Some of them became militant. Also, in retaining the outward signs of Catholicism in the parish churches, she turned some of the Puritans away, who became militant too.

Henry Compton conformed occasionally by attending the Church of England but nevertheless thought of himself as a member of the old Faith, the members of which now called themselves "Roman" Catholics to identify their difference. He numbered Catholics among his servants. The Jesuit priest, Robert Parsons, lists Henry Compton as one of those he had reconciled to the old Faith. It is unlikely Henry Compton ever attended worship in Saint Edward's Church for he did not live in Evenlode, but he would be aware of the tumult in the minds of his people and his Rector, William Farr, at Evenlode.

The Roman Catholics opened an English College at Rome and also at Douai in 1568. These sent secular and Jesuit priests to this country as missionaries. The missionary priests operated from the big houses that kept to the old Faith. They were pursued as traitors for they owed spiritual allegiance to the Pope. Many of the "Catholic" houses had a "priest hole" constructed to hide them. If caught, they were either exiled or imprisoned. Some imprisoned recusants were hanged to near death then drawn and quartered.

Evenlode House is reputed to have a priest hole. If the space considered a priest hole is indeed one, it would indicate that in these times a Catholic family occupied the house. Such a family usually employed Catholic servants. It was houses such as this that priests visited from time to time and the priest holes were for them to hide in should unwelcome visitors call.

At one time the Catesby family owned Chastleton House (though it seems they may not have resided there). Robert Catesby was one of those arrested in 1605 for the Gunpowder plot during the reign of Queen Elizabeth. It could be that the Catesbys were linked with whoever was living at Evenlode House. (This may explain the rather curious legend that a tunnel joins Chastleton House and Evenlode House. A tunnel is highly improbable, but the suggestion of secret communication is quite plausible.)

However the more likely link is with the Sheldon family who were a staunch Catholic family linked by marriage with some of the premier Catholic families in the north. The papers of Collection Two of the Evenlode Documents record that Ann Jones (nee Rook) had inherited a share in a "quartene" of land in Evenlode. She and her husband Richard gave this land to their daughter (also called Ann) as a marriage dowry when she married a William Sheldon who was a resident of Little Wolford. This land seems to have been in the vicinity of Evenlode House.

The Sheldons were linked with the Ingrams of Little Wolford and this brings the martyrdom of so many Catholic priests and laity during the reign of Elizabeth close to Evenlode.

John Ingram was an undergraduate at New Inn College, Oxford. He was expelled for recusancy. He escaped to the continent and first went to Douai and then to Rome where he was ordained in 1589. He returned as a missionary and worked in Scotland, but it is likely he visited his home in Little Wolford and may very well have visited Evenlode too.

After ministering in Scotland, he had to escape from persecution so he fled over the border to England in disguise. He was arrested at Gateshead, on the other side of the River Tyne from Newcastle. He was tortured but kept silent rather than betray anyone. John Ingram was then executed by being hanged to near death, his innards drawn out and finally his body quartered. This cruel martyrdom was carried out in the last year of Queen Elizabeth's reign.

Henry Compton and Mary Queen of Scots

Henry Compton found himself involved in the trial and execution of Mary Queen of Scots.

Mary had become Queen of Scotland on the death of her father when she was six days old. Her mother, Mary of Guise (who was French), ruled Scotland as regent. She was opposed to the growing control of the Church of Scotland by Presbyterians who followed the theology of the Swiss Protestant pastor John Calvin.

As a child Mary was sent to France to be educated. She was brought up as a Catholic, and as a child was betrothed to the Dauphin. They were married when she was fifteen and he was fourteen. Within a year of their marriage the King of France died and Mary's husband became King Francis II. Mary was now Queen of France by virtue of her marriage as well as Queen of Scotland in her own right.

Sadly her husband died and at eighteen she was widowed. She returned to Scotland without knowing the language or the country. She became involved in murder and matrimonial disaster and then even conformed to the Presbyterianism that had taken over the Church of Scotland to try to hold onto her throne. At which point the Pope disowned her.

In 1568 deprived from being Queen of Scotland she fled to England to throw herself on the mercy of Elizabeth. This was not a good idea as she had consistently argued that because Elizabeth was illegitimate she (Mary) was the rightful heir after Queen Mary to the throne of England. Her grandmother had been King Henry VIII's sister. Elizabeth imprisoned her in a fashion restrained for those days.

There were plots, and rumours of plots against Elizabeth. Some plots (such as the Gunpowder Plot) were set up by Elizabeth's agents to catch Catholics unawares. Mary Queen of Scots was involved in the plotting. She schemed and plotted and eventually Elizabeth brought her to trial.

Baron Henry Compton was summoned to be present at her trial. He was four years older than she was, so of the same generation. *The Victoria County History for Worcestershire* records that he took part as a peer in the trial of Mary Queen of Scots in 1587, and after her execution at Fotheringhay, was one of the four chief attendants at her funeral.

Queen Elizabeth was tough on those she saw as traitors and was infuriated when, after the execution of Mary Queen of Scots, the Armada was launched. In 1588 she rallied the people at Tilbury with her speech, "I know I have the body of a weak and feeble woman; but I have the heart and stomach of a king, and of a king of England too, and think foul scorn that Parma or Spain, or any prince of Europe, should dare to invade the borders of my realm".

The end of the Manorial Court of Evenlode

Courtier though he was, Henry Compton took his duties responsibly as a lord of the manor. He presided over a time of change in the Manorial system.

Evenlode is very lucky in that a description of the Court of the Lord of the Manor has survived and is in Collection Two of the Evenlode Papers. In small parishes such records are rarely found. The Court meets to record the granting by the Lord of the Manor of a tenancy of a farm in Evenlode. The tenancy being recorded was for land and buildings called "Baughtenement" and "Pounsy." "Tenement" is a word still used in legal language. In this document it does not have the same meaning as would be implied today. It originates from the French "tenir" and so "Baugh tenement" means the property once held by Baugh. The origin of the other name "Pounsy" is not clear. The property is the house and curtilage that later was known as Fletcher's Farm.

The full record of the Court reads:

> 10 December 1565. Court Roll of the manor of Evenlode (Henry Compton Esquire, Lord of the Manor).
> Admission of John Carter, on the surrender of Thomas Noke and James Langworth by a warrant dated 20 November 1565, to a messuage and two virgates of land with appurtenances called Baughtenement and other premises called Pounsy in Evenlode, to hold to the aforesaid John Carter and his son Richard and daughter Margaret for the term of their lives and each of them severally, according to the custom of the manor, paying an annual rent of twenty six shillings and eight pence and two capons at the feast of Pentecost, and other dues, customs, heriots and services due and customary by right.
> Carter pays the fine of twenty-six pounds and does fealty and is admitted as tenant.

The document records that two people, Thomas Noke and James Langworth, had held the property. It seems that tenancies ran for a fixed time and the duration of the tenancy was often quite long. Opportunity sometimes was given to renew the tenancy. For whatever reason (and whether voluntarily or not) Thomas Noke and John Langworth were surrendering it back to the Lord of the Manor.

The document shows that the Lord, Henry Compton, was renting this property for "three lives". These were the lives of John Carter, his son Richard, and his daughter Margaret. Such long tenures were clearly designed to enable farmers to develop the land without having to be constantly worried about being evicted. In fact the Carter family stayed on this land beyond this tenancy. William Carter (grandson of John Carter, and presumably son of Richard) bought the property from the Manor. His sale of it to Margaret Garner (Gardner) is recorded in 1651 in Collection Two of the Evenlode Papers.

The tenancy was for a "messuage" which is a house, outbuildings, courtyard and garden. It was also for two "virgates" of land. A virgate is one quarter of a hide so two virgates are one half of a hide. In fact therefore the farm was between thirty and sixty acres. The "appurtenances" are all the tools and equipment belonging to the farm.

In addition to rent in cash and kind, John Carter had to pay all customary "dues, customs, heriots and services". The customary rights referred to were mainly the right of the Lord to hunt on the land and to fish (the latter not relevant to this property) and to assert the authority of the Court of the Manor of Evenlode.

"Heriots" were a form of death duty payable to the Lord. Heriots were usually the dead man's best horse and his best clothes. The concept was already archaic. Heriots had arisen in the days when a farmer would have to go to war and wear armour. The war-horse and armour would be handed to the Lord after his death to be passed to someone else. In fact it is noticeable how archaic this formulation is when compared with John Carter's grandson's purchase of the farm. This later transaction was a deed of conveyance ("Bargain and Sale") with no mention of any "customary dues".

The "fine" seems to be a non-returnable deposit on entry into the use of the house, buildings and land. It is an unexpectedly large sum. It probably indicates that the house (among a number of houses that are the oldest in Evenlode, being dated to the sixteenth century) was at that time (1585) recently built and so quite a desirable residence. Which raises a question as to why Henry Compton as Lord of the Manor had it built. This will be considered later as it forms part of a surprising building boom in Evenlode.

The document concludes by recording that John Carter gave fealty to Henry Compton as his Lord. It was an act of obeisance that had been required of a man to his Lord for many hundreds of years.

This was the end of an era. After the death of Henry Compton, the title of "Lord of the Manor" lived on but by an Act of Parliament dated 1660, the Courts, their liveries, their demands of due customs and duties of a tenant to the Lord, and the elements of knightly service were abolished - except the right of the Lord of the Manor to hunt and fish throughout the land of the Manor.

Photo: The Evenlode Collection

Rich and Poor in Tudor and Stuart Evenlode.

Where the poor lived in the seventeenth century can only be surmised.
Cottages called "Bank Cottages" were built in 1751.
The above terrace replaced them at some time before 1841.

Chapter 7

Rich and Poor
in Tudor and Stuart Evenlode

The rich

Henry Compton died on 10 December 1589 and his son William succeeded to the Lordship of the Manor of Evenlode. In 1616, William became First Earl of Northampton. However by that time he had sold the Manor (in 1601) to John Croker, Gentleman. John Croker paid £1,700 for the whole Manor of Evenlode.

In 1603 John Croker died (about the same time as Queen Elizabeth). John Croker's son, also called John Croker, made a handsome profit of nearly 100% on 15 November 1604 when he sold the Manor to Edward Freeman for £3,200. The building of the first Batsford Hall is attributed to the Croker family and perhaps young John Croker needed money. In this way the Lordship of the Manor passed into the hands of the Freeman family.

Meanwhile, about the beginning of the seventeenth century, as the old Queen died and Charles I came to the throne, Thomas Habington made a survey of Worcestershire, a copy of which is included in Collection Three of the Evenlode Papers. In great flight of fancy he tells of Evenlode:

Emlod boundeth east on Chastleton, west on Bradwell, north on Morton Henmarsh, south on Adelsthrop
And here mee thinckethe I see our shyre as mounted as a Pegasus flyinge over the neyghboringe countyes, and as hee lately crossed Staffordshire, Warwickshyre, and Gloucestershyre so nowe coastinge to the confines of Oxford-shyre hee touchethe that memorable stone devydinge fowre countyes wheare Edmund Ironside, that English Hercules, overthrewe Canutus, the puissant and

worthy Kinge of Denmarke; and thence he caryeth the authority of our county about and over Coteswould, neaver strykinge the earthe but wheare hee produceth a springe w'ch beyond that of Helicon floweth w'th abundance of charity to heaven's eternity, as at Emlode w'ch the Bishop of Worcester dyd before the conquest of England bestowe on the Prior and his mounnckes of Worcester, but Emlode Church wanteth nobilitie of armes; her glory was in heaven.

In this passage there is an example of a growing awareness of the beauty of the English countryside, great loyalty to Worcestershire and a classical education. This would be read and appreciated by the rich.

(The only blot as far as Habington is concerned is that there are no coats of arms on display in Evenlode Church. This needs a word of explanation. It had become the custom for the gentry to have their coats of arms painted on a hatchment for use at their funeral. After the funeral these hatchments were then hung in the church permanently and some churches retain fine examples. The reason why Evenlode Church does not have any may be that at some time they were destroyed. An alternative plausible reason is that the emerging class of small gentry in Evenlode had not climbed sufficiently far up the social ladder to acquire a coat of arms and so merit a hatchment at their funeral. Whatever the reason, Habington bewails the fact that there are none.)

From swearing fealty to conveyancing property

In Henry Compton presiding at the Court of the Manor of Evenlode in 1565, there is an image of medieval Evenlode lingering on. John Carter had to swear fealty to his Lord. In the sale of the Manor by John Croker to Edward Freeman there is an image of a modern world where land is either conveyed upon sale or a tenancy agreement is drawn up. Perhaps it is not mere coincidence that this marks the ascent to the throne of the Stuarts.

The Deed recording the sale of the Manor is included in Collection Two of the Evenlode Papers. It makes interesting reading, giving a picture of some who dwelt at Evenlode during that time:

15th November 1604. Bargain and Sale.

Parties:

1. John Croker of Batsford (Glos). Gentleman.

2. Edward Freeman of Cutson *(Cutsdean)* (Worcs). Gentleman.

Consideration of £3200

Conveyance of the Manor of Evenlode with all rights and appurtenances in the town fields, precincts and parish of Evenlode, which Croker had lately purchased of the Right Hon. William Lord Compton, Lewes Mordant knight, Lord Mordant, Thomas Compton of London and William Atkinson of Inner Temple (sign as witnesses).

The document describes what Edward Freeman now owns as Lord of the Manor, but apart from farm land linked directly with the Manor House, the document notes that the rest of the land in the estate is let out to a number of tenants for periods of time. The tenants pay rent for their house and garden and farm. Though much of the land is unfenced, tenants know exactly what bit belongs to them for they have marked it. Little of this information is written down and Edward Freeman can only verify what is described by word of mouth and common village memories. The document continues:

Excepting to John Croker and his heirs the following:

A house and garden in Evenlode, two parcels of furze, and common of pasture for two beasts, now in the tenure of Margery Malyn.

Lands purchased by John Smith according to a deed of 10 June 1601, on which an annual rent of 13s 4d was reserved.

Lands lately purchased by Elliz Smith (deed of 10 June 1601), on which an annual rent of 32s was reserved.

Lands lately purchased by John Hardman (deed of same date) on which a rent of 10s was reserved.

Lands in the tenure of Joan Bliss, widow, which Margaret Farr purchased with the advowson of the church of Evenlode by a deed of 16 July 1601, with a reserved rent of 1d.

The above rents to be henceforth due to Edward Freeman.

It lists further exceptions:

Lease of part of the premises (ie part of the Estate) to William Freeman of Broadwell for 21 years from 30 January 1595 for a rent of £9.
Another lease to John Gunne for 21 years from 14 April 1595 for a rent of £10.
Another lease to Thomas Dudley for 13 years from 31 Jan 1602 for a rent of £10.
Another lease by John Croker and William Rudhall of Rudhall, Herefordshire to John Hardiman for 12 years from 1 April 1603 for a rent of £8.
An assignment by Croker to Rudhall of 23 Nov 1600 of a lease by Henry, Lord Compton to John Croker deceased (the father of the present John Croker) for a rent of £22.
The above rents to be henceforth due to Edward Freeman for the remainder of their several terms.

Thus it is to be noted that in buying the Manor, the new owner has to accept the continuation of existing leases and the validity of previous sales of land from the estate.

The houses these people occupied are not listed nor the amount of land they farmed so it is not possible to link names with places, unless other information is available. The other primary sources of information are St Edward's Church registers, Wills and the documents of Collection Two of Evenlode Papers.

Social Class

The sixteenth and seventeenth centuries saw wealth dividing society into Nobility (like the Compton family) and Gentlemen (like the Freeman family) who live on the rents and dues they receive from the land and properties they own, though often these are held with long leases by tenants. There are other classes too: Yeomen farmers, Husbandmen and Cottagers. Below them are craftsmen and labourers, and there are the paupers too.

At this time the rich gentry were busy amalgamating manors and exchanging land to create huge estates and hoping to be ennobled (like the Comptons). Wealthy merchants in the cities were gradually becoming great landowners. They acquired titles too and so moved into the ranks of the nobility. From this time on the doings of royalty and the rich gentry rarely affect normal everyday life in Evenlode.

Gentlemen (as opposed to rich gentry) were wealthy to a lesser extent. They bought and sold land. Examples are John Croker and Edward Freeman in the document above. Gentlemen also traded and bought and sold property. They were spoken to as "Mister" followed by their surname. Their families considered themselves "well-bred" as opposed to the yeomen's families. "Squire" originates from a title used by gentlemen. The richer in land or the greater in trade a gentleman became, the more he referred to himself as "Esquire" rather than "Mister," hence "Squire". In Evenlode the word "squire" never came into use.

"Small gentry" is a term used to describe working yeoman farmers with rather more land than others. Having acquired great possessions, they were able to rent some of their land out to others. But also they rented additional land from others to enhance their farm. Small gentry were likely to employ a greater number of men and boys for the land, and women and girls for the household and farmyard, and tended to spend their time supervising.

It is only in the case of John Carter that a record has been discerned of the size of the farm but it may be typical. If this is so, an Evenlode yeoman farmed between thirty to sixty acres and rented enough common land for six cows, three horses and fifty sheep.

The farmers

Some of the farmers of Evenlode in the seventeenth century can be identified.

John Carter became a tenant of what was later to be called Fletchers Farm, in 1565. He died in 1587 and his wife Alice died in 1610. His son Richard Carter then took over the farm. Richard died in 1636 and his son William bought Fletchers from the Manor, but in 1634 it had been let to William Gardner and he continued to farm.

William Gardner died and then his widow Margaret bought Fletchers from William Carter in 1651.

The following also farmed in Evenlode in this period. In some cases their land was scattered over neighbouring parishes and they lived there rather than in Evenlode parish. Two surnames emerged in earlier chapters:

Haynes: It was noted that the Haynes family held land from John and Philippa Petyt. In 1609 William Heynes' death is recorded and he is described as a yeoman. His son Richard farmed until his death in 1632. Thomas Haines was the last member of the Haines family to farm Horn farm. He died in 1765.

Pettyt: Also it was noted earlier that the Pettyt family (blood descendants of the Deyvilles) still farmed in Evenlode even though they lost the Manor after the War of the Roses. John Pettyt died in 1545 and a William Pettie lived in Evenlode until 1605. Pettits still lived in the area in the eighteenth century for one is an executor of Thomas Haines' Will.

The document above reveals these yeomen farmers: William *Freeman* of Broadwell, John *Gunne,* Thomas *Dudley* and John *Hardiman.* William *Gardner* farmed Fletchers after the Carters.

Thomas *Walford* farmed until his death in 1580 and then his son (also Thomas) ran the farm until his death in 1597. His widow died in 1607 and may have continued to farm after her husband's death.

Husbandmen

Husbandmen are a class below that of yeoman farmer. The distinction seems merely to refer to the amount of land farmed. This is a list of identified husbandmen in Evenlode at this time:

Bliss: John Blyssye was a husbandman. He died in 1538. His son John Blisse continued the work until he died in 1598. After his death his wife Joan Bliss continued to hold the land.

Darwen: Richard Darwen was a husbandman who died in 1587. John Derwhen (died 1562) and John Darren (died 1593) may be the same family.

Collett: John Collett was a husbandman (who died in 1566) as was Thomas Collett who died in 1608.

Rooke: The Rooke family were initially husbandmen. Later generations became yeomen and their daughters married into the small gentry in the late seventeenth and eighteenth century. At this time, John Rooke was married to Margaret. He died in 1573 and his widow in 1579. Richard Rock seems to be their son and he was a husbandman who died in 1587. Another Richard Rooke died in 1599. Thomas Rocke died in 1592 and his widow, Margaret Rocke, in 1602. The Rooks long continued in Evenlode.

Grene: Andrew Grene lived in Evenlode until 1583 and John Grune (his son?) died in 1609.

Maunder: Another husbandman was John Maunder who died in 1595 and his widow Joan in 1601.

Andrewes: Husbandman John Andrewes died in 1603.

Cottagers, Tradesmen, labourers and paupers

Cottagers. Only two widows give examples of cottagers, the class below the husbandman.

Malyn: Margaret Malyn had a house and a garden, two small pieces of poor grass land with gorse on it and she rented common land for two cows.

Farr: Margaret Farr bought land but the amount is not stated. As noted above, its ownership gave her the right of presentation of a priest as rector. This right cost her a rent of one penny a year.

Craftsmen, labourers and paupers do not appear in Deeds nor make Wills, but make up ninety per cent of the population of England at this time. With a number of cottagers and husbandmen living in Evenlode the percentage may not be so high, but it is reasonable to surmise that three quarters of the population of Evenlode would be members of labouring or craftsmen's families then as later.

Labourers and Craftsmen do not fit into the class structure above though it is possible for a labourer to rent land and move up to being a farmer just as it is possible for a craftsman to do the same. For example at this time the *Rooke* family were husbandmen but in 1756, William Rooke was described as a Gentleman. The *Fletcher* family was an example of craftsmen doing the same. The Fletchers in these years provided the village blacksmith, then moved into landownership and eventually became small gentry.

It is fascinating to read in the documents that Evenlode had a man who called himself a "falconer." He was William *Paxford*.

Only one labourer can be identified. His name was John *Rushall*. Other surnames are recorded in the parish registers. They are presumably the names of agricultural labourers's families.

Archer, Bartlet, Bramsgrove, Buntting, Freebury, Harris, Higgins, Humphreys, Hythe(Hyde), Keyte, Meadonsbury, Parret, Perrin, Robins, Slye, Smythe, Williams, White.

Agricultural work in late Tudor times

Farm work was gruelling and never-ending. There was a regular routine of ploughing, sowing, reaping, threshing and grinding. The horses had to be cared for. Cattle and sheep had to be tended and herded and cared for especially at times of calving and lambing. Animals had to be killed at the onset of winter and salted down for future use. There is also a regular round of shearing for the men and boys then spinning and weaving for the women and girls.

There were the daily tasks of milking and churning into cheese and butter. The poultry and pigs had to be fed and the eggs collected. The vegetables had to be tended and then harvested, as had the fruit. There was bottling and preserving to do. Beer had to be brewed.

What could be sold had to be, for always before them was the need to pay taxes, tithes and rent.

Market days at Moreton and Stow and local fairs brought breaks, Harvest and Christmas and Weddings gave opportunities for great celebrations.

Farming occupied the whole family's routine, though the amount and nature of the tasks each member had to do varied in accordance with the wealth and status of the head of the family.

Gentlemen lived in mansions, and supervised the farming of their own farms. They looked after their tenants, and received the rents they paid. Yeomen farmers had a fine house with a yard and barns and a garden and probably an orchard. Husbandmen and Cottagers had some land and a cottage with a downstairs room, perhaps an outhouse too, and two bedrooms, perhaps with an attic. Labourers' cottages were "one up and one down". All houses, even the labourers' cottages, had at least a small garden for poultry and vegetables and a pig.

The homes of the rich

Towards the end of the reign of Queen Elizabeth, and in the time of King Charles I, the families of the small gentry began to intermarry across wide swathes of the country and linked with the greater landowners in ties of loyalty and mutual support. Burying the dead brought them all into regular contact with each other. This network became exceedingly significant in the ordering of life over a county.

These county families vied with each other over their houses. The richer had large mansions with a great emphasis on a lovely garden and orchards. The less rich among the small gentry nevertheless abandoned the old houses to build new stone ones often with ornamentation.

Henry Compton, speculative builder
The fine stone houses of Evenlode

The houses of these richer families in earlier times in Evenlode had been typical of many parts of the country. The wooden frame was erected using trees felled locally and the spaces filled in with rubble. Inside the rooms were plastered with lime mortar mixed with cow hair to give strength. Roofs were thatched and attracted nesting birds. The whole structure was a haven for small mammals. These caused both damage and distress.

The initial building or re-building of all the larger houses in stone in Evenlode is dated to the sixteenth century. It is likely that the person responsible was the earlier Lord of the Manor, Henry Compton (who held the lordship between 1546 – 89).

There are several reasons why these houses should have been built or re-built in stone at that time. The first is the obvious one that the houses then existing being timber framed were old and ready for replacement. The second reason is that Evenlode was part of a much larger estate owned by the Compton family and it needed to make money for the family. By re-building the farmhouses for his tenants Henry Compton was able to re-let the tenancy at a hefty fine, as is illustrated above in the document relating to the letting of a house and farm to John Carter. Finally, in the middle of Queen Elizabeth's reign, for reasons connected with the war at sea with Spain, and with the profitable buying and selling of former monastic lands, and the emergence of a wealthy middle class, it was fashionable to re-build.

Henry Compton needed money. He was a courtier all his life and required a high income to support such a life-style. Making money out of his manors was a major way of achieving this. Building anew in stone he presumably judged was both profitable in terms of income from rents but also a wise investment for new houses would need less maintenance by the landlord.

His sixteenth century building activities have preserved a very interesting feature of Evenlode. The fine stone sixteenth century houses in the village of Evenlode reflect the times when a gentleman farmer rented a piece here, owned a lot there, ploughed a few strips in one area, and used common land and woodland in other parts. Very little of this was joined up. So the houses grouped together in a village and all the paths, bridleways and lanes lead out (as they still do) to the land.

It was with the Evenlode Enclosure Act of 1756 (that required the erection of fences across land and roads to be made) that farmland was collected together into cohesive areas. As a consequence, farmhouses after 1756 tended to be built where the farmland was. There are examples dotted round Evenlode where this is the case although some outlying farms such as Horn Farm and Heath End Farm pre-date this.

Both the *Victoria County History* and the Cotswold section of *The Buildings of England* written by David Verey and Alan Brooks list some of Evenlode's sixteenth century properties. The names given below are listed in these sources. The modern name is used, for the houses were initially identified only by the owner's or the tenant's name.

In *Manor Farm,* the west of the present house was the kitchen of the sixteenth century Manor House that preceded it. Only this part was retained in the re-construction of the eighteenth century. This re-construction included a noteworthy cantilever staircase.

The Poplars is dated to the sixteenth century. Some of the stone mullioned windows are original. Later in the sixteenth century, additions were made to the south.

Home Farm is similarly dated. The stone mullioned windows are original.

The original part of *Evenlode House* is dated to the middle of the sixteenth century with seventeenth century additions. It may have been rented about 1641 on a 99 years lease to Edward Poer, a Gentleman of Worcester, because the lease seems to have run out in 1740. By then, William Bricknell occupied the house. However, the lease may have commenced in 1671 (or renewed in that year).

Evencourt is mentioned in the *Victoria County History* as "a good example of a small sixteenth century house". The original character of the house is retained in the oldest part.

Most of the properties above and others have become sought after gentlemen's residences today.

The fine stone houses that Henry Compton built, the expansive farmland and the wide drovers' lanes, the well-bred society of the small gentry, and later the spectacle of the hunt, create a picture that is quintessentially English. Thomas Habington sensed this when he wrote his description of Evenlode. This picture gradually unfolds throughout the seventeenth century and the eighteenth centuries, making Evenlode a typical English village.

The Freeman family, the Manor House and Evenlode Park

The feudal rights of a lord of a manor were disappearing. With their disappearance the link between ownership of a manor and the title of "lord of the manor" begins to be loosened. Earlier in this chapter it was noted that in 1605 Edward Freeman bought the manor and the land and with it came the title of "lord of the manor". Later the Freemans will sell the Manor but the title "Lord of the Manor" will stay with the family and ultimately become a thing to be sold at will.

Edward Freeman was a member of the Freeman family of Batsford and other places in the area around. The Freeman family was numbered among the gentry and the county families. Their history is recorded in several entries in the *Victoria County History*. Edward's grandfather William Freeman (unlikely to be the William Freeman of

Broadwell who rented land in Evenlode at the time Edward became Lord of the Manor) had bought the Manor of Cutsdean in 1542. The Prior of Worcester had held the Manor of Cutsdean but at the time of the dissolution King Henry VIII gave the Manor to Richard Andrews. Richard Andrews then promptly sold it to William Freeman.

William Freeman held other property and settled the Manor of Cutsdean on his son John when John married Joan Bonner.

John and Joan had a son called Thomas. John Freeman died and John's father, William Freeman, tried to take the Manor of Cutsdean back. The widow Joan Freeman, on behalf of her son Thomas, took the case to the Court of Chancery and won.

By 1582 Thomas Freeman had married and had a son called Edward. He and his wife and his surviving mother (who seems to have retained an interest in Cutsdean) leased the Manor of Cutsdean in that year to Robert Ashfield and Francis Kettleby.

Thomas and his wife and family seemed to have removed to Bourton-on-the-Hill where his second son (another Thomas) was baptised in the church in 1590.

This younger son, Thomas Freeman, went to Magadalen College, Oxford in 1607. He graduated in 1611. After graduation he went to live in London where he wrote two volumes of epigrams. These he dedicated to Thomas, Lord Windsor. They included anti-puritan satire, catalogues of contemporary sins, and tributes to Shakespeare, Spenser, Donne and others. His work was published in 1614 in which year he died.

In 1604 the older son Edward Freeman (now married to Catherine Coningsby) rented or sold the Manor of Cutsdean to his brother in law, Humphrey Coningsby. As noted above he then purchased the Manor of Evenlode for his wife and himself in 1605. The Manor included the Manor House and the Manor farm and most of the other properties in the parish.

It seems probable that Edward and Catherine re-structured the Manor House at Evenlode to be their home. They are likely people to have built the very fashionable cantilever staircase in the house. However there are no records of any of their family in the Evenlode parish registers. This could be explained by their links with Bourton-on-the-Hill, but the absence of entries indicates that their residence in Evenlode Manor House may only be assumed.

Evenlode Manor House had a lovely setting looking south. To the west, unfenced meadow stretched down to the river (without of course any sign of a railway) and over to open countryside. The Freemans may have intended to create an Evenlode Park (as was the custom then) from some of the land of the Manor Farm. The evidence for this is that the field to the south of the Manor House still bears the name, "The Park", and the iron railings suggest this too.

To the west of the house and along the river is a field called Mill Pound (sometimes Mill Holme). This indicates the site of the mill that is known to have existed in Tudor times. Like the Manor House itself, the strong argument of continuity of use suggests that this mill would be on the site of the mill mentioned in Domesday Book. Although the course of the river may have changed over the centuries there is clear evidence of other channels now virtually filled in and a rectangular area of reed (next to the railway line) and other suggestive features that may relate to the workings of the mill.

However the mill ceased to operate in those times, and it is possible this was because Edward and Catherine cleared it away. There must have been a lane to the mill used by the people. Therefore they would have walked past the Manor House. This may have given offence to the occupants of the Manor. To remove the mill would remove any reason for the people to journey to the mill by a lane to the north of the house. Such a closure would create private space to suit the leisure of the Lords of the Manor and their Ladies and families.

In 1622 Edward and Catherine's son, Coningsby Freeman, married Beatrice. Edward handed over the estate to them though he retained oversight. By 1631 Edward must have died for Coningsby succeeded his father as Lord of the Manor.

Coningsby and Beatrice had four children. Unfortunately Coningsby died in 1639 and left Beatrice a widow. Their son (who is called Thomas in some sources and Edward in others) seems to have died young.

By the time of the death of Coningsby Freeman their daughter Joyce had married Thomas Owen, who farmed in Evenlode.

Their daughters, Elianor and Ursula inherited the Manor of Evenlode. Neither daughter lived in the Manor House. Elianor married Mr Lawrence, a gentleman of Cricklade.

Ursula married Edward Poer, a gentleman of Worcester. In 1641 (or 1671), he took a 99 years lease on Evenlode House and two yardlands in Evenlode as noted above. This land was mainly to the west of the house and seems to have been laid out as a small park.

Remaining trees indicate this and the deeds of Holly Tree House reveal that the area was originally known as "the garden".

As neither daughter intended to reside in the Manor House the Manor Farm was divided into two farms and rented out with the Manor House and other buildings.

In addition to the Manor Farm, the inheritance included the following properties occupied by tenants.

Seven messuages
(house, garden, ancillary buildings and land)
Seven cottages and seven gardens
A dovecote
200 acres of arable land
100 acres of meadow
200 acres of pasture
200 acres of heath

The details are in Collection Two of the Evenlode Documents and the story will be told in full later.

The vision of a Park around the Manor House of Evenlode never materialised, and by 1701 all the land had been sold either to farmers or to landowners who rented the farms and holdings to tenants.

The ordinary people of Evenlode

Whilst the small gentry and the Lord of the Manor lived in these fine stone houses the people still lived in small cottages. It may be that brick or rubble infill had replaced mud and wattle, but they were still lacking in basic facilities.

Life was still hard for agricultural labourers in late Tudor times. From mid-March to mid-September work began at five in the morning and finished not before seven in the evening, with two short meal breaks. In the winter work began at the first signs of light and continued until it was too dark to see. Labourers earned three pennies a day. Tradesmen earned about six pennies a day.

The children worked too. Their tasks were to pick up stones and carry them to the end of the furrow. They also guarded the sheep and the geese, with older boys herding the cattle. Small children were employed scaring birds away at seedtime.

Women and girls were employed in domestic chores and in milking.

However there was an opportunity to earn a little extra, killing vermin. An Act of Parliament in the reign of Queen Elizabeth enabled Churchwardens to levy a Rate to raise money to pay for vermin caught. The rewards in other places were as follows for there is no record of what happened at Evenlode. It may be assumed that in Evenlode, the rewards were the same as elsewhere. The list is taken from John Campbell-Kease' book, *A companion to local history research.*

Heads of rooks, crows and the like: 1 penny for three
Heads of owls: 1 penny for six
Unbroken eggs of the above: 1 penny for six
Hedgehogs: 10 pence each
Polecats: 4 pence each
Foxes and stoats: 9 pence each

Work was six days per week, but in some places the children had a respite on Saturday afternoons (if the Rector was resident) for, when he was, it was customary to summon the children to church a couple of hours before sunset for catechism lessons. The children were taught the Our Father, the Creed and the Ten Commandments, and the answers to the Catechism questions. Some enlightened clergy took the opportunity to teach the children how to read and perhaps write their names. In other places, perhaps more usually, this took place on Sunday afternoons.

The Civil Parish and the People

During the latter part of the reign of Queen Elizabeth, the Shires evolved into a county administrative system, but the Hundreds became less important except in relation to the Courts. The local administration of society was based on the civil parish. In most cases (as was the case with Evenlode) the civil and the ecclesiastical parishes were almost identical.

The churchwardens were given extra duties. It was the duty of the churchwardens to see to the property and finances of the parish church and report to the Archdeacon or Bishop, but by several Acts of Parliament in the reign of Queen Elizabeth they took on additional duties. It was their task to call together a number of the leading men among the people to choose three parish officers. This gathering of the leading men became the Vestry Meeting. It also dealt with village matters and fixed rates.

The first of the parish officers to be appointed was the *Parish Constable* whose task was to enforce the Law. It is interesting to note the assumption that it is the ordinary people who need to be made to keep the law. It is equally assumed that the gentry kept it without any accountability to anyone. The constables were first linked with the Hundreds but by the seventeenth century parish constables were becoming more usual. After 1617 the choice of parish constable was transferred from the Churchwardens and the people to the Magistrates of the County, though this seems not to have happened in Evenlode. Its isolation from the rest of the county of Worcester probably explains this.

The 1555 Highways Act required the appointment of a *Surveyor of the Highways* for each parish. This was an unpaid post. The task was to order the people to carry stones to mend potholes in roads and fords leading from their village to the neighbouring market towns. At Evenlode the Vestry Meetings continued throughout the nineteenth century to appoint a Surveyor, later, two Surveyors.

From 1572 the Churchwardens and the people had to appoint an *Overseer of the Poor*. The Overseer of the Poor had to work out how much money was needed in the parish to care for its poor. He then had authority to levy a "poor rate" to raise this money. He had to distribute alms and supervise the "poor house".

There is no indication when Evenlode acquired a poor house. These were Alms Houses. However an Archdeaon's Report dated some time after 1808 states that at Evenlode "the poor house is in good repair" so at some stage one was built or obtained by the churchwardens and the overseer of the poor. There is no indication where it was.

The eighteenth century parish registers refer from time to burials of a "poor widow", where the adjective seems to mean poverty rather than a word to induce sympathy. There are also occasional references to the burial of "paupers". These were often tiny children whose parents (presumably) had no means to pay for the burial.

The poor of Evenlode

The "poor" that the parish assisted from the "poor rate" (and charitable bequests) were the elderly and the infirm who had no living relatives. The parish also helped families in difficulties (because of lack of work or changing circumstances). In Evenlode, poor relief later took the form of coal for the winter. The poor house was for frail and elderly widows and spinsters (occasionally elderly couples) with no family to support them. Rarely would families be offered this. All these were considered the "deserving poor".

The parish did not care for any of the "undeserving poor". In the latter part of Elizabeth's reign there was a population explosion and a series of disastrous famines. As a result there was quick growth in an underclass of highwaymen, pickpockets, migrants and beggars. These were found mainly in the towns but sometimes they roamed the countryside looking for what they could beg or steal. The "poor rate" and Charities were designed to help the "deserving poor" not these people who were designated the "undeserving poor". One of the main duties of the Parish Constable was to escort these unwanted beggars and the like across the parish boundary.

In Evenlode, people knew who their own poor were and they administered the Evenlode Charities and paid the poor rate that was levied. Disputes could arise however so rules were drawn up to define who could potentially belong to the "deserving poor" should the need arise. Basically the rules defined who was "legally settled" in a village. Only someone legally settled would receive relief.

Poor people born in the village of legally settled parents were eligible as was a woman (and her children) who had come to live in the village as the wife of a man who was a legally settled resident. The same applied to those who had served an apprenticeship in the village and labourers who had been taken on for 365 days at the Michaelmas (October) hirings. A person was also eligible if he or she rented a property in the village that was worth £10 per annum. Also considered legally settled were people who came to live in the village because they had been appointed parish officers.

Others who came to live in the village were accepted as legally settled after they had lived there for three years, but after 1662 the Law allowed the village to prevent such settlement. It allowed the villagers to evict newcomers during the first forty days of living in the place. After 1691 this was made a little more civilised in that potential new settlers had to give forty days notice before moving in, during which the villagers could decide whether they wanted them or not!

Often someone leaving a village where he or she was legally settled (for example, to look for work) sought a "certificate of legal settlement". Such a person could show this at a new village where there was work and be allowed to reside there. This was allowed because such a person could be sent back to the village from which he or she had come, if they became poor. The receiving village would then have no responsibility for that person.

The intention of all this was to keep the poor rate as low as possible. This was always a good selling point to potential owners of land or property. A nineteenth century "Notice of Sale by Auction" of Davis's farm (now Poplars) drew attention to the attraction of a low poor rate.

This raises the question of who cared for this underclass of "undeserving poor"? Until King Henry VIII closed down the monasteries and the convents the monks and nuns cared for them. They were given a "dole" at mid-morning and evening, of a hunk of bread and a small flagon of ale. After the dissolution of the monasteries it seems nobody cared for them, although some of the very big estates (particularly those that held to the Old Faith) continued the practice of "dole" for those who were Catholics.

Photo: Susan Medhurst

Evenlode House

The priest hole and the link with recusancy and Chastleton House indicate support for the Royalist cause in Evenlode. The priest hole is hidden behind the fireplace in the room to the right of the door.

Chapter 8

By the sword divided (1603–62)

Roundheads and Cavaliers

Habington (quoted at the beginning of the last chapter) stretches the imagination in his flowery description of Worcestershire. He envisages Worcestershire flying like Pegasus to embrace land within its boundaries, but his dream-like look at the county does not herald the time of political division that arose during the reign of King Charles and the subsequent Civil War and Commonwealth.

During these times of turmoil, Edward Freeman was Lord of the Manor of Evenlode and then Coningsby Freeman.

As may be read elsewhere, the Civil War was about government and religion. It was the final struggle between the feudal concept of the King as the anointed of God with all authority (and the Church mirroring this) and the protestant view that every man is equal in the eyes of God (and therefore needs no bishop or priest but simply the Bible).

It was further complicated in that King James I and his son King Charles I were not only kings of England and Wales but also kings of Scotland (which had a separate administration, organisation and law as well as a Church that had become Presbyterian). Moreover, they were kings of Ireland (which also had a separate Parliament and a people that were predominantly Roman Catholic).

In brief, in 1603 Elizabeth died and was succeeded by King James VI of Scotland who became King James I. He reigned until 1625 when his son Charles became King Charles I.

The Stuarts believed in the divine right of kings and so acted as if this right gave them authority to rule and make political decisions. Their dilemma was that the Stuarts needed Parliament to pass laws to raise taxes, and the Puritans believed authority lay with the people by way of parliamentary rule. The scene was set for division.

Both King James and King Charles were dedicated to the Church of England. Charles believed that the Elizabethan Church of England (which kept its Catholic heritage yet accepted the need for reform of a number of controversial issues) was a good model for both countries. This gave great encouragement to those Church of England theologians who were busy creating a theology of the "middle way". These "Caroline Divines" saw this middle way expressed in an Anglicanism that was both Catholic and reformed.

A key figure emerged in William Laud, Archbishop of Canterbury from 1633 to 10 January 1645, when he was executed on Tower hill. Laud was High Church. He wanted a uniform Church of England. He insisted on the restoration in all churches of altars, crosses, candles, copes and communion rails. Under his leadership as Archbishop of Canterbury, new canons (church laws) for the Church were published requiring the re-introduction of these things. He was a firm supporter of the bishops and of the King and the Prayer Book. He was resisted by puritan clergy in the Church of England but welcomed by royalists who favoured the order and calm of the Prayer Book.

King Charles insisted that Scotland adopt the Prayer Book and accept Bishops, and follow Laud's lead so that the nations could be united in religion. A number of Scots people accepted the king's view and bishops were appointed, even though the Scottish Church was Presbyterian.

The majority of the Scots bitterly resisted this and took up arms. They were supported by the puritans in England, for these wanted the Church of England to become Presbyterian like the Scottish Church, and dismiss the bishops. In 1638 the Synod of Scotland produced a "National Covenant" in defence of Presbyterianism. Some notable Scottish people opposed this. Among them was the saintly Bishop Forbes of Aberdeen. In 1639 war broke out (the First Bishops War) between the King and Scotland.

Peace was patched up but in 1640 William Laud (Archbishop of Canterbury) published his canons as described above. The Scottish people declared them to be "popery" and Scotland's Parliament retaliated by abolishing the Book of Common Prayer and evicting the Bishops. The Second Bishops War resulted in Scotland in 1640.

King Charles very reluctantly recalled the English Parliament to raise taxes to support his fight against Scotland but the English Parliament was mainly puritan. When it met, it demanded submission to its will from the King, or no money. The King in great anger had to agree to the impeachment of William Laud and of his Chief Adviser (William Wentworth, Lord Stafford). In 1641 Parliament dismissed the Bishops and had Lord Stafford executed.

In Ireland King Charles had given "graces" to the Roman Catholic people to practice their religion without persecution. So they were Royalists. The Anglo-Irish nobility (who were Church of Ireland with the Book of Common Prayer and Bishops) were all Royalists too. The Roman Catholic people, the Anglo-Irish nobility and the Church of Ireland feared persecution by the puritans so they rebelled against the English Parliament and what it was doing.

In 1642 King Charles had had enough and entered the English Parliament in order to have five MPs arrested. Parliament was outraged at this flaunting of their privilege and voted to raise an army of its own.

The Queen went to France to seek help and King Charles raised his Standard in Nottingham on 22 August 1642. He called in the county families to provide officers and men. He also paid some professional soldiers to manage the war. The bulk of his foot soldiers were village labourers drawn in by their Squire or volunteers looking for rich pickings, but he had some brilliant officers.

The puritans also called in professional soldiers and a number of members of the county families joined them too, as well as riff-raff from London. As is well known many county families were "by the sword divided".

The raising of the King's Standard in Nottingham began the Civil War. Most of the nobility rallied to Charles, both Church of England (in the style Laud wished it to be that is, "High Church") and those who were recusants committed to the Old Faith.

The effect the Civil War had on Evenlode can be glimpsed in several events.

A divided Church: Gervaise Kecke,
Rector of Evenlode from 1626
and Ralph Neville, Puritan Minister of Evenlode

The first effect was that Evenlode had a divided church. In 1610 there had been a vacancy in the bishopric of Worcester and in the absence of a bishop the appointment of a rector for Evenlode had fallen to the crown. King James I was king and he appointed as Rector, William Holme. We know nothing about him but as the king appointed him, he probably followed the king in matters of religion.

In 1636 Gervaise Kecke was appointed Rector of Evenlode. A little more is known about him, for he faced the puritan attempt to change the Church of England into a Presbyterian Church. From the fact that he refused to comply it may be assumed that he was a follower of William Laud and the King, and so was a High Churchman.

The Kecke family seem to have originated in the Netherlands although there are Keckes in Wurtzenburg in Germany. The first immigrant was probably Johannes Kecke, whose name appears on a memorial in Marston Sicca (Long Marston) Church in Warwickshire (then in Gloucestershire). Other Keckes included Elizabeth and Thomas Kecke who were involved in a dispute over the manors of Bothamsall and Upton. The Kecke family also feature in law at the Middle Temple.

Gervaise Kecke was the son of John Kecke of Marston Sicca (Long Marston). The entry in Oxford University's *Alumni* reads:

Jervis Kecke, son of John Kecke of Marston Sicca in the County of Gloucestershire, plebian. Magdalen Hall. Matriculated 31 October 1623 aged 20. BA from New Inn Hall 27 January 1628/9. MA July 1633. Rector of Evenlode and Flyford Flavell in the County of Worcestershire 1662.

As Gervaise Kecke graduated from New Inn Hall, Oxford in 1628-9, and was made deacon in the same year he must have been a curate elsewhere. He became Rector of Evenlode in 1636. It may be assumed that Gervaise Kecke re-introduced further ornamentation into Evenlode Church as Archbishop William Laud advocated.

He was shaken in his pastoral care and shocked when in 1643 the English Parliament made their "Solemn League and Covenant" with the Scots and demanded that all clergy of the Church of England sign the declaration:

> that we shall all and each of us sincerely....endeavour the preservation of the true Protestant reformed religion in the Church of Scotland in doctrine, worship, discipline and government and the reformation of religion in the Church of England, according to the Word of God and the example of the best reformed churches.....

Kecke refused to sign. After the King's surrender in 1646 he and thousands of other clergy of the Church of England were deprived of their livings.

The implication of this declaration for the people of Evenlode must have been a shock. The puritans banned wedding rings as "popery." There could be no prayers for the dead for this too was "popery." In church the font was not to be used for christenings for these had to be performed in front of the people. The altar table had to be put in the middle of the church with no flowers, cross or candles. The communion rails had to be dismantled because they were "papistical". No Saints Days were to be kept, and neither Christmas nor other Feast Days. The minister was not to use any ecclesiastical garments. Bowing and kneeling were both forbidden as they were thought to encourage idolatrous respect for objects.

Evenlode refused to accept Gervaise Kecke's deprivation and apparently continued to pay their tithes to him. In 1647 a puritan Preacher was appointed as Parish Minister for Evenlode. His name was Ralph Neville. There is no record of him being ordained and in fact the Oxford record of alumni does not acknowledge that he is Rector of Evenlode until 1661, when he must have eventually received ordination from the bishop. His entry reads:

Ralph Nevill BA Merton College 1629 MA I July 1633 (son of Edward Nevill of Collom Berks, sometime of Sunninghill), Rector of Evenlode, County of Worcestershire, 1661.

As noted above Ralph Neville was refused the tithes and Evenlode continued to pay them to Gervaise Kecke. On 23 August 1660 Ralph Neville attempted to secure a "Decision" in the House of Lords to force Gervaise Kecke to hand them over. Part of this reads as follows. It seems that Parliament ordered the Sheriff of Worcestershire to collect the tithes until it be agreed to whom they belonged, Gervaise Kecke or Ralph Neville.

Upon reading the Petition of Mr Ralph Nevill, Clerk, Minister of Evenlode, in the County of Worcester; It is ordered, by the Lords in Parliament assembled, that the Petitioner giving Security by Bond to the Sheriff of the said County, who is to take Security in the names of Jervice Keck, to be responsible for the tithes of the said Parish of Evenlode if the trial shall go against him, that then the said Ralph Nevill is hereby empowered to receive into his custody this Summer's Tithes, Glebe and Profits; and the said Bond, so taken, shall remain in the Sheriff's hands, until it shall appear to whom the Right doth properly belong.

By this matter of the tithes, Evenlode in its own quiet way was affirming its loyalty to the King and the Church. After the Restoration of the King, Gervaise Kecke was preferred to the living of Flyford Flavell thus allowing Ralph Neville to become undisputed Rector of Evenlode. Ralph Neville had come as a puritan Preacher. He arrived in Evenlode as a young man, and a "Minister" full of enthusiasm for the Puritan cause. After the Restoration, he was ordained episcopally and conformed to the Church of England. There is no record that he ever received the tithes until that point.

There is one interesting episode in Evenlode's story from Ralph Neville's time as a Minister. There was a growth of quite odd little sects among the puritans. Often these consisted of one or two itinerant preachers with a handful of followers. One of these preachers was a man called Richard Coppin.

Richard Coppin had left the Established Church in disgust because of the careless lives of clergy and the casual way of taking services that he observed. He was delighted at the suppression of the Bishops and attached himself to the puritans who were advocating Scottish Presbyterianism. He then left them and joined the

Independents (who formed the Congregationalists in 1662). He then left them and joined the Baptists. In 1648 he claimed he had an "inward experience" during which he was commissioned to preach to everyone. His preaching caused great arguments in Berkshire where he was at the time and he was arrested for heresy and bound over to keep the peace. So he started writing and publishing books. By 1651 he was living in Burford.

The parishioners of Evenlode (to Ralph Neville's surprise) invited him to stay for a few days and preach for four successive evenings in the Church. Ralph Neville eventually acquiesced in this, but when he listened to Richard Coppin preaching that there was no heaven and no hell, he was horrified and as quickly as possible got a warrant to have him arrested for blasphemy.

Richard Coppin was tried at Worcester on 23 March 1652 and found guilty. He was then taken to the Oxford assizes and tried on 10 March 1653 and again found to be guilty. He was bound over to keep the peace. A year later on 19 March 1654 he was preaching in Stow-on-the-Wold. He kept preaching and writing book after book until 1659. Then no more is heard of him.

Divided in Battle: Spencer Compton, Royalist hero

The second effect of the Civil War in Evenlode was that there was much to talk about.

Although the Comptons had not held the manor since they sold it in 1601 there would be a number of elderly residents of Evenlode who would be pleased to hear and to re-tell the story of the heroism of a grandson of Henry Compton, once Lord of the Manor of Evenlode.

Spencer Compton was the grandson of Henry Compton who was Lord during most of the reign of Queen Elizabeth. He was educated as a soldier and had taken part in many continental battles. Henry's son William had been made First Earl of Northampton and Spencer Compton inherited the Earldom on the death of his father.

When the King raised his Standard, Spencer Compton, Earl of Northampton, joined him. It was in March 1643.

He was sent to Banbury to lead troops to relieve the Royalist forces at Lichfield but finding he was too late he turned to assist at Stafford. He met up with two Parliamentary Leaders, Brereton and

Gell at a place called Hopton Heath. Spencer Compton used his dragoons and cannon to good effect and the next day the Royalists discovered that the Parliamentarians had fled during the night. However Spencer Compton was killed during one of the cavalry charges. It is said that when he was given the opportunity to surrender he replied, "I take no quarter from base rogues and rebels as you are". The full story is found on the website of *The Sealed Knot Society.*

No doubt among the Evenlode folk the tale gained in the telling for it was as if they were there with the grandson of their old Lord of the Manor.

The London "Trained Bands"

Another tale to be told was of an event in the summer of the same year, 1643. The Royalists had shown initial success in the war and had taken control of most of the cities of the north and the west. The one exception was Gloucester, held by the Parliamentarians but besieged by Royalist forces.

The Parliamentarians decided to relieve this siege. Robert Devereux, Earl of Essex (one of the minority of the nobility who sided with Parliament) was instructed to march the "trained bands" of Londoners to the aid of Gloucester. These trained bands amounted to five regiments of foot soldiers. They were marched from London to Oxford then from Oxford to Chipping Norton. From Chipping Norton they took the ancient route to Stow and on to Gloucester. The weather was foul and the men were hungry, wet, cold and miserable.

In those days the road to Stow passed much nearer to Adlestrop than it does now. (It was diverted so that the Leighs could enclose their Park.) It can be discerned near the cricket ground, and the access roads to the railway station were the old road to the ford over the River Evenlode. They arrived at Adlestrop and were quartered there for the night. They probably camped in the meadows on both sides of the river. They may have been perfectly well behaved but the army quartermasters were very efficient at finding food. It may be that the farmers of Evenlode lost cattle and sheep to the spit that night, and many of the young Evenlode boys would have risked a beating to see the sight of such a large army encamped so near their homes.

The London regiments reached Gloucester on 5 September but the Royalists had withdrawn the day before. There was no food to be had. So the five regiments were turned round and marched back to London by way of Newbury. The Royalist forces harried them and some rode ahead and captured all the supplies. The London regiments therefore arrived back in London starving and exhausted, but were greeted like heroes.

Sir Joseph Astley

The Civil War created tales for telling and among the people of Evenlode the heroism of Spencer Compton would be remembered and the night the Parliamentarians camped at Adlestrop too. They would also re-tell the prophetic words of Sir Joseph Astley. This is his story.

In 1644 the Royalists had been beaten at the battle of Marston Moor and in 1645 Cromwell's New Model Army was ready. It was a devastating war machine compared with the daring young Cavalier squires charging on their hunting horses with swords flashing. By 1645 the Model Army had almost wiped out the Royalist forces and the king fled from the disastrous Battle of Naseby north for succour to Scotland, where he received none. There he was arrested and handed over to Parliament.

There was an attempt to rally the Royalist cause at Oxford. Sir Joseph Astley was marching there with two thousand untrained Welshmen with him when he met up with Parliamentarians at Donnington near Stow. The Welsh were beaten. At the end of the battle, Sir Joseph, who was elderly, was given a drum to sit on. He said, "Gentlemen, ye may now sit and play, for you have done all your works, if you fall not out among yourselves".

Their works were not all done. The New Model Army refused to disband on Parliament's order. A prisoner of Parliament King Charles sent a communication inviting the people of his Scottish kingdom to invade England and come to his rescue.

The Scots invaded in 1648 led by Scottish and English Royalist nobles but the organisation was disastrous. At one point the men were strung out along sixteen miles of road from Preston down to Wigan. The New Model Army attacked at Preston and was completely victorious. It demanded that Parliament put the king on trial and Parliament succumbed.

King Charles was executed on 30 January 1649. From the scaffold he proclaimed,

> I declare before you all, that I die a Christian, according to the profession of the Church of England, as I found it left me by my father, and this honest man I think will witness it. I have a good cause, and a gracious God on my side. I go from a corruptible crown to an incorruptible crown, where no disturbance can be, no disturbance in the world.

Some saw in him a self-willed man who would not bend with the times, but there were those who saw him as a martyr because he was executed for his beliefs.

But Sir Joseph was right. The puritans fell out with each other. Cromwell became completely frustrated by Parliament. On the 20 April 1653 he attended Parliament and addressed them all:

> Ye are grown intolerably odious to the whole nation; you were deputed here by the people to get grievances redress'd, and are yourselves become the greatest grievance. Your country therefore calls me to cleanse this Augean stable, by putting a final period to your iniquitous proceedings in this House; and which by God's help, and the strength he has given me, I am now come to do; I command ye therefore, upon the peril of your lives, to depart immediately out of this place, go, get you out! Make haste! Ye venal slaves be gone! Take away that shining bauble (*the mace*) and lock up the doors. In the name of God, go.

Cromwell ruled alone as if he had the Divine Authority he had denied to King Charles.

Photo: The Evenlode Collection

The Rectory

*The earlier part was probably built when
the Revd Charles Neville was Rector (1695-1717)*

Chapter 9

The Return of the King in 1660

The Neville dynasty

Oliver Cromwell died in 1658. His son Richard succeeded him but was neither soldier nor statesman. After a year he resigned leaving anarchy behind him. In 1660 King Charles' son was invited to return to the country and was crowned King Charles II.

Ralph Neville, once a puritan Preacher, conformed to the times and ministered at Evenlode in the restored Church of England and used the Book of Common Prayer. He had married Frances and according to the parish registers their daughter Anne was baptised in Saint Edward's Church on 8 September 1649 and their son Charles was baptised on 26 January 1650. This indicates that if Charles was then a baby, Anne had not been an infant when she was baptised. A plausible explanation for this is that about this time Ralph was mellowing in his views as a puritan, perhaps under the influence of his wife. Their son James was baptised in Saint Edward's on 18 April 1651.

Charles Neville, the elder son, was an undergraduate at Christ Church Oxford and, as recorded in the *Alumni* Records, was ordained priest in 1678. He succeeded his father as Rector in 1695. However, he was living in Evenlode from 1688 for from that date all his children are recorded proudly in the church registers. He must have been working as curate to his father. His children and the date of their baptisms are listed below:

Gratiana 9 October 1688
Harcourt 18 November 1689
Sarah 11 June 1691
Mary 29 June 1692
Ralph 2 November 1693
Charles 1 June 1696

Catherine 12 November 1697
Frances 13 March 1699
James 21 March 1700
Richard 11 June 1701
Henry 5 April 1703
Hester 22.3.1704
Anne 10 October 1706

Charles Neville's son, Ralph Junior, was an undergraduate at Merton College, Oxford. The same University records state that he was ordained deacon in 1715. Charles Neville had bought the advowson for Evenlode (right of presentation) and presented his son to the living. Charles then retired as Rector of Evenlode in 1717 and Ralph Junior succeeded his father as Rector.

In 1727, Ralph Junior left Evenlode and, having inherited the right of presentation to the benefice, he presented George Pye as Rector, and sold him the advowson.

Who built the rectory?

The original part of the Rectory was already built before 1756, for the garden (three acres) was enclosed prior to this. This is noted in the Tithe Apportionment Act of 1839. It seems highly likely, therefore, that it was built either by Ralph Neville Senior or Charles Neville. Charles Neville is less likely, as he was a family man and his father's curate, and possibly living in the Rectory before he was Rector. Also Ralph could afford to retire so he had wealth. Ralph Neville Senior seems the more likely person to have built the Rectory.

It is apparent from this that Ralph Neville had income other than the tithes and the glebe. If he built this house it would have been from his own resources. Moreover, in buying the advowson Ralph Neville indicated that he intended to create a Neville dynasty at Evenlode, which to some extent he did (being succeeded by his son and then his grandson).

Evenlode Place is the current name of what was the Rectory. In the new Pevsner, *The buildings of England* written by David Verey and Alan Brooks, it is said to be a nineteenth century house, but the *Victoria County History* says it has an eighteenth century core. It is not difficult therefore to place the building at the time when Ralph Neville was incumbent, but from where did the money come?

In attempting to trace the Neville family the entry for Ralph in the register of Oxford alumni proved unhelpful. There are no records of his father Edward Neville at either Collom or Sunninghill though the Register says that is where his father came from.

There was a "Thomas Nevill" who through his wife became connected with the Seymours, whose ancestor Edward Seymour, First Duke of Somerset, was Lord Protector to the boy King Edward VI. A link such as this, that connects both commitment to the puritans and also apparent wealth, is the sort of link that would need to be found, but it is elusive.

Prayer Book Priest

Whatever Ralph Neville Senior had once thought, he had to use the Book of Common Prayer when he became Rector of Evenlode. Archbishop Thomas Cranmer's vision of the Prayer Book priest was that of a scholarly man who combined daily public reading of the Prayer Book services and their lessons from the Bible, and also due adminstration of the sacraments, with pastoral care of all the people of the whole parish. In restoring the Book of Common Prayer to the Church of England in 1662, the king and the bishops intended to restore Cranmer's vision of the community life of a parish, led at daily prayer by a learned incumbent and guided by his Visitations.

This vision was fulfilled in some places but we do not know how Ralph Neville responded to this concept of care of the community given his puritan background with its core belief in individual conversion.

A picture of him can be sketched in one's mind. In those days a rector would not wear robes for worship. He would always wear black, both for normal use and for worship. In fact, the cassock had changed into a front buttoning frock coat that stretched down just to the knees. At his neck he would wear a white cloth band or kerchief. He would wear black breeches that buckled at his knee, white hose and black leather shoes. Outside he would always wear a shovel hat and, in cold weather, a black cloak over all.

The only exception to this mode of dress was at the quarterly Holy Communion service. On this occasion he would pull a white surplice over all.

So picture Ralph Neville if you will. Shoes and hose, buckled breeches and cassock-coat, standing in the pulpit proclaiming the scriptures and preaching constantly in season and out of season.

Internal re-organisation of Saint Edward's Church

The puritans inspired a re-organisation of church interiors and it is evident that this happened in Evenlode. It too can be pictured in one's mind.

The central feature became the pulpit. The altar that Gervaise Kecke had almost certainly restored would have been removed. Evenlode's pulpit would have been moved and centrally placed. The Rector preached from the pulpit. In some places there was a lower pulpit in front, from which the clergy would read the services. Where this was the case, a further desk in front of this was for the parish clerk who had to make the responses when required. This arrangement (the "three decker pulpit") fitted a church with a high ceiling. It is probable that in Evenlode Church the Rector both preached and led the Service from the pulpit whilst the clerk sat at a table below.

The table below was unadorned, though it was used for the quarterly Communion Service. It received no respect and frequently clergy used it as a table on which to put books and even hat and gloves.

The Chancel would in effect have become redundant. In some places it was even bricked up to form a separate room. Some churches kept the village hearse in it. Frequently it became a schoolroom in which the Rector taught the children (if he bothered to do so). There is no evidence to suggest that this latter was done at Evenlode.

On the south wall of Evenlode Church there is panelling. It is likely that this is the remains of "box pews." These became very fashionable and each family that was wealthy enough had its own box. In some instances a serving woman was sent ahead with hot coals in a container to warm the box for the family before the Service.

Like most other places Evenlode had a gallery, although the evidence for this is only found in a faculty of the Vicar General of

Worcester diocese, Joseph Phillimore. He granted to the churchwardens in 1840 a faculty to replace the pews, repair the roof and "restore the gallery". The gallery was for the use of musicians and singers.

Music in church

What did Evenlode folk sing at Morning and Evening Prayer? In 1562, Sternhold and Hopkins had produced a psalter of metrical psalms and canticles that was well used in churches. It was commonly known as the "Daye's Psalter". Although the rich hymnody of the Wesleys would not be written until the eighteenth century, the seventeenth century was not devoid of hymn writers. The hymns of Richard Baxter, John Bunyan, George Herbert and John Milton would have been sung, though the Church of England concentrated on metrical psalms and canticles.

A method of singing evolved for illiterate congregations. A line or a verse would be sung (sometimes by the Rector) and then everyone would sing it "after me". Thus the whole was sung in this way. It took a long time. Of course the canticles and some of the psalms must have been known by heart.

It is likely that Evenlode had (as in other places) a church band of musicians and singers. These would assemble in the Gallery. In recent years, some of this music has been re-discovered by an organisation called the "West Gallery Singers". The style of singing has been re-learned and, accompanied by appropriate instruments similar to those of the time, it is a really joyful sound raised to the Lord.

Although Thomas Hardy lived in the nineteenth century, he had a great fondness for the ways things had been. When he wrote, village church bands were probably mainly features of the past. It had become fashionable to have an organ or at least a harmonium. Hardy had talked with the old and knew their tales of the past and so his description of the village church band assembling in his novel *Under the Greenwood Tree* is probably how things were in Evenlode in the time of the Nevilles and later. In his novel he wrote:

Old William sat in the centre of the front row, his violincello between his knees and two bass singers on each hand. Behind him on the left came the treble singers and Dick; and on the right the tranter and the tenors. Further back was old Mall with the altos and supernumaries.

The same scene is evoked in Thomas Webster's wonderful painting of a village choir. This style of music was not supplanted until Victorian times when parish churches started copying the Cathedral style of worship. This introduced the chanting of the Prayer Book Psalms and Canticles by a robed choir.

The Legacy

Despite the division between the adherents of the Old Faith (now called Roman Catholics), the Established Church of England and the puritan Congregationalists, the seventeenth century was a period of great Christian growth and this would have had its effect on Evenlode.

Adherents of the Old Faith remained loyal to the Pope and, with the plausible evidence of a priest hole in Evenlode House, there may have been recusants in the Evenlode area, as was suggested above. It is likely that puritans continued to live in Evenlode too. Both groups, for different reasons, would shun the village Church, but the Prayer Book Church had found a place in many people's hearts.

One treasure from the puritan tradition crossed all boundaries and would have been known by everyone in Evenlode. It was *The Pilgrim's Progress* written by John Bunyan. This passage must have consoled many an elderly villager of whatever religious denomination,

Many accompanied him to the river side, into which as he went, he said, 'Death, where is thy sting?' And as he went deeper, he said, 'Grave, where is thy victory?' So he passed over, and all the trumpets sounded for him on the other side.

Political changes

In 1688 King James II (a Roman Catholic) fled the country and Parliament invited his protestant sister Mary and her Dutch protestant husband William of Orange, to become joint sovereigns. In 1715 the elderly King James II sent his son Bonnie Prince Charlie to recover the crown for the Stuarts. This venture ended in failure. In 1745 a much older man, loyally proclaimed "King Charles III" by his followers, again attempted to return, and again failed.

Charles died, perhaps fortuitously without a child. His brother, a Cardinal in Rome and therefore unmarried, became heir to the throne. Forlornly, some addressed him as "King Henry IX".

These things seemed to pass Evenlode by.

Map showing the position of the
five acres designated for the poor of Evenlode

Chapter 10

Enclosing Evenlode in 1756

Changing the face of Evenlode

Momentous things happened in England in the eighteenth century. The Hanoverians (disliked and ignored by many) were neither overthrown in the invasion of 1715 led by Bonnie Prince Charlie nor in that of 1745 led by the older "King Charles III", but no whisper of the attempts to do so can be heard in the history of Evenlode. Indeed in 1715 Charles Neville, Rector of Evenlode, swore the Oath of Allegiance to King George.

England lost its colonies in the American continent but no glimpse of this is found in this rural outpost of Worcestershire.

However, there was a momentous local change. It was the Enclosure of Evenlode Act of 1756.

Enclosure changed the face of Evenlode. Over the years, fields around the Manor House, Northfields, Heath End and Horn had been enclosed as had one or two orchards and some gardens, but by and large the rest was open land until 1756.

The poor people of Evenlode had never owned the land. These ordinary people feared Enclosure because it seemed to take away their independence. For centuries men such as they were had scraped their livings at subsistence level from the gardens and orchards of the cottages they rented, from the portions of strips of land here and there that they customarily used and from the cows and sheep they pastured on the common land. Everyone knew everyone else's boundary. The boundaries were marked by trees planted and stones erected.

It was after the sale of most of the land of the Manor by the Freeman heirs in and after August 1702 (when it passed into the ownership of several people) that enclosing the land began to make sense. The new landowners wanted to be precise about what they owned. Enclosure tidied up all the haphazard arrangements that were so familiar to the poor people.

The end of the Manor of Evenlode

The story of the sale of the Manor to the Freeman family and their subsequent history is related in the *Victoria County History* entries, not only for Evenlode but also for other places nearby, and is noted above.

Continuing this story, Coningsby Freeman as recorded above, died in 1639 leaving the Manor to his wife Beatrice in trust for their son Edward (later, often referred to as Thomas). Edward also had inherited the Manor of Neen Sollars some ten miles south of Ludlow. It was there that he chose to live in a similarly agricultural village. His mother chose to leave Evenlode too. She went to live in "Cotson" which may mean "Cutsdean" as it is often called "Cutson", but this "Cotson" is said to be in Shropshire. Edward died, apparently unmarried.

As well as their son Edward, Coningsby and Beatrice had three daughters. Joyce was the eldest. She had married Thomas Owen, a farmer of Evenlode. Ursula and Elianor jointly inherited the Manor.

The story now continues in various documents in Collection Two of the Evenlode Papers. The two sisters inherited the Manor House and farm, seven "messuages" (each a house, yard, garden, orchard and maybe a paddock) that were rented out and seven "cottages" that were also rented out. They also inherited most of the rest of the land of the parish (mostly unenclosed), for which they received rents from the holders. These lived in the messuages and cottages.

Elianor, who had married John Lawrence, Gentleman of Cricklade, was not interested in the Manor other than to receive income from it. John and she had one son, Robert Lawrence, like his father a gentleman of Cricklade. Robert Lawrence eventually inherited his mother's share.

Ursula had married Edward Poer (Power), a gentleman of Worcester. He owned land and property in various parts of the area and as described above in Chapter Seven, had leased "one messuage with two yardlands" in Evenlode for 99 years from Edward Freeman. (It is fascinating to relate that after 500 years the Poers were once again associated with Evenlode.)

Ursula's Will of 1682 indicates that by 1682, Edward Poer had died. In her Will, she left everything she owned personally, to her daughter Beatrice Katherine (named after her grandmother) with two small legacies to her sons John and Edward. Presumably they had inherited all the properties and lands of their father.

Ursula had been a wealthy woman. By her Will, her daughter, Beatrice Katherine, inherited "all her interests in Evenlode" and her "interest in a third part of the Manor of Neen Sollars" (which Ursula had inherited from her brother). Further, Beatrice Katherine inherited her mother's properties in Shropshire and Worcestershire.

Beatrice Katherine married Thomas Karver, like her father a gentleman of Worcester.

Thus Thomas Karver (on behalf of his wife Beatrice, daughter of Ursula) and Robert Lawrence (son of Elianor) came to have control of the lands of the Manor of Evenlode. They decided to make a legal agreement of what they owned.

The first thing to be done was to formally divide the Manor Farm that had been rented to two tenants jointly, Thomas Fletcher and John Parratt.

Dividing the Manor Farm

The Parties to the division are first listed and then the witnesses are listed:

Parties:
1. Robert Lawrence of Cricklade, Wilts. Gentleman, son and heir of John Lawrence late of Cricklade by Elianor his wife, both deceased
2. Thomas Karver of the City of Worcester, Gentleman and Beatrice Katherine, his wife, daughter of Ursula Poer late of the City of Worcester, deceased.
3. (Witnesses): Thomas Greenwood of Chastleton, Oxon, Gentleman; and John Sellwyn of Broadwell, Gloucestershire, Gentleman.

Then the document describes Manor farm as it was in 1699

The Manor (the Manor House and farm place) now in the occupation of Thomas Fletcher the elder and John Parratt or one of them, and an enclosure of pasture adjoining (10 acres) of which the south part is occupied by John Parratt and the north by Thomas Fletcher

Pasture called Broadleys (16 acres) occupied by Parratt

The Salley meadow (14 acres) occupied by Parratt

The meadow called Mill-holme (15 acres) occupied by Fletcher

Enclosed ground called the northfields (80 acres) divided in three parts, two occupied by Parratt and one by Fletcher.

Cottage and garden with pasture for two "rother" beasts adjoining occupied by Robert Howlett

The furzy grounds with meadow called the Langett (20 acres) occupied by Howlett

Cottage and land occupied by John Bliss

One yardland occupied by Ann, daughter of Richard Rooke lately deceased

Messuage and two yardlands occupied by Edward Poer, granted to him and Beatrice Katherine Poer now wife of Thomas Karver by a lease of January 1671 from Beatrice Freeman (Coningsby's widow) of Coston, Salop, widow, and Thomas (Edward) Freeman of Neen Sollars, Esquire, for a term of 99 years.

The Manor was then divided.
First to Robert Lawrence (son of Elianor Freeman):

To Robert Lawrence (son of Elianor), his heirs and assigns, the north part of the Manor House and court now occupied by Fletcher, with part of the apple orchard and lower orchard now used in tillage

The northfields

The Mill Holme

The cottage and land occupied by John Bliss. And various chief rents payable on lands formerly customary

Second to Beatrice (daughter of Ursula and her husband Thomas Karver):

To Thomas Karver and Beatrice Katherine his wife, the south part of the Manor House and court, part of the apple orchard and the lower orchard now used in tillage

The Broadleys
The Salley meadow
The cottage and garden with pasture for two rother beasts
occupied by Howlett
The furzy ground and the Langett meadow
The yardland occupied by Ann, daughter of Richard Rooke
deceased.

This arrangement left Robert Lawrence with the north fields and the meadow called Mill Holme (or Mill Pound). In 1699 he had built Northfields farmhouse and so he had a working farm to let or sell.

He also held John Bliss's cottage and land. John and others of his family before him (Joan Bliss is mentioned earlier) were tenants. John no doubt continued as tenant for the time being.

Robert Lawrence also had half the Manor House. This was rented out.

Thomas Karver and Beatrice had the land mainly to the south of the Manor House and the other half of the Manor House. This was a good unit to let to a tenant for income.

They also held the cottage and garden and the pasture for two "rother beasts" together with Langett's heath and meadow that Robert Howlett rented from them.

They also had the yardland rented by Ann, daughter of Richard Rooke.

In all, both parties probably felt that they had achieved a reasonable settlement of the Manor Farm to produce income for themselves.

As regards the land leased by Edward Poer (Ursula's husband), the division states:

The messuage and two yardlands granted by a lease of 99 years to Edward Power and Ursula Power (now Karver) to revert in equal parts to Robert Lawrence, his heirs and assigns, and to Thomas Karver and Beatrice Katherine, their heirs and assigns as tenants in common.

Ursula had left her "interest" in Evenlode to Beatrice. This "interest" must have been this house and land she shared with her husband that he had leased for 99 years (presumably as a summer residence for they had homes in Worcester and elsewhere). Although this was technically rented from the Manor, only Ursula had personal interest in it as her home. Her daughter Beatrice and her husband (Thomas Karver) would thus have had a personal interest too, (although Robert Lawrence would expect part of the rent after Ursula's death). As related above this lease ran until 1740. After this date the house known as *Evenlode House* passed into William Bricknell's hands. This coincidence of date confirms that the house leased by Edward Poer for 99 years was in fact *Evenlode House*.

The document relates the division of the lands of the Manor of Evenlode. It states that the following rights were to be divided:

An equal division to be made of all rights and privileges of the Manor, liberty of fishing, free warren and view of "frankpledge"

The document also says that the rents from all the properties, land and any other unspecified rents are to be divided equally too. It lists the "chief rents."

Seven messuages (ie farms and farm buildings)
Seven cottages and seven gardens
One dovecote
200 acres of unenclosed arable land
100 acres of meadow
200 acres of heath
£8 rent
free fishing and warren and view of frankpledge.

The unexpected sale

However, for reasons that are unknown, Robert Lawrence and Thomas Karver with Beatrice Katherine his wife decided two or three years later to sell the whole Manor. The date of the transaction was 25 August 1702. The purchasers were Mr Thomas Barker of Adlestrop and Joseph Phipps, Philip Woodman (though another document indicates another surname at this point) and John Bliss.

The bulk of the purchase was by Mr Thomas Barker of Adlestrop where he resided. The holder of the documentation for the deal is recorded in an unsigned document that clearly was drawn up by Mr Barker.

> Whereas Great parts of the mannor of Evenload with the lands there to belonging was lately purchased by me and by Philip Woodman, Joseph Phipps and John Bliss in severall partes and shares Of and from one Robert Lawrence and Thomas Karver and Beatrice Katherine his wife or one of them. And whereas my part being more and of greater value than that of any other of the said parties All the deeds and papers belonging to the Title of the said premises and comprized in this particular were by agreement deposited in my hands to be kept and produced att any time hereafter att the request and for the benefitt of every and either of the said purchasers and their heirs and Assigns respectively.

The title: "Lord of the Manor of Evenlode"

Mr Barker bought the greater part of the land of the Manor of Evenlode in 1702, but he sold the land to others, before the Enclosure Act of 1756. The title "Lord of the Manor of Evenlode" seems now to have become distinct from ownership of the Manor land. It was passed down in the Freeman family. The title passed from Coningsby Freeman's son Edward (known as Thomas) to one or other of his sisters.

It may have passed to Joyce Freeman who married Thomas Owen who farmed part of the Manor.

It may have passed to Elianor Freeman who married John Lawrence and so to their son Robert Lawrence.

It may have passed to Ursula Freeman who married Edward Poer and so to their daughter Beatrice who married Thomas Karver.

From one or other of these it passed to a descendant, Miss Milcah (surname unknown). It could have passed more particularly to this Milcah's daughter, also called Milcah. This Milcah (or daughter Milcah) married Thomas Greenwood who owned Brookend Estate. (Brookend was then a single farm and was a separate Manor. Lower Brookend had not yet been cut off.) Their daughter, Miss Ellen Greenwood, married the Revd Thomas Griffith Biggs, Rector of

Chastleton. Mrs Ellen Biggs eventually inherited Brookend Estate from her parents.

In the details of the 1756 Evenlode Enclosure, Mrs Ellen Biggs is described variously as "Lady of the Manor of Evenlode" and "Widow of the Manor of Evenlode" and received allotments of land under the new arrangements. These were farmed along with Brookend Manor where she lived. The fact that her land in Evenlode was Northfields probably means that the title passed to her through Elianor Freeman and her son, Robert Lawrence.

From Mrs Ellen Biggs, the title of "Lord of the Manor of Evenlode" and her land in Evenlode, as well as Brookend Manor, passed on to her daughter Ellen. Miss Ellen Biggs married Mr Thomas Fothergill. Thomas Fothergill's estate thus included land in both Evenlode and Chastleton.

In 1786 the Fothergill Estate, including the title "Lord of the Manor of Evenlode" and additionally the Lordship of the Manor of Chastleton was sold to Mr John Jones of Chastleton. He bequeathed it to his cousin, Mr John Henry Whitmore-Jones.

A picture of eighteenth cemtury Evenlode

Returning to 1702 and the sale of the Manor to Mr Barker, using these documents one can create a picture of Evenlode in that year.

There is *Manor Farm*. This is the Manor House, farm buildings and a number of fields already enclosed and named.

Separate from this after 1699 is *Northfields Farm*.

There is whatever property Joan Freeman and her husband Thomas Owen farmed. As *Heath End Farm* is an old enclosure this could be theirs, if not it is still a separate farm

It needs to be recalled that *Horn Farm* had long been independent of the Manor from the fifteenth century.

In addition to these, the document lists: "*Seven messuages* (farmhouse, buildings and land)". These have tenant farmers and are not identified.

Thus at the time of sale to Mr Barker in 1702, Evenlode consisted of eleven distinct farms (though the land for most would be in strips).

The document further adds: "*Seven cottages*" (cottage, buildings and gardens). Some or all of these may have been small farms of a few acres.

In addition, there was Edward Poer's *Evenlode House* with two yardlands, at least part of which were laid out as gardens with trees, and the Rectory with its three acres of leisure garden, and the Poor House.

The purpose of the Evenlode Enclosure Act of 1756

The Enclosure Act awarded all the unenclosed land to the various landowners in various "allotments". A copy of the full details of these awards made as a result of the Evenlode Enclosure Act is contained in book form within Collection Eight of the Evenlode Papers.

The process of the 1756 Evenlode Enclosure Act was to award allotments of land to individuals in lieu of strips and plots unenclosed yet owned by them. 980 acres were involved. The process enabled some form of rationalisation of the variously owned pieces of land, yet despite this, the Commissioners found themselves giving land to persons in perhaps two or three different places. This was mainly due to the facts that most wanted to keep in their hands the land that they had previously farmed and also to give fair shares of good and less good land. The Rector was of course awarded allotments for his unenclosed glebe land.

One of the tasks of the Enclosure Act was to remove the hated obligation to pay tithes to the Church. As described previously these tithes were originally divided into four parts. One part was to pay a due to the bishop and diocese, the second to maintain the chancel of the parish church, the third to give relief to the poor and the fourth to maintain the clergy and the clergy house. In effect the tithes had become further income for the Rector in addition to the profit from the glebeland. To replace the tithes, the rationalisation allotted additional glebe land to be given to the Rector to make up for the loss of tithes.

The purpose of the Tithe Apportionment Act of 1839

In 1756, some parts of Evenlode already had been enclosed. The reason for the 1839 Tithe Apportionment Act was to remove the obligation to pay tithes on the old enclosures (pre 1756) just as it had been removed from the new enclosures of 1756. The full details and a map (too large to reproduce) are in Collection Eight of the Evenlode Papers.

The obligation to pay tithes was removed not by giving extra glebeland to the Rector but by fixing rents for these old enclosures. This rent was to be paid to the Rector.

In the calculations of the commissioners in 1839, the names of the then owners of these pre-Enclosure Act lands are listed alongside the rents to be paid to the Rector. These names may be compared with names of people who were awarded allotments of land in the Enclosure Act (and also names of people mentioned when the boundaries are described). In some cases this enables ownership of farms to be identified. However it may not be assumed that land listed in these Acts as belonging to a particular farm remained so. Land in Evenlode has been sold and bought, rented out, inherited and given as a wedding dowry more frequently than might be imagined.

The farms of the "Old Inclosures" (before 1756)

Northfields

Mrs Ellen Biggs owned Northfields with land around that was already enclosed by 1756. The house was built in 1699 by Robert Lawrence (husband of Elianor Freeman) and no doubt had a yard, garden and orchard as seems to have been a common pattern. She lived at Brookend and farmed Northfields with Brookend Manor Farm.

Caldicote Heath Farm (Heath End Farm)

Heath End Farm also pre-dates the 1756 Evenlode Enclosure Act. The property linked with Heath End Farm consists of a yard with the house and an orchard and a coppice. The fields are easily identified today. Along the lane to Moreton there is Great Meadow and Long Ground. Also there are Oak ground, East of Oak ground, West of Oak

Ground, Barn Close and Bogs Meadow. Also listed is "Little Meadow" which name seems to have slipped out of use although it may be the "Little Meadow" in Chastleton. Access to the House was on a track from the Moreton Road.

Horn Farm

Horn Farm was enclosed long before the Enclosure Act. It may be recalled that in 1451, John Petyt, Lord of the Manor by his marriage to Philippa (daughter of Peter Deyville, the last of the Deyville Lords of the Manor) gave arable land and fourteen acres of meadow to one Heynes (Haynes, Haines). In 1609 William Heynes' death is recorded and Horn Farm passed to his son Richard.

Some time later a Thomas Haines owned the "old inclosure" at Horn. This information is gleaned from his Will, a copy of which is in Collection Nine of the Evenlode Papers.

Thomas Haines is not mentioned in the Enclosure Act, but shortly afterwards he must have bought newly enclosed land for ultimately he owned land adjoining Horn Farm and land to the west between Horn Lane and the Adlestrop Road. He would have continued to pay tithes on the old enclosure land. By 1765 he had died. He left his land to his son Thomas Haines for his life. From the Will, it was not expected that Thomas would have children probably for mental or physical incapacity. The Will charges his sister Johanna ("Sister Willson") to care for his son and after his death the land was to go to his rightful heirs. The execution of the Will was to be by his kinsman Thomas Pettit. It is interesting to note that in his Will he names his home Horn House.

Landowners and householders after the Enclosure Act

The Enclosure Act gives this information:

Ellen Biggs

As recorded above, she owned and lived at Brookend and held Northfields in Evenlode that was already enclosed.

She also owned the two detached fields, Near Yarnborough and Far Yarnborough and other pieces that were not enclosed. So in the awards of the Enclosure Act she was awarded four allotments. Two of the allotments awarded were on the east side of the Four Shire Stone road. One was of five acres and adjoined the Yarnboroughs. A further plot was of 15 acres and began after the little brook.

In return for her unenclosed land to the south of the parish, she was awarded two further allotments. The first was of 53 acres and had as its boundary the Chastleton road and parish boundary to the north and east and the Horn Brook to the south. Adjoining this was a second allotment of 26 acres also bordering Horn Brook. These allotments must bear some resemblance to the land that later belonged to the Jones Estate.

Clearly she needed access to the river. Apparently, the meadows near Northfields House were unenclosed so she was awarded a rectangular field of 14 acres that ran from the house to the river.

Mary Evans

Mary Evans was awarded 2 acres near her own "old inclosure". It has not been possible to identify where this was but it was adjoining Mrs Biggs' "old inclosure" at Northfields and may have been land Mary Evans purchased from the Northfields "old inclosure".

Rector's Glebe

It is a surprising thing to discover that after the work of the Enclosure Act and taking into account the amount of land in the "old inclosure", the Rector was by far the largest landowner in Evenlode. The glebe amounted to 323 acres.

Of the old enclosure, the Rector had three acres of pasture for his "pleasure garden" attached to the Rectory opposite the Church. He also already owned as an old enclosure 97 acres of farmland.

He was awarded four allotments of land. There was an allotment of 97 acres bounded to the west by the river, to the south by the Adlestrop boundary and adjoining the new Adlestrop road. By 1756 it had been the custom for generations of Rectors to let the glebe rather than farm it. This allotment was rented out and evolved into *Evenlode Grounds Farm*.

There was an allotment of 23 acres immediately on the north side of the Longborough Road where it leaves the lane to Moreton. There was an allotment of 85 acres off the Four Shire Stone road and stretching to the Brookend grounds. This seems to have been allotted partially in lieu of tithes. To this was added a further 17 acres, in lieu of tithes.

To whom these acres were rented is unknown.

Allotment for the Poor of Evenlode

The allotment given to the poor by the Enclosure Act was five acres. This lay north of Heath End Farm's access track. The poor were also awarded grazing rights on the green and on all the road verges in the parish.

Concern for the poor was also evident in the two bequests made and recorded on the boards in the Church. It may be noted that in 1756 William Bricknell, the Churchwarden was also overseer of the poor. In a small parish like Evenlode this was a regular pattern of appointment. The Board reveals his bequest:

Mr Thomas Barker of Adlestrop in the County of Gloucester gave to the Poor of Evenlode ten shillings per annum, to be paid at Christmas annually for ever out of certain lands called the Eastwells in the Parish of Longborough, in the said County of Gloucester. 1701.

There is an additional bequest on the Board:

By a deed dated 11 June 1756 and made between William Mullis alias Rooke of Evenload, Gentleman, of the one part and Edward Phillips, Clerk, Rector, and William Bricknell, Churchwarden and Overseer of the Poor of Evenload, of the other part, a piece of land then called Campden's Close now forming part of an Inclosure called Illes's Piece, now the property of Mrs James 1865, was charged with the annual payment of the sum of forty shillings for the Poor of Evenload for ever.

This is the allotment awarded to *Henry Iles* (an allotment of rather more than 4 acres). This allotment is described as "Iles piece" formerly known as "Campden Close". It appears to have been to the north at the beginning of the Longborough Road. It seems to have been bought for the Poor originally but then sold with annual payment of forty shillings to the Poor Fund as part of the agreement.

Fletchers Farm

Detailed documentation is available from Collection Two for the further story of Fletchers Farm on Horn Lane. In summary, as noted above, in 1625 Edward Freeman sold the ancient property of

Baughtenement and Pounsy on Horn Lane to William Carter, whose grandfather had rented them from Sir Henry Compton, Lord of the Manor, and sworn fealty to him. Although now a landowner, William Carter did not occupy the property but rented it to the Gardners to farm as his tenants. Margaret Gardner bought it after her husband's death.

It passed into the Higgins family and in 1709 or 1710 the Higgins family sold the farm to Joseph Fletcher. He was the son of Thomas Fletcher, the village blacksmith. This Thomas Fletcher died in 1696 and he left a Will. In it he left "iron and materials of trade, three horses and four cows, farming implements and straw" to his son Joseph Fletcher. Given the date it may be assumed that the Fletchers lived and worked at the house now called "The Old Forge" in Horn Lane. As well as being smiths they held land and had the use of common land for the animals.

In addition Thomas Fletcher was not only a blacksmith and a farmer but also he loaned money. There are a number of documents giving details of loans such as two loans together worth £50 to John Humphreys. His son Joseph Fletcher continued to do the same.

Joseph Fletcher married Joan Rooke. She was the daughter of Richard Rooke. There were a number of families of Rookes in the village at that time. They were husbandmen and the name was already common in the parish in the sixteenth century.

Her sister was Ann Rooke who farmed the yardland belonging to the Manor Farm. Ann had married Richard Jones, a yeoman farmer of Evenlode, and no doubt her yardland was added to whatever else he rented.

In 1713 a Thomas Rooke, whose relation to the two women Ann and Joan is unknown, left them a "quaterne" of land. It was land that he had purchased from Richard Stanley who had also sold (or his father had) a part of an orchard to John Higgins in 1653. It is reasonable to presume that this "quaterne" was in the same area of Horn Lane as the orchard had been and next to Fletcher's land.

The "quaterne" had to be divided equally between Joan Fletcher (nee Rooke) and Ann Jones (nee Rooke). The two husbands, Joseph Fletcher and Richard Jones, agreed the division.

As far as Joseph Fletcher was concerned he simply added this to the growing amount of land he owned at "Fletchers Farm".

As related earlier, Richard and Ann Jones, however, gave their share of the "quaterne" to their daughter also called Ann, as a marriage dowry when she married William Sheldon of Little Wolford. Later in

1741 Joseph Fletcher junior bought out the Sheldon interest and added it to "Fletchers Farm".

The commissioners carrying out the Evenlode Enclosure Act made two awards to Joseph Fletcher junior, who had inherited everything from his father, Joseph Fletcher:

25 acres, 1 rood and 5 perches bounded on the south by Horn Brook, on the east by Thomas Davis's new allotment, on the west by Mr Bricknell's old Inclosure, an old Inclosure of John Davis and by a new Allotment of Mr William Bricknell and a new Allotment of Richard Noble.

18 acres, 3 roods and 31 perches, bounded on the south by Cook's new Allotment, on the west by Moreton Heath and Darke's Close, on the north by the new Allotment of John Hobbins and on the east by the new allotment of John Davis.

Joseph Fletcher junior had risen considerably in the world from the times of his grandfather with the Forge, three horses and four cows. He owned land and was numbered among the landowners but he also rented land so was operating a larger farming business. He paid £30 per halfyear rent to Thomas Greenwood of Brookend for what must have been a considerable acreage. The receipts have been kept for the years 1741 – 49.

By the time he died and his son Thomas Fletcher inherited he not only owned Fletchers Farm and rented land from the Greenwood Estate but also rented land for grazing stock at Milton-under-Wychwood.

The Fletchers (like other farmers in other parts) also rented some of the Rector's land. The actual receipts still exist. They are on scrappy bits of paper, written in ink and sometimes with blots! On one is the signature of "Ralph Nevill" (spelt thus). (He was grandson of the Ralph Neville of Civil War times.) Other signatures are George Pye who was inducted in 1727 and Robert Dagge who was inducted in 1735. There is also a receipt in a very educated script signed "C Loder" who elsewhere is named "Charles Leader".

Thomas Dibble

Thomas Dibble had held land in the unenclosed area to the east of Green Lane. He was awarded two allotments under the Enclosure

Act. One was of 35 acres. This was bounded to the east by the Chastleton boundary and to the north by Mrs Bigg's enclosure of Near and Far Yarnborough. He also was awarded 94 acres behind the seven cottages on the Bank above the Green that had been built in 1751 by the parish.

William Bricknell

Among the awards of new allotments made to William Bricknell in the Enclosure Act, reference is made to two "old inclosures". One mentions "his home house farm." Fletcher's Farm boundary is identified to the west by "Mr Bricknell's old inclosure". This indicates that William Bricknell's house, yard, orchard, garden and paddock were to the west of Fletchers Farm in Horn Lane. This clearly identifies his home as Evenlode House with the land mainly in front, over the lane, and also on both sides.

The second "old inclosure" of William Bricknell's, mentioned in the 1756 Act can be identified. His presumed relative, George Simcox Bricknell, is listed in the 1849 Tithe Apportionment Act as owning the fields called Howlett, Langate and Square Ground that were an old enclosure. These had been rented to Thomas Howlett before the dispersal of the Manor. This land was presumably William Bricknell's by 1756.

In addition to this second lot of "old inclosure" lands that seem to have once belonged to Manor Farm, William Bricknell was awarded 46 acres near Four Shire Stone (but not adjoining the coach road), and a further six acres nearby. He also received 83 acres of land to the south of the new Adlestrop Road and bordering the Adlestrop parish boundary to the south. This was beyond (but adjoining) land awarded to the Rector, on the corner of the new road to Adlestrop and the road to Stockbridge.

John Hobbin

He was awarded 38 acres at Stockbridge next to the newly awarded glebe land.

Thomas Fox of Four Shire Stone Farm

Thomas Fox had awarded to him under the Evenlode Enclosure Act of 1756, two allotments of land. One allotment was of 14 acres adjoining the main coach road at Four Shire Stone. The other was of 21 acres adjoining Horn brook.

Thomas Davis of Davis's (Poplars) Farm

Thomas Davis had three allotments of land awarded to him. There was an allotment of 5 acres near Four Shire Stone and, further in towards the village, an allotment to the west off the Moreton Road of 13 acres. He had 27 acres awarded to him off Green Lane to the east and this was the core of what became known as Davis's Farm (later Poplars Farm).

In St Edward's Church registers, there are records of two families of Davis. There is the family of John and Mary Davis and there is the family of William and Sarah Davis. Both these men will be relatives of Thomas Davis.

<u>Thomas Rook</u>

Thomas Rook was awarded 37 acres north of the land of Mr Dibble and this land adjoined an orchard on its west side. He was also awarded 27 acres on the north side of Four Shire Stone road. In order to have access to water he was awarded 5 acres of land on the riverbank. This was on the south side of the Longborough road just before Stratford Bridge.

The surname "Rook" (also Rooke, Roke, Rooch) is an old Evenlode name going back to before the Reformation. Little by little the family seems to have become a little more prosperous as they eventually own 69 acres rather than rent land. Thomas Rook was a Churchwarden with William Bricknell as their names on the Charity Board reveal.

A limestone chest tomb of a "Thomas Rook" lies four metres east of the east end of the Church. The Rook family were well liked if this epitaph on one of Evenlode's gravestones represents them all:

"Here lieth the Body of
Leonard Rooch, in this Ground;
He was as Good a Neighbour.
As Ever Liv'd in the Town."

It is recorded in Peter Drinkwater's Collection *Epitaphs*

<u>Thomas Bricknell</u>

Thomas Bricknell was awarded four allotments. 22 acres were on the south side of the Horn Brook near the new allotment for glebe. The other three allotments formed a cluster, 8 acres and a further 2 acres adjoining this to the north of the Four Shire Stone road and 5 acres next to the Northfields "Old Inclosure" in one direction and the allotment for the poor in another.

<u>John Freeman</u>

John Freeman was awarded 23 acres off Horn Brook to the south and a further 8 acres along the Moreton-in-Marsh road and Four Shire Stone road. He (or his family, later) rented a further 14 acres to the north of his allotment off the Horn Brook (the Far and Near Horn fields).

John is likely to have been a descendant of the William Freeman who, it was noted, rented land in Evenlode in the early seventeenth century and who lived at Broadwell. As there are no records of the Freeman family in the church registers, he probably lived at Broadwell too.

Alicia Somerscales

At the time Mrs Somerscales was awarded allotments of land by the Enclosure Act, the Revd Joseph Somerscales was curate at Saint Edward's Church. He must have been her husband or her brother. He certainly was married. His son graduated from Oxford.

Alicia had land in her "old inclosure" but this cannot be identified. She was awarded two allotments. These were first, 12 acres between the Four Shire Stone road and the Moreton Heath opposite the track to Heath End Farm. Second, she was awarded 11 acres fronting the river.

James Cook

James Cook was awarded two allotments. One was of 6 acres and the other of 15 acres. Both adjoined Mrs Somerscales land.

William Bartlett's and Thomas Bartlett's land

William Bartlett was awarded 12 acres north of the Horn Brook and 10 acres next to the glebe off the Four Shire Stone road. Thomas Bartlett was awarded 10 acres on the other side of the Horn Brook and 6 acres south of the Longborough Road.

The relationship between these two is unknown. The Bartletts feature in the church registers over several generations. Towards the end of the eighteenth century, the family of (another?) Thomas and Ann Bartlett is recorded.

Smallholders/Husbandmen

As noted above, Henry Iles was awarded 4 acres. John Davis was awarded 4 acres off the Four Shire Stone road.

Richard Webb was awarded 2 acres off the Green Lane. This may have been an orchard.

Private residents

John Harris was awarded half an acre. Richard Fletcher was awarded half an acre.

Buy to let

Evenlode must have been noted as a place to invest money in land. From the Enclosure Act of 1756, it is related that James Leigh was awarded two acres of Evenlode land. He rented it to William Collin. Sir Hildebrand Jacob owned a new allotment of 3 acres on the riverbank. Probably for fishing, for it seems that salmon came up the Evenlode in those days and trout were a good size.

It must not be assumed that the landowners farmed the land they owned and even if they did, they may not have lived in Evenlode, but elsewhere.

A Road Map of Evenlode

With the Enclosure Act it is possible to describe a map of the roads of Evenlode for the new boundaries are allocated with reference to the roads.

For the easy movement of carts and cattle, the Act details the widths of the roads to be twenty-five feet and requires all roads to have ditches on both sides for drainage. The mounds thus created by digging the ditches are land boundaries on which walls or hedges were to be built or planted. Thus the face of the countryside was changed from open common and long ploughlands, to hedged fields and hedged roads.

The Act says that suitable bridges had to be built at Stock Bridge, also on the Longborough Road at Stratford Bridge and on the Moreton Road at the boundary. All these would have been wooden bridges initially. Prior to that, access across the river could only have been by ford or by earlier bridges by then destroyed.

The Moreton Road. The bridleway to the east of the Church between it and Church Farm is reckoned to be the old road to Moreton which continues over the fields, across the bridleway to Longborough, then along the river bank on the line of the present way-marked footpath. The Road described in the Enclosure Act is what we have now.

Starting at Saint Edward's Church, the Moreton Road heads east as it does now, bends north at what is now Poplars Farm, and continues past the stables as it does today.

Before reaching there, a track leads off to the west. This may have been called the "Meadow Road" in 1756 though this is not confirmed.

At the stables a track still leads off east leaving Heath Farm (present day Stubbles) on the left to join the bridleway. In Saxon times and earlier this linked Four Shire Stone to Chastleton. This "Four Shire Stone to Chastleton Road" provides the eastern parish boundary.

Returning to the Moreton Road, this bends at the stables as it does now then continues. There is a bridleway signed to the west and in 1756 this was known as the Longborough Road. This road leaves the Moreton Road in a westerly direction, crosses the old Moreton Road creating a cross roads, then passes over the river at Stratford Bridge. It then runs to the Fosse Way near the present road to Longborough.

The Moreton Road continues to where the Four Shire Stone Road turns off as it does now (leading to the coach road to Worcester and Oxford). The Moreton Road then passes Heath End lands and the five acres allotted to the poor of Evenlode. Beyond that the road enters Moreton Heath and Moreton parish.

In the village, the Green Lane is as it is now. Leaving Poplars farm it heads south. Immediately past the old School there is today a bridleway to the east. This bridleway merges into the bridleway leading to Chastleton. In 1756, this bridleway from Green Lane and on into Chastleton was known as the Chastleton Road.

Green Lane continues as now to Horn Lane. Horn Lane follows the route it does now and after Grange Farm continues along Horn Brook to Horn Farm. It passes Horn Farm and then turns sharp right up the side of Harcombe Wood on what is now called Conygree Lane to Chastleton Park.

Back at Saint Edward's Church, the Broadwell Road heads south. It is joined by Horn Lane as now then continues to Stockbridge. It may be that the present Adlestrop Road turn was created in 1756 to make access easier to the Rector's glebe on the right (the modern Evenlode Grounds Farm).

People on foot, on horseback and with horse-pulled carts would have used these roads to travel to Moreton, to Four Shire Stone (and so to the coach road), to Longborough, Chastleton, Adlestrop and Broadwell. The surveyors of the highways would have ordered the people periodically to collect stones to fill in wheel ruts and holes. Despite this, journies in winter would have been tedious and would have taken a long time, and even in summer, after heavy rain, both people and horses would have found the roads heavy going in places. The roads flooded then (as now) at Chosely brook on the Moreton Road and Sow brook on the road to Stockbridge.

The People of Evenlode after the Enclosure

By the eighteenth century the church registers become readable and informative. This is a list of families. Some are still having children. Some are elderly and only have one child left at home. Some are newly married and so only have one or two children. The list is incomplete for these registers do not include single person households nor those without children living at home in this period.

The Rector is listed: Revd William and Ann Horton, Rector, 8 children.

A private resident is listed: John and Susanna Harris (house owner), 2 children.

Ten farmers are listed:

Thomas and Ann Bartlett, farmer, 5 children, Joseph died aged one week.

William and Mary Bartlett, farmer, 1 child.

John and Mary Breakspeare, tenant farmer, 5 children.

John and Mary Davis, farmer, 2 children. (John Davis lived in one of the two houses then owned by John Brandish on the corner facing the present Rose Terrace.)

William and Sarah Davis, farmer, 3 children.

John and Mary Fletcher, farmer and blacksmith, 5 children.

William and Hannah Fletcher, farmer and blacksmith, 5 children.

Robert and Hanna Garner, tenant farmer, 4 children, Susanna died aged two years and two months.

Thomas and Ann Kibble, farmer, 5 children, one died. (This may be the "Dibble" family of the Enclosure Act.)

Thomas and Hannah Rook, farmer, 2 children, John died aged 7 years.

The *remaining families* are:

Edward and Elizabeth Allen, 4 children.

Richard and Ann Allen, 5 children. John died aged 3 months.

Thomas and Jane Bayliss, 6 children, Hannah died aged 10 months.
Thomas and Sarah Betts, 1 child.
Joseph and Mary Braggington, 1 child.
John and Jane Bridgewater, I child.
Robert and Rose Brooks, 1 child.
William and Sarah Butler, 6 children.
Thomas and Ann Carter, 1 child.
William and Mary Edwards, 6 children.
Edward and Elizabeth Gibbins, 1 child.
William and Mary Gough, 1 child.
William and Sarah Gregory, 8 children, Joseph and Anne were twins. Anne died at 1 year and 11 months.
Joseph and Sarah Hill, 7 children.
William and Mary Hope, 1 child.
Robert and May Humphreys, 4 children. John died aged 9 years.
Richard and Mary Jacques, 2 children.
William and Margaret Lane, 2 children.
William and Sarah Milcock, 5 children.
Joseph and Elizabeth Randall, 1 child.
John and Hannah Ripman, 1 child.
Joseph and Susanna Stevens, 2 children.
William and Elizabeth Tate, 2 children.
William and Sarah Walker, 5 children.
John and Mary Watson, I child.
Thomas and Elizabeth Whiten, 4 children.
George and Sarah Yeatman, 6 children, George died in infancy.

The high death rate among children will have been noticed in the above. It is highlighted in this list. The following children died in Evenlode in the Millennium Year 1800, two were infants.

Edmund Allen
Hannah Bayliss (9 months old)
Hannah Butler
Susanna Garner (aged two years and two months).
Francis Horton
Sarah Milcock

As was described above, Ralph Neville Junior resigned the living of Evenlode in 1727 and presented George Pye. Ralph Neville then sold the advowson to George Pye who presented Robert Dagge in 1735 and then Charles Leader in 1737. George Pye sold the advowson in 1744.

The *Revd Charles Leader* was a graduate of New College, Oxford. He became Vicar of Chesterton and rector of Abbott Stoke in Dorset in 1727 as a newly ordained man. In 1737 he became additionally rector of Evenlode. He remained Rector until 1767 and saw the implementation of the 1756 Enclosure Act.

Charles Leader seems to have retained his previous incumbencies and may have lived there. However Mrs Judith Leader (presumably his mother or his wife) presented a fine silver chalice and paten to Saint Edward's church. This indicates some affection for Evenlode so he probably visited regularly. During his incumbency, the following names are noted in the church registers as curates taking the services and the occasional offices:

Joseph Somerscales.
W E Baker
S Paget
W L Bennett

Joseph Somerscales lived in Evenlode and after ordination was a curate at Evenlode until his death. He died on 1 May 1765. His mother, Hannah Somerscales had died in 1751 but his old father had lived on until 1763. Alicia Somerscales, who was awarded an allotment of land under the 1765 Act, was either Joseph's wife or his sister. Joseph's son went to Balliol College, Oxford.

During the time Charles Leader was Rector, the Parish Clerk was Edward Durham. Edward Durham died on 17 January 1760.

In 1767, the *Revd Edward Phillips* was inducted as Rector. He was a graduate of Pembroke College, Oxford. He was an absentee rector. He was, additionally, Vicar of Feckenham from 1767 to 1786 and there he resided. In 1782 he also became curate of Bradley. During his incumbency, the following names are noted as curates taking the services and the occasional offices:

Thomas Horne
John Williams
John Hughes
Miles Tarn.

From 1782, Miles Tarn was also curate of Longborough where he resided. He was paid £28 per annum and took the fees for his ministry at Evenlode.

In 1786, the *Revd William Horton* became Rector. He was a graduate of St Alban Hall, Oxford in 1771. He then studied at All Souls Oxford. He was made a deacon in 1774 and priest in 1776. He was Vicar of Saint George's Bloomsbury until his induction as Rector of Evenlode in 1786. He was married to Anne and they came to live in Evenlode. William and Anne had eight children. Shockingly, George died aged 8 months, Elizabeth died aged 5 years, Sophia died aged 7 years and Mary Ann died aged 18 years. The other four children grew into adulthood. They were Helen, James, William and Thomas. Their deaths are recorded along with their parents. William died aged 51 on 19 July 1804. Anne died aged 73.

There is a memorial in the Church tower to the Horton family but parts of the above can be found in Collection Three and the rest is from the *Church of England online database.*

Photo: Jenny Hill Exhibition

The Church as it was in the Nineteenth Century

Chapter 11

The Archdeacon visits Evenlode (1808)

The Bishops' fear of Revolution

At the beginning of the nineteenth century the Church of England Consistory Courts still administered the Law of the land concerning family life and inheritance, in addition to church matters. The Vestry Meeting in each parish controlled local affairs. In theory, anyone could attend the Vestry Meeting, but it tended to be controlled by members of the Church of England.

Those who belonged to the Methodists and other denominations wanted their voices to be heard. This was coupled with demand for change at every level from the mass of ordinary people.

A need for change was recognised by the Establishment but every rich man was terrified that the mass of the huge underclass in English society would rebel and create an English Revolution like the French one. The bishops of the Established Church were one with the rich in their anxiety.

The French Revolution was in everyone's minds. In the early years of the nineteenth century England was in the middle of the long war with France. Both English patriotism and hatred of the French Revolution were rife, as was gross ignorance. In Hartlepool they hanged a monkey mistaking its chattering for French. In a few years, Nelson would fly his famous "England expects" message and all the illiterate, ragged, ill-fed, abused and pressed sailors would cheer their hearts out. Yet it could so easily have been a cry of mutiny. This actually happened in the naval dockyards at Chatham at one point in the period.

The Church of England's reaction to the times was to hold on to its powers in Law and its place in Society. But the bishops were aware that in their dioceses it was the laity of each parish (not the bishops) that had responsibility through the Vestry Meeting for all matters in the parish concerning education, the poor, the church building and its property. Also, that the churchwardens had secular responsibilities (such as appointing surveyors of the highways) as well as church responsibilities. Moreover, the bishops were equally aware that, in many industrial places, the old method of administration by the Vestry Meeting was beginning to collapse. With laity in control in the country parishes, and collapse impending in the cities, there was the possibility of revolution. The wealthy and the bishops were fearful.

.

Local government in Evenlode

In Evenlode the Vestry Meeting system continued to work correctly. Evenlode men governed Evenlode. The Evenlode Vestry Meeting Minute Book exists for this period in the Gloucestershire Archive. In it can be read how the Vestry fixed a Rate for the Poor (which presumably included money for the Poor House), a Rate for the Church for repairs; later a Rate was fixed for the School. The Vestry organised stone from Broadwell for the highways in Evenlode.

From the Evenlode Vestry Meeting Minute Book it is apparent that educated men attended the Annual Meetings (they could sign their names in the book). There were several farmers but also one or two tradesmen. The people's churchwarden was chosen at the Vestry Annual Meeting and the Rector announced his appointment of the Rector's warden. The Vestry Annual Meeting appointed two Surveyors of the Highway and two Overseers of the Poor. Later, the Evenlode Vestry Meeting acted as school managers for the school. The parish clerk attended all the meetings. For a few years the Vestry appointed a Collector of the Rates that had been fixed by the Vestry.

Neglect and Abuse in the Established Church

The bishops were not to know that in many places like Evenlode things continued satisfactorily as they always had done. Thus through ignorance their fears of revolution remained but there was anxiety and concern over a number of other things too.

There was an additional anxiety over the problem of absentee rectors (though the bishops themselves were as guilty as the clergy in this respect).

For example, in 1805 William James was inducted as Rector of Evenlode. He was a graduate of Magadalen Hall, Oxford. He had been ordained priest in 1791 after which he was on the staff of Saint George's Chapel, Windsor. He was not resident at Evenlode. He was additionally Rector of Harescombe with Pitchcombe in Gloucestershire and was not resident there. The rents from the glebe in both places were simply extra income for him. The rectories were either rented out or served as his residence when he came to collect his money.

William James appointed a curate for Evenlode, who was a priest called William Jones. He would have been paid a minimal stipend to do the work. In order to increase his income, he was also curate of Bledington, where he ministered for another absentee rector at this time. He was not a graduate but had the Bishop's Licence.

He was inducted as Rector of Evenlode in 1825 after William James died and remained Rector until 1830 when he had to give way to Charles James (William James' son) who by then was legally old enough to be ordained (23 years) and so could hold the living of Evenlode: a sad comment on the use of patronage.

There is no reason to suppose that William Jones was other than a faithful curate but the prevalence of rich clergy holding several benefices in order to have a huge income (whilst paying only a modest stipend to a curate to do the work) was a scandal. However, the tithes and rents were not always paid to the absentee rector until he visited the parish. There are receipts in existence for rents for glebe used by Fletcher's Farm. These reveal delays of up to three years before payment was delivered and receipted. They are in Collection Two.

It is not surprising to reflect that with so many absentee clergy receiving the fruits of parishes, little was expected of them.

There was further worry for the bishops. The general state of the parish churches and churchyards was scandalous. Many had not been maintained for well over one hundred years and were in very bad condition. Similarly it seems that worship in these churches was being badly neglected.

However, the ecclesiastical issue that was causing most concern to the Bishops was the rise of Methodism and leakage from membership of the Church of England.

John Wesley is believed to have said that the world was his parish and he had acted that way. He and George Whitefield had preached in the fields and established an alternative way of being a Christian, the Methodist way. The Methodists had introduced singing hymns as a popular devotion and Anglicans (used to the Canticles and Psalms sung by the village choir in the church gallery) did not like their "enthusiasm."

John Wesley had advocated a return to the high standards of the Book of Common Prayer. He shared the vision of Cranmer and wanted to restore it in the nation's parishes. His followers (Wesleyan Methodists) used the Prayer Book. They should have been welcomed in the Church of England but were rejected, thus feeding the clamour for change.

However, his colleague, George Whitefield had preached Calvinism and taught that those who experienced "assurance" of forgiveness of sins in a moment of "conversion" were predestined to enter into heaven (even if they subsequently sinned) whilst everyone else was predestined to hell. This "evangelical" way of "assurance" was taught among the Primitive Methodists and was becoming popular.

So, with the Church of England asleep, the need for change, the possibility of neglect and abuse, and the fear of dissidence, the bishops sent out the archdeacons to visit the parishes. And in 1808 the Archdeacon of Worcester came to Evenlode.

The Visitation of 1808

The Visitation undertaken by the Archdeacon of Worcester in 1808 gives a unique glimpse into Evenlode. It reads thus:

48 families. I Baptist.
Divine Service: On Sundays, twice.
Holy Sacrament quarterly. Communicants 14.
Money to the poor by the churchwardens.
Catechism on Sundays during Lent.
Church, chancel and poor house in good repair.
No school.
The interest of £60 given to the poor.

Patrons: Mary Hughes presented in 1767 and 1786.
George Perrott of Fladbury Esq., presented in 1805.

Those familiar with Archdeacon's Visitations are aware that prior to the Visit, the churchwardens are given a list of questions to answer. This Report is a list of the answers and it is easy to work out what the questions were. The questions do not relate just to church matters, they relate to matters concerning the poor and education also. These answers and the questions that led to them can be grouped.

Questions and answers about education
Questions and answers about caring for the poor
Church related questions and answers

Education

It will not be until 1826 that Anthony Ashley Cooper (who was born in 1801, and was later to inherit the title of Earl of Shaftesbury) will enter the House of Commons with an enthusiastic call to end social abuses. One of his main themes will be the building of schools for poor children.

That type of enthusiastic programme does not spring out of nothing. It must have been the case that as Ashley Cooper was growing up, thoughtful people were discussing these things and concluding that there ought to be education for the poor. No doubt the Archdeacon of Worcester who visited Evenlode in 1808 was one of these thoughtful people. His comment "No school" carries with it an accusatory tone. There were 48 families living in Evenlode, yet there is no school for their children.

It is true that the Catechism was being taught on Sundays in Lent but there was no regular "Sunday School". Robert Raikes had initiated the idea of Sunday Schools in Gloucester in 1781. He was a dedicated member of the Church of England and so these schools taught not only stories in the Bible but the Catechism too. Scholars were expected also to attend adult worship. For most children this process began with teaching them to read and to write. There was no evidence to indicate to the Archdeacon that anything was being done to teach the poor children of Evenlode how to read and write and do simple arithmetic.

Caring for the poor

How does the parish care for the poor? Are there Charities for the poor? Is the poor house maintained satisfactorily? The answers given to these questions by the churchwardens prove to be satisfactory to the Archdeacon and their accuracy can be verified by the Minutes of the Vestry Meeting.

The Vestry appointed annually two Overseers of the Poor. The Vestry's Collector of Rates also collected the rents for the lands for the poor and this was used to provide coal each week (later twice each winter).

As described above, the pieces of land that are displayed on the Charities Boards in the Church comprised the five acres off the Moreton Road next to Heath End Farm that was awarded after the Enclosure Act. There was the piece of land known as Campden Close or Ile's Piece. At the time of the Archdeaon's Visitation this latter formed part of Davis's farm and Mr Davis paid a charge of forty shillings annually. An annual sum of ten shillings was received from the land at Eastwells in Longborough donated by Mr Barker. The road verges were also rented for grazing. These were divided into twelve lots and various farmers and smallholders rented one or more lots.

The accounts were meticulously kept and the amounts of coal and the dates of delivery carefully recorded. No doubt the Archdeacon inspected these and was satisfied.

The Archdeacon's comments about the poor house were apposite. Even if it were satisfactory at the time of his visit in 1808, the times were calling for change. Evenlode Vestry opted, when the Act of 1834 allowed it, to join with Stow-on-the-Wold and other villages in a Union to build a workhouse.

Church related questions

When is public worship held? How often is the Holy Communion administered? How many communicate?

When the Archdeacon posed these questions the Churchwardens answered that the frequency of worship was twice each Sunday. Perhaps we should not doubt them but one of the parson diarists of the eighteenth century, Parson Woodford, records with some frequency how he despatched his maid to the church door with a note to put on it that said "No Service" when he was suffering from the gout, or had a bad cold, or, on one or two occasions, when he judged it was too cold to be in church for a service.

The Archdeacon does not however ask the more difficult question "How many people attend worship on Sunday?"

There are no records of church attendance for these times. It may be that the answer to his next question about the number of communicants is revealing. The fact that there were only 14 communicants at Evenlode Church in 1808 when the Archdeacon visited is very surprising.

There is a folk memory that churches were always full but given that the Catechism was taught during each Lent, there must have been at least several young people each year eligible for confirmation (given the numbers of babies baptised per year). Yet only fourteen people in the whole of Evenlode communicated on the four occasions the Holy Communion was celebrated: Christmas, Easter, Whitsunday and Michaelmas. From the registers it is evident that most babies in the village were christened, but otherwise was there much participation in the life of the Church? The Church of England was asleep.

The Archdeacon judged the Church building (and presumably the churchyard) to be in satisfactory condition.

Are there dissenters in the parish?

The state of church life at Evenlode revealed nothing to equate with revolution (as the authorities feared), though attendance at Saint Edward's Church by the poor may have been quite limited (judging by the number of communicants). The Archdeacon was told that there was only one dissenting family in Evenlode and they were Baptists (presumably worshipping at Stow-on-the-Wold Baptist Church).

Photo: Jenny Hill Exhibition

The Bell Inn and its patrons

Photo: The Bob Sharpe Collection

The Workhouse at Stow-on-the-Wold

Evenlode joined the Stow Union of Parishes to build a Workhouse

Chapter 12

The effect of the Corn Laws (1815–41)

After the final defeat of Napoleon, at Waterloo in 1815, there was a danger of cheap imports of corn flooding into the country from Europe. The Napoleonic Wars had prevented this. In order to preserve British agriculture Parliament had put a huge import duty on corn from abroad. These Corn Laws preserved the price of corn to keep farming viable, but had a disastrous effect on the cost of bread, the staple diet of the poor in England.

There was an even worse effect in Ireland, as Irish corn was shipped to England to obtain these high prices for the landowners. The Irish poor consequently lived on potatoes. When the potato crops began to fail many Irish died but thousands of young Irish men and women, both single and with young families, sailed from Cork for America. A large, though lesser number, sailed from Dublin to Liverpool, seeking to work in the Lancashire mills and London. Many of these settled in the dreadful slums.

The flood of Irish settling in England coincided with a population explosion. This exacerbated the rise in the price of bread. In the country, the farmers could not meet the requests of the agricultural labourers for higher wages to feed their families. Sometimes the parish Vestry Meeting had to top up wages from the collections for the poor. This put stress on the system of caring for the poor.

Work was hard to find on the farms for labouring men. Men and women and their families walked away from rural hunger to look for work in what William Booth, the founder of the Salvation Army, dubbed "darkest London", or in the "black country" of Birmingham and Wolverhampton where the constant flames of furnaces lit up the sky by night and the early mists of morning were thickened by smoke into yellow smog.

It is perhaps not surprising, though unexpected, to discover that Evenlode men found themselves in prison and transported to the colonies. Their crimes are unrecorded and may have been merely hunger-driven. In Collection Three of the Evenlode Papers are extracts from the records of Gloucester Prison. In 1819 Thomas Bragg, or Braggington, was admitted to Gloucester Prison. He was a farm labourer aged 24. He was sentenced in August of that year and was deported for life on the ship *Neptune I* to New South Wales in Australia. In 1830 Joseph Payn was admitted to Gloucester Prison. He too was a farm labourer aged 52. He was sentenced in April 1830 and was deported for life in July on the ship *Persian* to Van Dieman's Land (Tasmania).

Selling up

This state of misery after the war saw the sale of land. In 1815 *Four Shire Stone Farm* was sold by auction. The sale notice gives a picture of the farm as it then was. It can be found in Collection Three of the Evenlode Papers.

A valuable inclosed Freehold and Tithe-free Estate, called by the name of Four Shire Stone, in the parish of Evenload, desirably situated adjoining the turnpike road leading from Moreton to Chipping Norton, two miles from the former and six from the latter place, five from Stow, and six from Shipston; consisting of about 64 acres of rich Arable and Pasture Land, the greater part Grass, with an excellent and convenient Farm house, a good garden, planted with choice fruit trees, a good barn, stable, cart-house, cow-sheds, pigsties, and other conveniences thereto belonging. The purchaser may be accommodated with cow commons, adjoining the farm upon reasonable terms.

The state of misery of these times also brought about bankruptcy among farmers. In 1832 Farmer Davis, who then owned *Davis's Farm* (now known as *Poplars*), became bankrupt. The farm included land at Chastleton and Horn Ground. It was put up for auction at the White Hart Royal Hotel in Moreton-in-Marsh.

LOT 1. Orchard Ground. 4 acres
LOT 2. Four Headlands. 8 acres

LOT 3. Hovel Ground. 8 acres

LOT 4. Horn Ground. 9 acres

LOT 5. Campden's Close. 3 acres. Held under a lease for 999 years in return for an annual payment of 40 shillings for the poor of Evenlode and a peppercorn rent.

LOT 6. A very desirable compact Freehold Estate, comprising a commodious Dwelling House, Brew-house, Wash-house, Yard, Barn, Stables, Cart and Waggon houses, Cattle Sheds, and every requisite Out-building, in excellent repair; together with a large productive Orchard and 5 fields of very superior Arable, Meadow and Pasture Land, in a high state of cultivation, containing about 41 acres.

LOT 7. Arable land. 19 acres

LOT 8. 3 roods adjoining LOT 7

LOT 9. Adjoining LOT 7, a newly erected barn, Stable and Feeding Pens with a commodious Yard and 5 fields of superior Arable land, in a high state of cultivation. 35 acres. (1)

In 1850 the properties and land of LOT 6 and LOTS 5,7, 8 and 9 (at least) were settled in the name of the Rector the Revd Charles James on behalf of his second wife, Mary Sandys by her family. Mrs James was younger than Charles James and lived 26 years after his death. Her name as a farmer arises in a number of contexts. The name of the farm remained Davis's Farm. The Rector rented it to tenants.

A couple called William and Mary Davis became paupers as recorded in the 1841 Census and it appears went to live in the Evenlode poor house. It may be that this William Davis was the bankrupt farmer of Davis's farm.

Subsistence farming

The bankruptcy of Evenlode Farmer Davis in 1832 was indicative of the state of rural life in the years after the Napoleonic Wars. Evenlode farmers were mainly dairy and beef farmers. Of the 1,619 acres in the parish over 1000 acres were under grass. The arable land amounted to 322 acres. Half of this was given to barley and oats.

Of the remaining, two thirds was given to wheat. The rest was given to peas and beans though a very small amount of land was given to potatoes and turnips. It seems that few farmers prospered during these years.

The workhouse

Caring for the poor had become increasingly demanding for the Evenlode churchwardens and the Vestry. It was hard to increase the rates when farmers were struggling and with one even becoming bankrupt.

In the large towns and cities the concept of a parish caring for its own poor had now broken down, and, as noted above, in 1834 the government passed an Act to allow parishes to form a Union to build a workhouse.

Evenlode, and other villages around, combined with Stow-on-theWold in a Union to build a workhouse for the area. (There had been an attempt to associate Evenlode with a workhouse in Moreton-in-Marsh. Three Evenlode signatures are appended to the request: The Rector Charles James, Richard Davis and Jonathan Keightley. The Evenlode Vestry however decided to join the Stow Union.)

In essence a workhouse was a factory. Those who were too old to be employed, or those families (even young ones) where the adults could not find work, would be admitted to the workhouse. There they would receive enough food to stem starvation and a bed space for sleeping. Families were split up. Children were all herded together. The men and the women were separated too. Everyone spent the daylight hours engaged in some form of manual work under strict supervision. The picture Charles Dickens paints of workhouses is part of the folk memory of English people. Everyone remembers Oliver saying, "Please, Sir, I want some more."

Even after the Second World War, when workhouses were converted into geriatric hospitals as a consequence of the change of thinking, the elderly poor pleaded not to be sent to the place they still thought of as the workhouse. The elderly of Evenlode would have had the same feelings towards the workhouse at Stow.

Inability to restore the Church

Shortage of money in Evenlode is further indicated by the failure to restore the Church even though a faculty to do so was granted by Diocesan Chancellor Joseph Phillimore to the churchwardens. The plan was to give the Church a new ceiling and new stone floor, and to restore the West Gallery. (2) This implies that the box pews and the gallery of the time of the Nevilles had gone prior to this.

If Evenlode were typical of other places simple benches would have replaced these. To avoid the possibility of a man choosing to sit close to a woman who was not his wife the custom was begun whereby women sat on one side of the Church and men on the other.

The vision to return things back to the "good old days" of the West Gallery singers and band (and perhaps even the box pews) was there, but there is no evidence that any of the work was ever attempted. The churchwardens were Richard Kibble, who was farming Horn Farm and Richard Anchor, who had rented land and had created his own Anchor Farm.

A school for the children of the Poor of Evenlode

The vision was there for a school too, but presumably because of the financial situation Evenlode was slow to provide one. However, as 1840 approached, things began to improve. The first record of a school building in Evenlode is in the conveyance of land. In 1840 the Lord of the Manor was John Henry Whitmore Jones of Chastleton House. He and John Arthur Whitmore Jones (his heir apparent) conveyed land under the statute of Queen Victoria for a schoolroom for the education of the poor "in the principles of the Established Church". The signatories to the conveyance were the father and son, Messrs Whitmore Jones, the Rector Charles James, the churchwardens Richard Kibble and Richard Anchor. The signatories included the overseers of the poor. These were John Fletcher and Richard Anchor who thus signed twice. (3)

The school opened in 1844 as a Church of England National School. It was a simple building. There was just one classroom. There are no records giving information about this school, except that in the Census of 1841, Miss Emma Gilbert is listed as Schoolmistress. Perhaps she taught in her home until the school was built. This was not unknown.

Cottages

After the miserable period of the Corn Laws, the population exploded as remarked above. In 1800, 227 people lived in Evenlode and in 1841, 325 people lived in the parish. Statistics record that there were 66 residences in 1841. Some of these were farmhouses and some farmhouses had a cottage or two but how many cottages were there in 1841 in the village for the increased number of families?

In 1701 (only) seven cottages were listed. They belonged to the Manor and the occupants subsisted by way of their gardens and use of the common land. Some of these were probably still occupied (perhaps all). In 1751 cottages were built on the bank to the west of the Green (Bank Terrace). It is not known how many. Judging by the architecture, the four cottages of Vine Terrace were built in the second half of the eighteenth century. These are not enough to house a population in 1841 of 325, even though a number of these lived in the farmhouses and farm cottages.

Some effort was made to house everyone. The cottages on the bank were pulled down and, by 1841 a terrace of seven brick and tile cottages was built. By 1841 also, Portland terrace and Rose terrace were built, but even if one includes these there is discrepancy between the number of buildings and the number of residences.

An explanation as to how this number was housed can be found in Collection Five of the Evenlode Papers. This Collection relates to two cottages at the end and corner of Horn Lane facing Rose Terrace.

Collection Five contains the Will of John Brandish dated 1763. He owned considerable property, at least some of which was in Oddington. In describing his Evenlode cottages (only a part of his possessions) he says they are in the occupancy of John Smith and John Davis. One of the cottages is the present one (Springside) and the other was at right angles to it facing the present Rose Terrace.

At the time of the Enclosure Act John Davis was married to Mary and they had a little family. John was a husbandman. There seem to have been an orchard and some land attached to his cottage. He was awarded four acres under the Enclosure Act. John Smith is not mentioned in the Act so presumably he did not hold land. Clearly both cottages pre-date the Enclosure Act of 1756.

In 1821 another John Brandish inherited the dwellings. He was a great-grandnephew of the previous John Brandish and was servant to Joseph Marie Xavier Maguenett of Moreton-in-Marsh who clearly was a French exile from the Napoleonic Wars. By this time both dwellings had been halved into four residences.

In 1841, they had been further divided into five residences. By 1859, they were divided into six residences. This increased the amount of rent the landlord could collect but it also explains how the exploded population was housed.

A residence for some families may have been only a single room.

Five families occupied the two cottages in 1841. They were: Thomas and Flora Bartlett with one child, James Sedgeley (family unknown), John and Elizabeth Gregory with a twenty year old daughter and her baby, William and Ann Gregory and two children and Stephen and Elizabeth Bartlett and four children.

Note:
(1) The Sale Notice is in the Evenlode file at Stow on the Wold Public Library.
(2) Gloucestershire Archive
(3) Gloucestershire Archive

Photo: Jenny Hill Exhibition

The Old School today

Evenlode school, opened by the Victorians of Evenlode.
The large room to the left housed most of the children
The infants met in a small room facing the front door
The teacher lived to the right of the building

ADLESTROP STATION 3

Photo: the Bob Sharpe Collection

Adlestrop Station

The Victorians laid the railway through Evenlode
Adlestrop was the nearest staion

Chapter 13

What the Victorians did

Victoria became Queen in 1837 and remained so until she died in 1901. Her reign began after a time of general misery, but as the Empire expanded wealth became greater and a sense of wellbeing filtered down to Evenlode too. The people of Evenlode celebrated her Diamond Jubilee in 1897 with unrestrained enthusiasm. The 207 inhabitants drank 500 pints of ale (with the children consuming 150 bottles of lemonade). The village ate a huge feast. There were consumed four bushels of potatoes, 12 dozen cabbages, 208 pounds of meat. A huge 12 pounds of suet was used to make the traditional suet pudding eaten with gravy as the starter.

Queen Victoria's reign was an era of re-discovery, revolution and reform. The art of classical times was re-discovered. New "Gothic" buildings like St Pancras' Railway Station were built and modern "classical" statues erected.

Factories invented the production line and economy of scale. Methods of transport were revolutionised. Mobile steam engines moved goods and passengers across the land. Steam-propelled ships crossed the seas to the Empire, bringing in raw goods and taking back manufactured goods, to great profit.

Yet, even as wealth was being created, there was still poverty and ignorance. Gradually, reformers fought for change in caring for the poor, in educating the young, in supplying clean water and building sewers. In the years of Victoria's reign these were addressed, and in religion, the Church of England at long last woke up. It began to re-discover itself and its rich heritage.

Directly and indirectly, what the Victorians did affected life in Evenlode.

The Corn Laws had created misery for the poor and hard times for the tenant farmers, but good profits for those who owned the land. Landowners thus had wealth and time enough to spend on country pursuits. Often such pursuits were led and organised by the Squire or Gentry if there were such in a place.

Although the significance of the position of the Lord of the Manor of Evenlode had dwindled after the sale of the Manor by the Freeman family, in one respect its significance was retained. The Lord of the Manor of Evenlode had retained the right to hunt over the old Manor land. Thus the Jones family of Chastleton and their guests no doubt joined by farmers of Evenlode would hunt and shoot over Evenlode.

These country sports included wildfowling for migrant ducks, shooting birds, hare coursing and hunting for the fox. Evenlode agricultural labourers were paid to help and were glad of the extra money. They enjoyed blood sports too, though their blood sports tended to be cockfighting until one was killed, baiting badgers with small dogs (the badgers frequently wounding or killing the dog), and ferreting for rabbits.

Hunting in Evenlode in earlier centuries had been hunting for stags. Harcombe was a favourite place for both beast and hunter. It is said that in 1762 the Fifth Duke of Beaufort had an unsuccessful day with his staghounds so he had put the hounds to hunt a fox. He had such an exhilarating chase that henceforth he concentrated on foxhunting. Until 1835 the Beaufort hounds were brought up to Heythrop in mid-September and hunted in the area until just before Christmas, they then returned to Badminton. In 1835 a separate pack of hounds was established under the Heythrop name. Lord Redesdale (the first Master) ensured they were carefully selected.

A feature of life in Evenlode therefore was the regular sight of the Heythrop Hunt and the hounds. The undulating grassland of the Evenlode side of the Vale and also of the Sezincote side of the Evenlode Vale was, and still is, fine for the fox and for the riders. The Hunt met once a month on Evenlode Green. They would set off with a crowd of children from the village school running behind as the surviving school log book relates. "Play time" was always extended that morning.

Those on a shoot sought partridge and pheasant. Apparently the easy to way to shoot a plump partridge was for a man to fly a kite. The partridges imagined this was a bird of prey and clustered together in a field making easy targets. However, the marksmen shot down rooks and pigeons for fun. The locals knew that these made fine eating in pies so they were happy to be given them. They were happy also to eat the rabbits that nobody else wanted.

Rustic Sports for other Evenlode Victorians

The Fairs at Stow and Moreton were ostensibly designed for the purpose of hiring men and women for work. They also served a great function in maintaining links between extended families. They were a venue to meet a potential husband or wife. In addition they gave great pleasure to the ordinary people, and the opportunity to both farmer and labourer to buy and sell produce and animals.

This report of Moreton Fair appeared in the *Moreton Free Press* for the 13 October 1860. Although referring to how things were in 1860 it is probably a good glimpse of how things had been for several generations:

Moreton October Cheese and Cattle Fair was held on Tuesday last and may justly be considered as regards the show of cattle and cheese, the largest fair that has ever been held in the town. Nearly 3000 sheep were penned, and a very large stock of cattle was exhibited, but trade was not brisk owing to shortness of keep. Upwards of 100 tons of cheese were offered for sale at prices carrying from 70 shillings to 80 shillings per hundredweight.

This was but one aspect of the Fair. J Arthur Gibbs tells of the Fairs in his book *A Cotswold Village*. There were many opportunities at the Fair for rustic fun and for young men to show off. Among the sideshows was the greasy pole to climb in order to win a leg of mutton. There was racing to win a pig or a cheese. Sometimes there were donkey races for a flitch of bacon. Popular too was singlestick (fighting with wooden staves) until one man knocked the other's head so hard that this laid him out. He was roused with a bucket of water.

Evenlode Victorians: The Census of 1841

The Census of 1841 was a great leveller. It recorded both masters and men, and rich and poor, for all were the new Victorians. There are two disappointments about the 1841 Census. First it does not record addresses so for most people the address is unknown. Second it only records those residing at a certain date so names of some of the Victorians of Evenlode may be missing if they happened to be away at that date.

Although the Census does highlight some families that had lived for generations in Evenlode the surprising thing is that there was a continuous movement of population. It seems that agricultural labourers and domestic servants moved regularly to find a better master or mistress. This must be related to the system of hiring servants and labourers at the Fairs. People may not have travelled huge distances but intermingling between the villages was normal. Families living in Evenlode were linked to family members in Longborough and Broadwell in particular.

The returning officer for Evenlode put himself and his family down first in the Census Return. He was *Ernest Tidmarsh*. He was 45. His wife was called *Agnes*. She was aged 40. Neither was native to Evenlode. However their three daughters were all born in the village. They had a small boy lodging with them called *Richard Horn*. Ernest Tidmarsh must have had other employment but only recorded his status as Recording Officer.

The Rector in 1841 was the Revd *Charles James*. He graduated in 1824 and had become Rector in 1830. His age is recorded in the Census as 26 but this would mean he was only 15 when he became Rector. In fact his memorial in the Church states that he was born in 1805, so he was 36 years old. The Returning Officer must have misheard.

He had married a widow who was 23 years older than he was called Esther Carruthers. The date of this marriage is not known. Esther died at Evenlode in 1838 when she was 56 years old. It seems that two of her children (by her previous marriage) died in early

169

adulthood whilst living at Evenlode. These names are recorded in a memorial in the Church Tower.

Charles James had then married *Mary Christina Sandys* whose name is in the Census. She was the daughter of Richard Sandys Esquire of The Slade, Stroud in Gloucestershire. In the 1841 Census she was listed as being 25 years of age. The Census says that they have a child, aged 5, called Ann Maria living with them. As Charles James' first wife had died only three years before aged 56 the parentage of this child is unclear.

They employed three female servants, *Elizabeth Britten. Lavinia Smith* and *Sarah Bluett*. They also employed two men servants, *George Boulde* and *John Godson*. All the servants lived in. Apart from the little child who was born in Evenlode none of the others were born in the village.

Those of independent means

The Census lists the occupation of people and some Evenlode residents are listed as being of independent means. Among these is *Robert Bricknell* and his wife, *Jane Bricknell*. He is aged 76 and she 60. Robert and Jane employed two resident servants, *Elizabeth Pedley,* aged 50, and *William Corbet* aged 15. All were born in Evenlode. It is likely that they lived in Evenlode House. The Enclosure Act indicates that William Bricknell lived there and it may be assumed that Robert is his descendant. Under the Tithe Apportionment Act *Jane Bricknell* owned an orchard that owed church tithes (commuted to a rent of eight shillings and one penny per year). As the orchard was next to Evenlode House, this probably confirms that she and her husband, Robert, lived there.

Their son was probably *George Simcox Bricknell* but he seems not to have been resident in Evenlode. George Simcox Bricknell is listed in the 1839 Tithe Apportionment Act as owning the fields called Howlett, Langate and Square Ground as has been noted. Linked with these fields was the cottage called Howlett's Cottage. In 1839 it was being rented to *John Brakespear*. From the Enclosure Act it can be worked out that additionally the Bricknells owned much land between Northfields and Manor House.

Another resident of Evenlode of independent means was *Richard Davis,* aged 78. *Thomas Bliss,* aged 70, and his wife Mary, aged 60, were also of independent means. Thomas was not born in Evenlode though Bliss is a well-known Evenlode name. The surname goes back to before the Reformation. Mary was born in Evenlode. Thomas Bliss still farmed a little. He rented what used to be called Ralph's furlong from *John Horsley.* It is not known which house he lived in but it had an orchard and garden. These owed Church tithes. This duty was commuted to seven shillings and five pence per year under the Tithe Apportionment Act of 1839.

There was also *Joshua Bricknell,* aged 70. He employed a manservant who lived in and who was called *Jacob Sedgley,* aged 20. Neither was born in Evenlode. How this man is related to the other Bricknells is not known.

Ann James, aged 75 was probably the widow of the Revd William James who was Rector of Evenlode from 1805 until his death in 1825. She was therefore the mother of the Revd Charles James who became Rector in 1830. She had two servants who lived with her. *Sarah Rodgers* was aged 30 and *Anne* was aged 15. None was born in Evenlode. In the negotiations for the conveyance of land for the school Mrs James is noted as a landowner with a field at the rear of the school. In the census she is listed as a woman of independent means.

The census records *Charlotte Eaton,* aged 35. She was not born in Evenlode and nothing else can be discerned about her.

As noted above, the 1841 Census records a schoolmistress in the village even though the National School was not opened until 1844. She was *Emma Gillett* aged 30. She was not a native of Evenlode.

Non-resident landowners

Among the non-resident landowners that the Census records, was *Thomas Phipps.* At the time of the Tithe Apportionment Act of 1839 he owned the Manor House and its yard and garden, with the orchard and a paddock. He also held 22 acres of old enclosure pasture (perhaps as well as 1756 enclosure land). The old enclosure fields were called Daniel's field, Brock meadow, Oak meadow and Mill Pound where the mill had been. There was in addition a wooded area called Blind Pool. With the exception of Mill Pound these names do not relate to current names, though the field he calls Brock Meadow is likely to be the one now known as Brook Meadow. Which tenant farmed his land is not known.

Evenlode land called the Ridgeway fields and the Cart Gap fields and other land towards Chastleton and south to Horn Lane formed part of *Fothergill's Estate*. This estate also included *Heath Home Farm (Stubbles)*. The tenant here farmed Chastleton land and Evenlode land around Stubbles and the Ridgeway Fields.

Thomas Horne (who died in 1861) lived in Moreton-in-Marsh but he owned land in Evenlode. He was a wealthy grocer, a respected philanthropist and a devout *Congregationalist*. He owned the stretch of fields from Big Horn and Little Horn west to Dairy Ground and south to the Adlestrop border and Road. His tenant is likely to have lived in *Grange Farm*.

A puzzle is a stone built into Grange Farm with the initial R and FH 1625. This is likely to refer to Richard Haines who farmed Horn Farm then and may give a date for the building of Grange Farm, presumably initially as part of Horn Farm. At what date the Haines family acquired all the land to the south of Grange Farm is not known. Thomas Haines owned it at the time of his death in 1765 as recorded in his Will. This, as recorded above, is in Collection Nine of the Evenlode Papers.

A most unexpected non-resident landowner (a man who is still internationally renowned) was *John Henry Newman* who became a Roman Catholic Cardinal. In 1800 there was a Sale of land in Moreton and Evenlode and someone bought five acres in Evenlode known as Darke's Close. This land adjoins the brook to the north of what is now Wells Folly. The land became part of the glebe of the parish of Saint Mary, Oxford.

However this land continued to owe tithes to the Rector of Evenlode and in 1839 when calculations were being made to allocate rent in lieu of tithes, the Tithe Map notes the owner of Darke's Close as the parish of Saint Mary Oxford, and then in another part names the then Vicar of Saint Mary's Oxford *John Newman*. (Darke's Close was actually rented to *William Garner*).

The Census lists those who farmed Evenlode land. Twelve farmers are listed. Only three can be identified as owner-farmers and only four tenants can be linked to particular farms or land. It is striking to note how many had been born elsewhere and were not Evenlode natives.

John and Elizabeth Horsley, aged 65 and 60, farmed *Heath End Farm* at the time of the Census. They had four daughters and two young male lodgers called *John Allison* and *Warner Castle*. None of them were born in Evenlode. In the survey after the Tithe Apportionment Act of 1839, it was noted that John held 36 acres of arable land, 21 acres of pasture and 4 acres of woodland. He had a yard with the house and an orchard and a coppice.

Access to his house was by a cart track, with the land for the poor of Evenlode on the right as one enters. He also owned land adjoining the river near Stockbridge. This seems to have been what is now called Meadow Bottom. In Horsley's time it was called Rowes Furlong. This is a very ancient name that goes back to the ninth century when it was called "Ralph's furlong". In fact, as noted above, John Horsley rented this land to *Thomas Bliss*.

Fletchers Farm was owned and farmed, as it had been for over a century by the Fletcher family. *Joseph and Hannah Fletcher,* both aged 45, years farmed Fletcher's Farm in 1841. They had two sons resident, Thomas and George. They employed a servant aged 20. She was called *Ann Sandles*. None of these were born in Evenlode.

Richard and Jane Sophia Kibble aged 40 and 35, farmed *Horn Farm* in 1841. Richard and Jane had three children. Richard was born in Evenlode but his wife was not. The children were. They had a servant called *Jane Hunt* who did not come from Evenlode. From the Tithe Apportionment Act of 1839 Horn Farm land consisted of Far Ground, Spring Ground, Barley Fold, Harkum, Park, Butts, together with house, garden and yard. "Harkum" is clearly a phonetic rendering of Harcombe, which means "the wooded valley of the deer". The Butts is still a recognised fieldname that surely indicates where, by order of the king, the men of Evenlode practised archery. This was in the times of King Edward III (who trounced the French at Crecy). Spring Ground is likely to have been what is now known as Spring Hill. The

Park is now associated with Manor Farm land to the west of the road to Stockbridge so it must have been bought at some stage. Richard Kibble is probably a descendant of Thomas and Ann Kibble who lived in Evenlode in the latter part of the eighteenth century. They had a number of children who were baptised in Saint Edward's Church. In keeping the registers, names were written down phonetically so "Kibble" is sometimes spelt "Keble". The Kibbles sold the farm to Mary Ann Clemans (elsewhere Clements). She lived and farmed at Milton-under-Wychwood. After her death Mary Ann's last Will and Testament (proved in 1860) ordered Horn Farm to be sold.

The land farmed by four other farmers (all tenants) can be identified. *Joseph and Judith Harrison,* both aged 65, (neither of whom was born in Evenlode) were tenant farmers of *Evenlode Grounds Farm.* Their son *Isaac* lived with them and he was not born in Evenlode either. They had a female servant *Ann Roff* and a manservant *William Jacques.* Neither of these was born in Evenlode.

Richard and Elizabeth Anchor, aged 60 and 55, are listed as tenant farmers. *Mary Teal* was a servant in their household. From the information gathered for the Tithe Apportionment Act, it may be noted that *John Wishaw* (a non-resident) bought seven acres of land from the bottom of the Rector's garden down to where Rose Terrace is now. This he rented to Richard Anchor for £2/-/10d per annum. Richard farmed other land too. Richard and Elizabeth Anchor's farm buildings still bear their name.

Thomas and Esther Bryan, both aged 30, had two sons. Neither parent was born in Evenlode but the boys were. A parish (not yet identified but likely to have been Chastleton) had bought Horn ground for glebe and had rented it to *George Freeman* and then to *Thomas Brian.* Thomas Brian (Bryan) paid £5/5/6d per annum rent to the relevant incumbent. Thomas also rented from the same parish a field described as "Midlane." He paid the Rector for this a rent of £1/11/-d. Thomas Bryan was on the way to calling himself a farmer rather than an agricultural labourer. He was probably related to the two tenant farmers of Evenlode listed below, George Bryan who may have been his father, and William Bryan his brother.

William and Fanny Lord, aged 46 and 31, (neither of whom was born in Evenlode) were farming *Four Shire Stone Farm.* The Recording Officer makes a convenient note against their name to remind him of where they lived, otherwise which farm they farmed could not have been identified.

Unfortunately it has not been possible to place the remaining five tenant farmers into particular farms.

John and Charlotte Cluff, aged 60 and 50, and their daughter *Martha* are listed. They were not born in Evenlode. The agricultural labourer Edward Cluff is probably their son.

Stephen and Martha Brain, aged 41 and 39, and their five children are listed. They were not born in Evenlode.

George and Ann Bryan, aged 70 and 65, are listed. Neither was born in Evenlode. They had a son aged 25 living with them who was born in Evenlode and a daughter aged 20 who was not. Clearly they had moved to Evenlode as a married couple, then moved away, then they had returned. They had two small children living in the house whose surname was Bryan too.

William and Ann Bryan, both aged 25, are listed. Neither was born in Evenlode.

Richard and Sarah Heath, aged 33 and 35, are listed. They had a small baby. Neither parent was born in Evenlode. *John Heath* lived with them who was aged 81 and was born in Evenlode. Also living with them was *Ann Trinder* aged 76 and described as of independent means. They had a servant, *Rebecca Becham.* Neither of these was born in Evenlode.

The Bell Inn

Robert and Elizabeth Betts were both aged 40 at the time of the 1841 Census. Robert was a publican and landlord of the Bell Inn. They had four children and lived in the Inn. In the Census it is noted that *Joseph and Martha Betts* were aged 70 and 75 and that Joseph was a brewer. Probably Robert's father, his cider and beer would have been barrelled and sold in the Bell. Neither Joseph nor Martha was born in Evenlode. Another family of Betts was that of Thomas and Sarah. Thomas was an agricultural labourer.

From Collection Five of the Evenlode Papers it transpires that in 1859 the neighbouring cottages to the Bell Inn (namely the cottage facing Rose Terrace that was divided into four dwellings and the present Springside Cottage by then divided into two dwellings) were auctioned at the White Hart at Moreton-in-Marsh and Robert Betts bought them. After Robert's death his wife continued at the Bell then after her death they were sold. Robert's Will had envisaged that the properties would pass to his two sons John and Charles and to his daughter Naomi who married Mr Cook of Long Compton. An equal share was to go to William Lane though his relationship to William is not stated.

None of these wished to live in the properties, so John Betts sold them all to William Phipps who was the blacksmith at Longborough and they shared the proceeds.

It is interesting to note how the family dispersed. John Betts was a grocer in the High Street at Solihull. Charles Betts was living in Bishop Auckland in County Durham. Naomi Cook lived in Long Compton. William Lane's address was the "Golden Cross" at Rickmansworth. A classic example of how the railways enabled movement of the population.

By 1899 the Bell Inn was owned by Flower's Brewery.

The Evenlode blacksmith

John and Mary Breakspeare were aged 41 and 39 respectively at the time of the 1841 Census. John was the blacksmith. They had three children all born in Evenlode though neither of the parents was born in the village. John and Mary would have lived in Horn Lane in the house now known as The Old Forge. John also farmed. He rented from George Simcox Bricknell (his neighbour in Horn Lane, at Evenlode House) the fields called Howlett, Langate and Square Ground. This was the "old enclosure" between Manor Farm and Northfields Farm.

Tradesmen and shopkeepers

Thomas and Sarah Hayward, aged 33 and 30, had two children. None were born in Evenlode except the baby. Thomas was a sawyer.

Thomas and Dorcas Bartlett, both aged 30, had two children. Dorcas was not from Evenlode but the others were. Thomas Bartlett was a carpenter.

George and Ann Rustall were aged 40 and 45. He was a gardener. Neither came from Evenlode.

William and Rebecca Bryan, aged 45 and 49, were also trades people but their trade cannot be identified. They had three children. The last two were born in Evenlode but none of the rest of the family was born in the village.

There were three (possibly four) shops in Evenlode in 1841. This is a surprising number of shops, though in most cases the shop was likely to have been a room in the front of the house in which they lived.

Sarah Boswell, aged 41, kept a stationery shop. She was not born in Evenlode.

Sarah Bartlett aged 26 kept a grocer's shop. *Emma Bartlett* aged 20 was a dressmaker. It seems probable that these two were sisters and perhaps shared a cottage. Stephen Bartlett and Thomas Bartlett may have been their brothers. These two men were both married living in Evenlode and were agricultural labourers. The parents of all four Bartletts are likely to have been William and Mary Bartlett. William was a young farmer in 1800 when the baptism of his child is recorded in the parish registers. Ann Bartlett who is listed as an elderly pauper must be a relative but what the relationship was, is unknown.

Thomas and Elizabeth Hobley were aged 56 and 60. He was a hatter or possibly a slater. It is impossible to discern from the handwritten Census return which profession he was as the writer formed "Sl" in identical fashion to "H". Neither was born in Evenlode.

The Agricultural Labourers of 1841 and their daily lives

Most of the new Victorians of Evenlode were agricultural labourers and their families. A few labourers eventually found full time employment on the railway. Unlike the farmers and trades people a number of the labourers were natives of Evenlode. A few surnames indicate that the family had lived in Evenlode over several generations but as has been noted above, family links spread to villages round about.

The labourers and servants were poor in the rural economy of those days, but they were clean and decently clothed. The men wore tough corduroy trousers, a scarf round their neck, tucked into their collar-less shirt, a jacket and nailed boots. The girls did wonders with bits of ribbon and careful needlework.

The cottages too of the labourers of 1841 were poor but clean, with scrubbed stone floors. Washing was done communally in a building at the end of the row in some places called the "hovel." Hovel Field may be where the washing was hung out to dry. Water was free and plentiful from the well.

Baking day was very important for bread was the staple diet. Most men went out into the fields having eaten bread and butter for breakfast and took with them bread and bacon and an apple for their midday dinner (or bread and cheese and an onion). A workingman ate one pound of bread a day. That is half of a modern large loaf. He came home to his tea. This included bread and pastry. His drink was tea or beer.

When the gentry went after game, rabbits, rooks and pigeons were given to the men assisting. Rabbits gave body to the cottage stockpot. All three, rabbits, rooks and pigeons, could be turned into tasty pies with onion, carrot and a bit of fat bacon. Beef and mutton were less affordable. In Evenlode there was fruit from the orchards. Most cottages had a garden in which cabbages and carrots, onions and potatoes were grown. Also grown were a wealth of flowers.

Children had the same diet, but in the morning their bread might be softened with a little warm milk, or milk eked out with hot water. Those children who lived too far away from school to go home at midday took something with them for their midday meal. In winter a favourite to take with them was a hot jacket potato and a twist of salt. This not only fed them at midday but also kept their hands warm on the way to school. In 1841 it was likely that many children walked barefoot in the warmer months.

The agricultural labourers and their families in Evenlode at the time of the Census of 1841 were these. They occupied 41 residences.

Edward and Elizabeth Allen, aged 75 and 72. Neither was born in Evenlode.
Richard and Elizabeth Allen, aged 45 and 30, and their four children. All were born in Evenlode except Elizabeth who was born in "either Scotland, Ireland or foreign parts" (the alternative to England in the Census form).
Thomas and Rachel Allen, both aged 45. Thomas was born in Evenlode but Rachel was not. Neither were the six children living at home born in Evenlode except the baby, John, who was only three months.

Stephen and Elizabeth Bartlett, aged 35 and 30, and their four children. The parents were not born in Evenlode but all the children were.

Thomas Gilies Bartlett and Flora Bartlett, aged 38 and 26, and a child, Ann. All were born in Evenlode.

Jacob and Mary Bayliss, aged 36 and 35, and three of their children. All were born in Evenlode.

Samuel and Mary Beag, both aged 29, and their four children. All were born in Evenlode except the two youngest children, aged 3 and 1.

Mary Beal, aged 46, who described herself as an agricultural labourer. She may have been a widow for she has three young children. They were born in Evenlode but she was not.

Thomas and Sarah Betts, aged 65 and 60. They had three adult children living at home and a girl of 10 years, *Mary Allen.*

Edward and Ann Cluff, aged 40 and 35. Neither was born in Evenlode but their six children were. *Edward* may be a son of tenant farmer *John and Charlotte Cluff.*

John and Eliza Dobney, aged 28 and 25, and their three children. None were born in Evenlode except the baby, aged 1.

James and Margaret Gardner, aged 50 and 45, and seven children. All the children were born in Evenlode but neither of the parents was born in the village. The surname is however found in Evenlode in the seventeenth century.

Thomas and Ann Giles, aged 67 and 63, and Emanuel Giles, aged 14. All were born in Evenlode.

John and Hannah Golsby, both aged 35, and their seven children. Hannah came from Evenlode and their last two children were born in the village. All the others were born elsewhere.

Charles and Elizabeth Gregory, both aged 20, and their two children, Mathew and Alice. All were born in Evenlode except Elizabeth. It seems likely that Charles was a son of James and Sarah Gregory.

James and Sarah Gregory, aged 49 and 38. James was born in Evenlode but Sarah was not. There were four children living at home. The eldest was Joseph, aged 19, and the youngest Eliza who was aged 4. All were born in Evenlode except Henry who was born elsewhere in 1828.

John and Elizabeth Gregory, aged 45 and 40. John was born in Evenlode as was their daughter Sarah, aged 20, who was still at home and a baby, aged 1.

Richard and Ann Gregory, aged 40 and 30, and four children. All except Ann were born in Evenlode.

Thomas and Rhoda Gregory, aged 55 and 56. There are two boys living with them Simon, aged 15, and James, aged 9. All except Rhoda were born in Evenlode.

William and Ann Gregory, aged 30 and 35, and their two children. William was born in Evenlode, as was the youngest child.

John and Sarah Harris, aged 24 and 40, and their three children. All except Sarah were born in Evenlode.

William and Elizabeth Harris, aged 53 and 43, and four of their children. All the children were born in Evenlode but neither of the parents.

William and Mary Harris, aged 35 and 30, and their six children. William and all the children were born in Evenlode.

Sarah Hill, aged 36, described herself as an agricultural labourer. She had two children born in Evenlode though she herself was not.

Richard and Ann Hirst, both aged 30, and their three children. Only Ann and baby Mary Ann, aged one month, were born in Evenlode.

John Jacques, aged 43. He was born in Evenlode.

Richard and Dina Jacques, aged 40 and 30, and four children. All were born in Evenlode except Dina the mother. Another *Richard Jacques* was also lodging with them.

Thomas and Mary Jacques, both aged 40, and the four children living with them. Neither parent was born in Evenlode. The three youngest children were John, Elizabeth and James.

John and Hannah Hope, both aged 30, and their three children. All were born in Evenlode except Hannah the mother.

James and Sarah Langer, aged 45 and 44, and their six children. All were born in Evenlode except James himself.

Henry and Elizabeth Mills, aged 40 and 43. They had a girl called Priscilla, aged 15, living at home. There was a baby Jane, aged one year. Priscilla and the baby were born in Evenlode.

Samuel and Mary Moss, aged 50 and 55. He was not born in Evenlode but Mary was. They had a fifteen years old daughter Sarah, born in Evenlode, living at home and there was a baby.

Sarah Mulcock, aged 75, is listed as an agricultural labourer and living with her was Eleanor Mulcock aged 30. Both were born in Evenlode.

William and Hannah Mulcock, aged 40 and 30, and their four children. All were born in Evenlode except one child born elsewhere.

Thomas and Elizabeth Newman, both aged 30, and their four children. All except the 6 months old baby were born elsewhere.
William and Ann Saul, aged 65 and 50. Neither was born in Evenlode.
William Saul and *John Saul,* aged 35 and 30, shared a cottage. Presumably the sons of William and Ann Saul, they obviously valued their independence. They were both born in Evenlode.
Edmund and Sarah Tidmarsh, aged 40 and 35. She was born in Evenlode but he was not. They were probably relatives of the Recording Officer.
Richard Tustin, aged 60, born in Evenlode.
Gregory and Sarah Wilks, aged 45 and 46, and two adult children. All were born in Evenlode except Gregory.
Thomas Witham, aged 75. He was not born in Evenlode.

Paupers

Evidently the Stow workhouse was not open before 1841 or else the people of Evenlode had allowed their own deserving poor to remain in the village poor house to the end of their days. The paupers were:
Ann Bartlett, aged 70, born in Evenlode
Ann Butter, aged 70, born in Evenlode
Mary Beag, aged 66, born in Evenlode
William and Mary Davis, aged 75 and 67, not born in Evenlode. William may be the bankrupt whose farm was sold.
Mary Davis a child born in Evenlode. She may have been resident to help William and Mary.

Victorian Evenlode and the railways

The greatest means of providing work and wealth for the Victorians was the railway. Evenlode may not have had a Railway Station but the new fangled "Puffing Billies" hissed and chuffed along Evenlode's riverbank with increasing frequency. The Puffing Billies hauled goods and conveyed people and brought change. The journeys they made gave opportunities to poor men to settle elsewhere with their families and make a fresh start where there was money. Every family in the land was affected in one way or another. The railways eventually replaced the canal system. They took on the same tasks but did them much more quickly. Less time meant cheaper transport. Also they were able to take on a greater variety of tasks than the canals.

Two generations earlier, the building of canals had made a massive contribution to the industrial revolution. They enabled coal to be moved to power the stationary steam engines that drove the machinery in the factories and mills. They also enabled non-perishable goods to be transported from place to place. After the expense of building a canal, the cost of running it was initially quite small. A narrow boat was worked by whole families, husband, wife and children, and powered by one horse. It was only later that the cost of maintenance of a waterway began to become clear.

The canals had other drawbacks. Travel on them was slow and in winter the canals were sometimes frozen. The narrow boats and "butties" (the boat that was towed behind) were often locked in ice for weeks. Neither could they carry perishable goods or animals. So animals were still driven to the cities and sold to the butchers. The drovers drove the animals along the old drove roads with their wide verges.

The introduction of railways promised great wealth to the owners for they could move people and animals and every kind of goods, not only non-perishable but also perishable, swiftly and regularly. However, the canals gave a language to railway engineering. Canals had to be built on the "level." If there was a rise in the ground a "cut" had to be made to take the canal through. The canals were called "navigations" and those who built them became known as "navvies." So the railways had levels and cuts too, and navvies built them also.

The genius of the railway was to design a steam engine small enough to run on rails and yet still powerful enough to pull wagons. Several attempts were made to achieve this and observing these attempts George Stephenson designed and built the first passenger railway (track, engines and rolling stock) between Darlington and the river wharves at Stockton-on-Tees in 1825. He had built many tracks from the collieries along the Tyne down to the river and had the requisite engineering skills. The width of the tracks was the length of his walking stick and the wagons were built to fit the track. His walking stick was 4 feet 6 ½ inches long.

At the height of railway mania, a railway was decided upon to link the black country of Dudley and Wolverhampton with Oxford and beyond. The suggested route passed through Evenlode. The company that was set up to build it was called the Oxford, Worcester and Wolverhampton Railway Company. The company opted for Isambard Kingdom Brunel's wide gauge rather than Stephenson's.

The OWW Railway Company was authorised on 4 August 1845 to construct the railway. It was to leave the Oxford and Rugby line at Wolvercote junction and then proceed to Worcester and so on to Wolverhampton by way of Stourbridge and Dudley. The Great Western Railway's engineers were employed to oversee the project and Isambard Kingdom Brunel was appointed the chief consultant engineer.

The route had to be surveyed and the most economical line chosen. This involved much work for gradients had to be calculated so that the "levels" were not too steep for the engines and the "cuts" (expensive to dig) not too many. Whilst this was being carried out the Company began the construction of the tunnel at Chipping Campden. Twice the company tried to evade its commitment to the GWR and this caused considerable controversy. The contractor Francis Tredwell died, with the company owing him money. Work was stopped for several years because of the ensuing litigation. In 1850 Peto and Betts were appointed the contractors (still under the supervision of Brunel's brothers) but the gauge was changed to what was by then the standard gauge (Stephenson's). By 1854 the Company was in a very bad financial state but was taken over by the West Midlands Railway Company. In 1862, the GWR took over the West Midlands and with it the OWW.

However, this was in the future. After the survey sometime after 1845, the OWW had to purchase the land over which the line ran.

The conveyance of glebe-land, owned by the then Rector of Evenlode (Charles James) in his right as Rector, has survived in Collection Eleven of the Evenlode Papers. The land he sold ran alongside the river. It was surveyed and valued by James Webb and William Woodward. The final indenture was dated 5 June 1849 and signed by the Rector and representatives of the OWW.

The Rector was paid £560 for the land needed for the level and this included any minerals and mines discovered below the surface when construction began. He was paid £45 for permission to build a road from the lane to give access to the site for workmen. He was additionally paid £540 compensation for his "severance" from his land. The land concerned was part of Evenlode Grounds Farm. The tenant was Joseph Harrison. It is not recorded whether he received any of the severance money!

Ralph Mann quotes a description of the "navvies" who built the line, in his book *The Rectors of Kingham*. They were rough and tough men who were best kept occupied, for if there was no work for whatever reason, they made for the public houses and trouble ensued.

It is possible that the arrival of the "navvies" at Evenlode is connected with the fact that in 1849 and 1850 a number of Evenlode men were sentenced to imprisonment in Gloucester. The details are in Collection Three of the Evenlode Papers. In 1849 Robert Jordan, aged 17, a labourer and Richard Frederick Gregory, aged 20, also a labourer were imprisoned. In 1850 Robert Jordan was again imprisoned together with two other men, Daniel Gregory, aged 20, a soldier and Frederick Gregory, also aged 20, a labourer. That year William Mulcock, aged a mere 15 years, also went to prison.

When the railway opened the nearest stations for Evenlode were Adlestrop and Moreton-in-Marsh. Moreton-in-Marsh Station had large pens for both cattle and sheep. This meant that animals could be driven to the market at Moreton sold by auction to butchers from the cities, and other farmers long distances away, and then be transported speedily and humanely in cattle trucks by train.

The opening of the Oxford, Worcester and Wolverhampton Railway enabled men without work to move from Evenlode into factories in Stourbridge, Dudley and Wolverhampton. This becomes evident in the school logbook that records the absence of a pupil who was visiting relatives in Wolverhampton. For an Evenlode child to travel to Wolverhampton must have seemed an enormously long journey, to a black and grimy place.

There were problems with the OWW. There was a serious accident at Round Oak Station between Stourbridge and Dudley some three miles before Dudley Railway Station when travelling towards Wolverhampton. The Inspector said it was the worst railway accident he had attended. The OWW was nick-named "The Old Worse and Worse." Yet, the line enabled Evenlode people to travel in a way never before even dreamed of, horseless coaches pulled on rails by a moving steam engine!

Most of the early passenger trains ran between Wolverhampton and Oxford where they terminated. Eventually, it was decided to run an "express" train to London. It ran in the early afternoon so that passengers could spend the next day engaged in their business activity. The journey time from Moreton-in-Marsh to London was a very respectable two hours and five minutes.

Victorian Evenlode and Education

The most notable of the great reforming Acts of Parliament during the reign of Queen Victoria was the Education Act of 1870. Aware that this Act was impending, the Vestry in the 1860s was anxious that, unless it improved the school a School Board would be created with powers to impose a compulsory school rate.

The Vestry was by this time a group of men who clearly were socially conscious. The spirit of Victorian religion had obviously spread to Evenlode. It seems that their anxiety was not about having to spend money on the school, but about keeping it under the village's control.

The Minutes of the Vestry during the 1860s are heartening. In 1866, there are recorded the regular appointments of two surveyors, two overseers of the poor and four constables. The increase of constables from two to four is interesting and puzzling. They were John Bartlett, a carpenter, George Fletcher, Thomas Fletcher and George Bryan, all farmers. Joseph Gregory was appointed as village poundsman and attendees at the meetings included John Phipps, blacksmith, and George Payne, gardener. They decided that year not to give coal to non-resident poor and this seems to have been a consequence of the decision taken the previous year, not to give coal on a weekly basis but to have twice-yearly deliveries. They agreed to fix a Church Rate of 2 pence in the pound and an additional Church Repair Rate of 1½ pence in the pound. They used this to build two buttresses on the north wall of the Church. They abandoned charging rates to the inhabitants of the rented cottages (the labouring families) but charged the rates to the owners of the cottages at a 30% reduction.

The Vestry was clearly well aware of the educational needs of Evenlode. It had received some form of ultimatum and a response had to be made by the 1 January 1871. The members agreed to collect from the ratepayers the sum of £15 to repair the schoolroom and to collect a further £21-6s-0d annually towards the Mistress's salary. For whatever reason, their industry in attempting to retain the school was not rewarded. The School went to the Board. The documents are held at the Gloucestershire Archive.

The conveyance was "made between the Revd Thomas Holford Buckworth, Rector of Evenlode, John Timms and Edward Harrison, farmers and churchwardens, and Charles Fletcher and George Bryan, farmers and overseers of the poor – the Trustees and Managers of the National School" and the new Board. It reminded everyone that John Henry Whitmore Jones and John Arthur Whitmore Jones (his heir in law) had in 1840, given land for a National School conducted in the principles of the Established Church, "for children and adults of the labouring, manufacturing and other poorer classes in Evenlode". Then it went on to state that the school was conveyed to the Board on 11 September 1876 to be a school "as provided within the meaning of the 1870 Education Act". The Chairman fixed the Common Seal of the new School Board. His name was John Timms.

John Timms was the churchwarden so the Vestry had thought this through and come to the conclusion that it was more sensible to fall in line and have a School "under the Act" but with one of their own as Chairman. This proved wise. As soon as the conveyance was made, more land was acquired from Miss Whitmore Jones. On 14 October 1876, Newman and Sons Builders, of Evenlode, were awarded the contract to convert the existing School House and site into a school and teacher's residence, erecting a new class room, porches, out offices, boundary walls and forming play grounds.

The "new classroom" is the large room on the north of the current residence called "The Old School." It is 30 feet long and 16 feet wide and was designed for 40 children to be taught by the Mistress. To the Mistress' left hand were the children of Standards 1 and 2 (7 and 8 years old). In front of her were Standards 3 and 4 (9 and 10 years old). To her right were Standards 5 and 6 (11 and 12 years old). Children left school for employment on their thirteenth birthday.

Also in the School was a small room sized thirteen feet by thirteen feet. This was designed for 14 infants taught by an assistant.

The School Board ordered a rate to be paid. In 1876 James Newman was appointed as Rate Collector at an annual salary of £8 per year. He had to collect the Poor Rate, the School Board Rate, a "Sanitary" Rate and "any other rate required by law".

The Evenlode Charities in Victorian times

The concern to raise money for the Coal Charity was ever present. The "Poors" land was no longer used by the poor (if it ever had been) but was rented to tenants. The money thus collected paid for the two big deliveries of coal over the winter. Charges were also collected from the pieces of land associated with the charity, Eastwells in Longborough and Campden's Close on the corner of the "road" to Longborough.

All the verges were rented out too. The rents for 1902 are recorded in the Vestry Book in the Gloucestershire Archive. They are likely to have been similar in Victorian times, though the names of the farmers in this list are those of 1902:

Broadwell turn to Adlestrop. Mr Wooliams 6/-d
Bell Inn to Stockbridge. Mr Whittingham 10/-d
West of Hambidges' House to the Bell Inn. Revd Kelsall 5/6d.
Portion of W. Hunt's land. W Hunt 5/-d.
Portion of G W Ralph's land. W Hunt 6/6d.
Village Green to Evenlode House. W. Hambidge 11/6d.
Village Green to Evenlode House (second). W Hambidge 12/-d.
Midlane (enclosed portion). W Collins 14/-d.
Portion by W. Whittinghams' land. G Jacques 8/6d.
Moreton bridge to Evenlode bridge W Hands £1/10/-d
Evenlode bridge to village. W Hands £4/4/-d.

The village green was used for grazing too and the consequences of this, and the renting of the verges for grazing, require little imagination. The scene must have inspired the joker to invent the jingle revealed at the 2000 Millennium Exhibition:

Adlestrop for beauty
Oddington for wit
Broadwell for money
Evenlode for ____.

Under the Constabulary Act of 1839, a local constabulary had to be established to replace or enhance the traditional Parish Constables elected by the Vestry. From 1839 to 1841 the Gloucestershire Quarter Sessions repeatedly tried to get Evenlode to pay for constabulary services. This highlighted the problem of Evenlode being in Worcestershire, whereas services like the constabulary emanated from Gloucestershire.

As residents of Worcestershire, Evenlode refused to pay Gloucestershire for a constabulary and presented a petition in 1841 asserting that a paid constabulary was quite unnecessary in Evenlode anyway. However, given the arrests referred to above around the 1850s, it seems that Evenlode eventually succumbed.

By an Act of 1872 each Poor Law Union was enabled to re-style itself as a "Local Board of Health". This, the Stow Union (which Evenlode had joined) proceeded to do. It took on concern for sewage disposal. The reason for a "Sanitary Rate" in Evenlode is connected with this formation of a Stow Local Board. This became Stow Urban District Council in 1895. In 1935 the UDC became part of the North Cotswolds Rural District Council.

A footnote: The Victorian Penny Bank

An encouraging sign of aspiration for the future among the poor and young of Evenlode in the reign of Queen Victoria was the beginning of saving money. The Moreton branch of the YMCA founded the "Moreton Coffee Room Bank." The records are in Collection Three and disclose that there were more than twenty depositors in the Bank from Evenlode.

Photo: The Evenlode Collection

Evenlode Congregational Chapel

Photo: Evenlode Collection
Restored for High Church worship

190

Chapter 14

Church and Chapel
in the Nineteenth Century

The Catholic connection

Before 1840, Darke's Close, near Wells Folly, became part of the glebe of Saint Mary's Church, Oxford. As noted above, the recipient of the rent was the Vicar of Saint Mary's Oxford, John Henry Newman.

John Henry Newman became one of the most well known of Victorian clergy. He was an Oxford graduate clearly heading for a distinguished academic career. Anyone aspiring to a Fellowship in those days had to be unmarried and ordained. John Henry Newman was both. He became Vicar of Saint Mary's Oxford. Together with men like John Keble, Newman began the "Oxford Movement" which attempted to bring back Catholicism to the Church of England in a way that rejected the jurisdiction of the Pope.

After a soul-searching period in which he wrote the hymn "Lead kindly light, amid the encircling gloom" he left the Church of England and became a Roman Catholic to great consternation and shock in the world of Oxford University of the 1840s.

When a Roman Catholic priest, apart from a spell as Vice Chancellor of the Catholic University of Dublin, he founded the Birmingham Oratory, where he lived a scholarly life. He was a theologian and writer of great erudition. All his sermons (both Anglican and Catholic) have been edited in many volumes. They are readily available in libraries. Many know him as the author of the words of Elgar's Oratorio "The Dream of Gerontius" with its wonderful hymn, "Praise to the holiest in the height".

As an elderly man, he was made a Cardinal. Since his death his writings have become more and more significant, and his theology shaped the work of the Second Vatican Council. His "cause" is now being considered in Rome and at the time of writing it is believed he will soon be given the title "Blessed". Many people pray that after this, he will be given the title "Saint". It is suggested that he will also be declared a "Doctor" of the Church.

Evenlode's Congregational Chapel

John Henry Newman publicly became a Cardinal of Rome. This publicity would have been unheard of in years gone by. In Queen Victoria's reign other denominations, and even religions, were allowed to prosper.

The Methodists continued to build chapels in every parish. In Evenlode, it was the Congregationalists of Moreton-in-Marsh who built the Chapel. George Whitefield, the great Methodist preacher in the early days, did not preach in Moreton and the surrounding villages. He believed his Calvinist version of the Gospel was being well taught by the Congregational Christians at Moreton-in-Marsh. So when Evenlode received a chapel, it was a Congregational foundation.

The Congregational Chapel was opened in 1865, but there must have already been a potential congregation to merit building it. People must have been walking or riding on horseback to Moreton to make the idea of building a chapel in Evenlode desirable. The Minister of Moreton Chapel travelled around all the villages visiting contacts and welcoming people into the Congregation. Congregational Lay Preachers travelled into the countryside to take Sunday services.

Thomas Horne is almost certainly the one linked with establishing Congregationalism in Evenlode. He did not live at Evenlode but he farmed Evenlode land and employed a number of people on his land.

The Moreton and Disrict Local History Society records details of Thomas Horne He was born in 1786 and was the son of Joseph and Ann Horne who owned the White Lion Public House in the High Street of Moreton-in-Marsh (now White Lion Cottage). He began his working life as a carrier and soon was buying and carrying and selling all the produce of the grocery trade around the north Cotswolds and south Warwickshire. Then he moved into land and eventually owned and farmed 700 acres.

In the Moreton-in-Marsh Congregational Church registers, it is recorded that he was:

admitted to the church 1 April 1840 and died in the faith and hope of the gospels on 23 January 1861 and was interred in the (Moreton) Chapel ground. By the consistency of his character he commended the gospel and by his great liberality he did much to sustain the ministry for many years. The cause of God at Moreton and the surrounding villages was greatly aided by him.

Although he was a resident of Moreton-in-Marsh he owned and farmed 139 acres at Evenlode. This was *Grange Farm,* the land stretching from Horn Lane across to the Adlestrop Road. He also had land at Oddington and Bourton-on-the-Water making the total amount of 700 acres. He employed one farmer for all this land but also twenty-five men, twelve women and fourteen boys. A number of these lived in Evenlode and worked on his Evenlode land. It is not known who his managing farmer was or where he lived. It is quite possible that he lived at Grange Farm.

He also established a distribution network for farm produce and other groceries. This supplied goods to the four counties round about.

This rich landowner who aided the "cause of God" in Moreton's "surrounding villages" is likely to have ensured the building of the first chapel at Evenlode. No doubt he anticipated that those who worked for him would attend. Even though he died in 1861 it would be surprising if, in his latter years, he had not been connected with the enterprise of building a chapel.

The *Gloucester Chronicle* obituary reads:

Moreton-in-Marsh 2 February 1861
The late Thomas Horne, senior
This old and much respected inhabitant died after a long affliction borne with Christian resignation on Wednesday evening last having reached the age of 74 years. The deceased was the founder of the extensive business bearing his name in this town, which he successfully carried on for more than half a century, and was a noble illustration of what may be accomplished by strict integrity, thorough business habits, and indomitable perseverance. He

commenced business on a small capital in a cottage adjoining the present Assembly Room and by indefatigable industry lived to become the possessor of ample fortune, the owner of a considerable part of his native town, and the head of a firm whose commercial transactions are not to be equalled in the four adjoining counties. The deceased gentleman will long live in the memories of the inhabitants of Moreton. The British Schools were we believe erected and mostly maintained at his expense; the elegant Congregational Chapel, now in course of erection, owes its existence to his generosity; and he also contributed most handsomely to our Church Building Fund, the local charities, reading room and in fact every object designed for the benefit of Moreton without regard to party or sect.

Evenlode Chapel was built in 1865 but later was demolished to make way for the Village Hall. It was a plain building, 22 feet long and 17 feet wide. It was furnished with seating, three desks or tables, a pulpit and a harmonium. Three oil lamps provided light. Outside there was a garden somewhat larger, 34 feet long and 26 feet wide, with an outbuilding. It may have been planned as a burial ground but was never used as such.

The restoration of Evenlode Church

In the 1840s, the churchwardens Richard Kibble and Richard Anchor had a vision of a restored church. What they had in mind seems to have been a classical restoration in the Georgian style. This never happened, and by the 1840s it was becoming unfashionable.

The Restoration was carried out during the time that Charles Peach was Rector (1877–95). It was in two phases.

In 1878–9, J F K Cutts restored the chancel and added the vestry. He reshaped stone where he could and replaced much stone especially in the window frames. He placed an aperture in the wall beside the Rector's stall presumably for books. It is possible that he may here have re-used stone from an aumbry or a piscina that would have been in the south wall of the sanctuary.

In 1884–5, Cutts tackled the nave and the south aisle. He re-used stone where possible and during this restoration an aperture was made in the south wall which cannot be in an original position. The stone sedilium was removed from the sanctuary and placed in the south aisle. The plastering over of the medieval painting of the Doom was carried out.

In his restoration he re-used a stone for the sill of the eastern most southern window in the south aisle in which holes for "Nine Men's Morris" have been made. Early notes about the Church say that this was done by "the monks" but as we have seen there were no monks at Evenlode. In the same windowsill is the base of the piscina that would have been set in an aperture in the wall. It would have drained into the earth outside. The piscina was where the priest washed his hand before saying Mass and where water unused in the Mass was poured away. Cutts also saved a small millstone and housed it near this particular windowsill. The suggestion has been made that this was used to make flour for the bread for Holy Communion, but it is more likely that it belonged to the village for use by the poor, and kept in the Church so all knew where it was.

J F K Cutts is regularly criticised for his severe restoration, but what this Victorian architect did was to provide a refreshed, clean church of shaped stones and fine timber such as the Deyvilles built in the twelfth century and extended in the fourteenth century. It was architecture re-discovering the medieval style.

High Church worship

What was also being re-discovered was the old ritual of the pre-Reformation Church. Churchmen excitedly talked about vestments, liturgical colours, cross and candles on the altar (the Laudian two or the Roman "big six"), mixing water with the wine in the chalice, using wafers rather than a slice of bread, even incense. This appealed to the romanticism of the Victorians, and some or all these features came into use in many churches.

Charles Peach's list of church fittings in 1880 indicates his personal preference for "high church" worship. The list is in the Gloucestershire Archive.

For the altar in St Edward's Church there are:

Brass gemmed altar cross
Pair of candlesticks
Pair of three branched candlesticks
Dorsal and side hangings (curtains around the altar)
3 sets of altar frontals red, green and violet
3 richly illuminated altar panels (visible on feast days – white)
2 super frontals – red and violet
For the chalice there are:
Burse and veil in violet, red, green and white
1 lawn chalice veil

In addition in the sanctuary are:
Credence table
2 cruets
Candle extinguisher
Oak desk for office book
2 oak chairs

In the nave are:
Litany desk
Oak lectern
Ante-pendia in violet, red, green and white for pulpit, lectern and litany desk
Alms bags in violet, red, green and white

Also in the list are general items such as oil lamps, brass vases, linen, kneelers, curtains, furniture for the vestry and a harmonium. Charles Peach would own and use his personal stoles and other priests' vestments. As Archdeacon Slope remarked in Thackeray's novel, "It is not only in Barchester that a new man (incumbent) is carrying out new measures and carting away the useless rubbish of centuries. The same thing is going on throughout the country".

There is no list indicating what Charles Peach threw out but not everything was thrown out for the Church still has its plate. This is a description of the precious chalice presented by Mrs Leader:

A large chalice with Paten cover, bearing the hallmarks of 1753 and illegible maker's marks on both pieces. The chalice is 9.25 inches in height and weighs 16 oz. 15 dwts; the bell-shaped bowl measures 4.5 inches in diameter, 4 and seven-eighths inches in depth, and rests upon a stem that which carries a large pear shaped knob. The Paten cover is 4 and five-eighths inches in diameter, 1 and three-eighths inches in height and weighs 6 oz. 10 dwts. Both cup and cover are inscribed

The gift of Mrs Judith Leader to the Parish of Evenload

This and other church related documents are held in the Gloucestershire Archive.

Evenlode's Victorian Clergy

The *Revd Charles James* became Rector on 20 January 1830. He had graduated from Christ's College Cambridge in 1824. He saw through the arrangements for the Tithe Apportionment Act of 1839. He sold glebe land to allow the railway to pass through Evenlode. He remained Rector until 1857. He was resident at the Rectory.

The *Revd Henry Worsley* became Rector for just over a year on 27 August 1857. He had graduated from St Mary Hall Oxford in 1789 so was an elderly man. His daughter Mary married Windsor Edmund Hambrough.

The *Revd Windsor Hambrough* was born in 1830. He was in direct descent from the Plantagenets by way of Alice, sister of King Richard III. He graduated from Christ Church Oxford. He married Mary Worsley in June 1853 and became Rector of Evenlode upon the death of her father. He died on 3 November 1899 his wife having predeceased him in April 1895. However, he resigned the living of Evenlode in 1867.

The *Revd James Meaburn Stainland* became Rector on 5 July 1867 for a short while.

The *Revd Thomas Everard Buckworth* became Rector on 22 September 1868. He continued the disastrous custom of selling glebe land because of a need for cash. He sold meadows adjoining the river. Charles James had sold land to the OWW Railway, but the reason was commercial. The reason for this sale is unknown but it may have been linked to the nineteenth century additions to the Rectory. In 1875, the Revd Thomas Holford Buckworth succeeded him. He was Rector only for a short while.

The *Revd Charles Peach* became Rector on 12 February 1877 and remained Rector until 1895. He presided over the severe restoration of St Edward's Church and the beautifying of it with many new fitments associated with the re-discovery of the Catholic roots of the Church of England by the men of the "Oxford Movement".

Photo: Jenny Hill Exhibition

Evenlode School pupils in 1901

Chapter 15

Before the War (1897–1914)

In Queen Victoria's Jubilee year of 1897

The Vestry met as usual in 1897. Prior to the arrival of the new Rector, the Revd Henry Kelsall, in 1895, there had been a dispute over the appointment of the People's Churchwarden. A public meeting was called and a vote demanded. A date was fixed and the polling station was open at the school from 12noon to 2pm and from 6pm to 8pm. All adults were expected to vote. It seems that many did for the total population (including women and children) was only 248 and 86 votes were cast. The lot fell on Mr Bricknell.

The new Rector had caused a stir when he came. One of the first things he did was to make some money by selling the church elms as standing timber for £11/8/0d. The vestry noted this but saw that new trees replaced them.

The bells ring out for the Queen's Jubilee

The Revd Henry James Kelsall presided over the renovation of the bells and new machinery to hang them in order that a peal in honour of the Queen could ring out over Evenlode. Evenlode's five bells in the tower of St Edward's Church rang out gleefully with a peal in honour of the Diamond Jubilee of Queen Victoria in 1897. The details of the Appeal to renew the bells are in the Gloucestershire Archive.

Bagely's Catalogue of 1732 had noted that there was already a peal of five bells at Evenlode. This may have included the present tenor bell because this is dated from the seventeenth or eighteenth century. This bell (which weighs 7cwt and 2qrs) was re-hung for the Jubilee.

200

The second and fourth bells were newly cast for the Jubilee. H. Bond & Sons of Burford, Bell Founders, were awarded the contract. The second bears the date 1897, the name of the Bell Founders and the names of the Churchwardens, C. H. Collins and H. Hunt. It weighs 3cwt and 2qrs. (Charles Collins farmed Home Farm and Henry Hunt farmed Coldicote Heath Farm for Mr Barnsley).

The fourth weighs 5cwt and 2qrs. It also bears the date 1897, the name of the Bell Founders and the bell's name: "The Victoria Jubilee Bell." In addition it gives the name of the Rector, Henry James Kelsall MA, and the following verse:

"Many years may I tell
Victoria reigned well"

John Rudhall had cast the treble bell in 1831 and it weighed 3cwt and 1qr. This was re-hung for the Jubilee.

G. Mears of the Whitechapel Bell Foundry had cast the third in 1858. It weighed 4cwt. It too was re-hung for the Jubilee.

H. Bond & Sons fitted new gearing and re-hung all five bells (probably in a new frame) in time for the peal in honour of Queen Victoria's Jubilee.

So, in 1897, the year of Queen Victoria's Diamond Jubilee, the bells rang out and joined those of the surrounding villages in thanksgiving to God. There were special services in St Edward's Church and no doubt in Evenlode Congregational Chapel too. The people feasted on huge portions of meat, eaten with vast quantities of potatoes, cabbage and savoury suet pudding washed down (apparently) with five pints of beer each.

Evenlode Life "Before the War"

Glimpses of Evenlode in the years before the First World War reveal a peaceful way of life. It was more leisurely and perhaps more religious (if church going be the criterion) than today. It is no wonder that those born during the reign of Queen Victoria (looking back) saw this as a golden age "before the War." They meant of course the dreadful First World War with the slaughter in the trenches.

Articles from that period in the *Cotswold Journal* are interesting to read. On Christmas Day in the year 1900 the Rector, the Revd

Henry Kelsall, held two services. He preached in the morning, but in the evening of Christmas Day there was a special service. The Church Choir (augmented by the children of the Sunday School) performed, "A Service of Song with Carols" written by Bridge and Stainer. A reporter for the *Cotswold Journal* noted that both the services were "cheerful and hearty" and that the Church was "tastefully decorated".

Sunday Schools were a major part of Evenlode village life. There were two Sunday Schools in Evenlode. One was organised by the Church and the other by the Chapel. Both seem to have been well attended. In 1905 the *Cotswold Journal* reported the summer outings of both Sunday Schools.

The Congregational Sunday School outing took place first on 5 August. It was organised by the Longborough Chapel. The Evenlode Chapel Sunday School members joined the Longborough Chapel children. Others came from the Moreton Chapel Sunday School too. The report reads:

On Wednesday week the children attending the Congregational Sunday School at Longborough had their annual summer treat. Children, teachers, and friends, about 90 in all, met at the Chapel and were conveyed in wagons, kindly lent by Mr J Stokes, the Superintendent of the Sunday School, to Adlestrop Hill, some seven miles distant. Arriving there, they were joined by the school children from Moreton and Evenlode Chapel Sunday Schools. The weather being very hot, and after the somewhat long ride all were ready to do ample justice to the excellent tea, which was provided by the Moreton friends. After tea, various games were indulged until about 7-30pm when the call for home was sounded.

On 19 August it was the Evenlode Church Sunday School treat. The report reads:

The children attending the Evenlode Church Sunday School had their annual treat on Friday. They arrived at the Rectory at three o'clock and received a hearty welcome from the Rector (the Rev. H. J. Kelsall). At four o'clock tea was served on the lawn, and at five o'clock the parents and friends also partook of tea. The weather was delightful and the various games and amusements were thoroughly enjoyed. The whole of the party numbering about 50 had a very pleasant time. The National Anthem was sung and hearty cheers were given for the Rector and Mrs. Kelsall.

No doubt the children eagerly compared notes as to which was the better "Treat"!

It might seem odd to think of the journey from Longborough to Adlestrop Hill as "long" but the great horses pulling the carts were gentle giants who proceeded at a casual walking pace, so it probably took almost two hours to make the journey.

In 1906, the Bishop of Worcester held a Lenten Mission at Evenlode. The Cotswold Journal reports:

The Bishop of Worcester's Lenten Mission has taken place at Evenlode during the week, when his Chaplain, the Rev. C. Pepys, preached on Sunday morning, held a children's service in the afternoon, and conducted another service during the week, all of which were well attended. On Monday morning the Bishop arrived from Northwick. He visited the church and was much interested in the chancel arch, which is early Norman, the old oak pulpit and font, both of which are pre-Reformation, and the Norman sedilia, which is very similar to the one in Canterbury Cathedral. He then inspected the altar plate and registers, which are very complete and date back to 1561.

Mr Yells (the Churchwarden) was much concerned with nightingales, mayflies and (presumably) fishing:

Mr C Yells, of Coldicote Heath, Moreton-in-Marsh, calls our attention to a statement in one of the "yellow" newspapers that there is a scarcity of nightingales this year, and that there are very few May fly. He says that in the Evenlode cover at least half a dozen of these lovely songsters can be heard, and he adds that on the Evenlode River mayflies were rising by hundreds on Tuesday. Whatever may be the cause in other parts of the country, there seems to be no diminution in the number of nightingales in the neighbourhood.

There was crime! The *Cotswold Journal* reveals that the driver of a horse and cart got into trouble with the police. The newspaper reported in 1902:

Oliver Hine, a labourer of Evenlode, was summoned for riding on a cart while in charge without reins on August 15. Defendant pleaded guilty. PC Jones said at about 4.15pm he was on duty between Four Shire Stone and Evenlode. He saw defendant riding on the shaft of a cart while in charge. He had no reins. Defendant said there was another man with him who was equally in charge, but was a little way behind the horse. He thought he was nearer and was fined 1s including costs.

A Romantic view of the countryside

The Victorians had begun by admiring the raging furnaces and the amazing machines of the industrial revolution. After the Queen's Jubilee people began to realise what destruction industry had wrought in the countryside, not least in encouraging the departure of the young for work in the industrial areas. This movement of population meant that customs that once passed down from mother to daughter or father to son, were fast becoming lost, though it is probable that these traditions of the past were not missed by country folk.

In the early days of the twentieth century the countryside started to receive "romantic" visitors searching for a culture about to be lost. By accident almost, Cecil Sharp and others became aware of the tunes and dances called Morris Dancing. They came by train and brought their bicycles with them to reach remote villages and search out these tunes and dances, and write them down for publication. For example, Cecil Sharp cycled in Gloucestershire (sometimes with a "phonograph" resting on his handlebars) to record old people singing the old songs passed down over many generations. He visited Harry Taylor in Longborough and John Mason in the Stow Union workhouse and the Hathaways (father and son) at Bledington and others round about.

Many of the tunes and songs are simple and charming and tell of love and courtship, though in all there is a tinge of sadness, for the paths of love never run smoothly. Most children in the 1930s and early

1940s learned to sing the "Raggle Taggle Gipsies-O" in a polite version. George Butterworth (who died in the First World War) and, supremely, Vaughan Williams, wove the old tunes into moving new pieces of music that now feature regularly in the repertoires of musicians.

To what extent Evenlode witnessed this invasion is unknown, but the tales of visitors persuading locals to sing and play the tunes and recall the dances must have been passed round.

The truth is that although there was a distinct possibility these tunes and dances might have been lost without the research of these romantic musicians, the chapel-going villagers had mixed emotions about Morris Dancing. Morris Dancing was associated with a culture of "binge drinking" and an eager willingness to swing into action with fists at the slightest provocation. Early photographs reveal that the dancers were not delicate. They were large, well muscled, rough, working men!

Evenlode and the Arts and Crafts Movement

This romantic view of nature and the country spawned the Arts and Crafts Movement. This is associated with William Morris and his wallpaper designs based on the themes of nature. Other names such as the artist Raphael Rosetti (brother of the hymn writer, Christina Rosetti, who wrote the hymn "In the bleak mid-winter") are also well known. The return to using natural themes and natural materials and traditional skills moved also into the world of architecture. The north Cotswolds became a centre for the Arts and Crafts movement. In the world of architecture, Guy Dawber's name was prominent.

Coldicote Heath Farm on the Four Shire Stone Road (later to be known as Wells Folly) was replaced by a new house and associated buildings designed by Guy Dawber in 1904–5. This was done for the then owner Mr Milne Barnsley. He called the new house Coldicote House. It is featured in *Country Life* for 22 October 1910. It is also featured in Mary Greensted's book, *The Arts and Crafts Movement in the Cotswolds,* where she writes that Guy Dawber's handling of mass and material was shown to good effect.

The article in *Country Life* relates:

The pictures of Coldicote show that Mr Dawber had adopted coursed rubble as the most suitable treatment for the thin stone layers in which the local quarries, only two or three miles away, provide the stone. It is built without any dressing or cutting beyond what is needful, to make the pieces roughly rectangular. By this means, and by raking out the joints deeply when the mortar is partially dry, a quality of surface and a texture are secured which not only suit the material, but are of the essence of the local traditions.

The quarries Dawber used to obtain the thin stone were at Eyford, one mile beyond Upper Slaughter, towards Cheltenham. The article goes on to say that no dressed stone was used anywhere and that the angles and windows were constructed using ordinary walling stone.

It remarks that the chimneys are brick, both to save expense but also to prevent too bulky a structure. It also acknowledges that in the arches there is the influence of Lutyens. The article concludes that Dawber has paid as much attention to the back of the house as the front and it confidently states, "Coldicote can be surveyed with pleasure from every point of view".

These extracts are contained in Collection Three of the Evenlode Papers. Coldicote House was sold to Sir Geoffrey Shakerley around the year 1930. Colonel Shakerley changed the name to Wells Folly.

Evenlode Grounds "before the War"

Coldicote House was a unique building venture in Evenlode in 1904. The working farmers of Evenlode lived in the traditional farmhouses and the labourers in the cottages. In Collection Eleven of the Evenlode Papers there is a detailed description of Evenlode Grounds Farmhouse and its fittings. This is probably typical of all the Evenlode Farmhouses. It creates a picture of life in an Evenlode Farmhouse of those days "before the War".

Evenlode Grounds Farm was part of the Evenlode glebe land. In the winter days of 1896–7 Henry James Day, the tenant farmer, had died. After his death the tenancy was awarded to Walter Harvey Woolliams. However, though the land and the house belonged to the Rector everything else belonged to the estate of Mr Day.

The extremely meticulous details recorded in the agreement on changeover, give a fascinating view of a tenant taking over a farm from a previous tenant. The agreement was made between the new tenant Mr Walter Harvey Woolliams, and Thomas Franklin and James Tayler (acting on behalf of the estate of Henry James Day). There was an Umpire, Mr C F Moore.

As far as farm activity was concerned the value was calculated of stacked hay and straw, crops planted and growing (including the cost of seed and manure) also the harrowing of 17 acres. Also valued were seed, calf racks and barbed wire, and a number of other items in the farmyard. Mr Woolliams agreed to pay for these.

The fixtures in the house and in other buildings that had been bought and fitted by Mr Day are written in neat handwriting in a large document. It was anticipated that Mr Woolliams might purchase these too. The fittings were:

Drawing Room: 2 rolling blinds and fittings
    1 patent spring blind
    Bell with crank and wires
    Brass curtain cornice and rings
    Tiled hearth, and brass kerb
    Set of china doorknobs
    4 brass fingerplates
    Mantel board and iron rod
Lobby: Brass rod over cellar door
Dining Room: Grate as fixed (broken)
    Stone mantelpiece and board
    Tiled hearth and ash pan
    2 roller blinds and fittings
    2 shelves in recess
Hall: Rail and two pegs
Kitchen: 2 shelves in recess
    Deal dresser with drawers
    2 cupboards
    Iron plate rack over range

Cupboard door in fireplace (not allowed)
Closet under stairs, a cupboard and painted screen (not allowed)
Dairy: Shelves as fitted in recess
2 shelves and brackets
5 birch supports for leads (not allowed)
Shelving with side supports
Large zinc fronted meat safe
Iron grating (not allowed)
Scullery: Tin spouting, 5 shelves and benches
Stone D trough
Wash House: 50 gallon copper furnace
Force pumps and lead piping
2 iron brackets and supports
Courtyard: Iron furnace and fittings
Bake House: Making fireplace in lieu of oven (not allowed)
Staircase: 2 mahogany handrails in supports (not allowed)
Bedroom 1: 2 roller blinds and racks, small grate
2 brass curtain rods, bells crank and wire
Passage: Roller blind and moveable steps
Bedroom 2: Roller blind and fittings, small grate
Closet door (not allowed)
Bedroom 3: Roller blind and fittings
Bedroom 4: Roller blind, Deal partition (not allowed)
Bedroom 5: Roller bind etc, mahogany pole, rings, grate as fixed
Cellar: Wine cupboards, 3 shelves
Yards etc: 6 stone troughs
Granary: Brick partition (not allowed)
20 iron hurdles in front of house and summerhouse
4 line posts
2 iron bars in waggon shed
2 doors to boxes in stable
Partition, boarded ceiling, 1 floor and doors in Gig house (not allowed)

Some of the items in the list were "not allowed" by the Umpire. This means that he had judged that they had become part of the fittings of the house and could not be described as possessions of Mr Day. The rest were believed to have a value that could be realised. Mr Woolliams' notes are written in pencil on the back of this list. These notes show the price he agreed for some of the items. For example, he paid £2/10/3d for the roller blinds, £3 for the kitchen dressers, £2 for the force pump in the washhouse and £1 for the 12 stone troughs.

It is not too far back for older readers to picture in the mind, china doorknobs, the bell for the servant and the wooden slats of the window blinds. Those little bedroom grates with a cast iron surround (perhaps with tiles set in) and a mantelpiece painted black, together with a coy painted screen in the corner, come easily to mind too. The dressers in the kitchen with rows of plates and the big range, black leaded every morning, for heating water and for cooking are in the memory too. Also the big copper in the washhouse with the fire underneath recall memories of long Mondays of "possing" with the "poss stick" and "wringing" in the wooden mangle and "pegging" out to dry and ironing with the heavy black irons heated by the fire in the range.

Harvey Woolliams farmed Evenlode Grounds Farm until 1913 when it was let to Albert Edward Douthwaite. The details of this tenancy agreed with the Rector were likely to be similar to the details of Mr Woolliams tenancy.

In the agreement, the farm was described as embracing 160 acres with a fine farmhouse and convenient buildings. The rent required by the Rector was £240 per half year (he settled for £230). Rates were £4 an acre. The tenant was required to farm "according to the custom of the country but not to mow more than one third of the grassland". The Rector reserved to himself all the timber on the farm, any potential mines and quarries, and the shooting rights. There was a fine threatened of £30 per acre for any land ploughed without the consent of the Rector.

At some time this glebe land was sold to Mr Douthwaite though the date is not known. For whatever reason, having bought the farm, Mr Douthwaite decided to sell it. Evenlode Grounds Farm was sold in March 1919 to Mr Robert Woolliams.

Evenlode cottages

In 1919 Mr Robert Woolliams not only bought Evenlode Grounds Farm he also bought five cottages in the village. Although the date is after the War was over, the description of the cottages is likely to be identical to what they were like "before the War". This means that from this information a picture can be created of the housing occupied by the labouring families of Evenlode.

These particular cottages were the five between Rose terrace and Stockbridge Farm. There were two larger cottages facing the road and these now comprise Holly Tree House. The other three smaller cottages were east of Holly Tree House and at right angles to the road (Westwold).

At the time of the purchase they had been owned previously by several members of the Roberts family and Mary Ann Clements and were rented to tenants. Then they had become the property of Mr Thomas Clements of Swindon. It may be that here there is an example of people moving away from Evenlode to find prosperity in thriving Swindon with its railway "works". In 1901 this movement of population was very evident for 11 houses were unoccupied in Evenlode in that year.

When Robert Woolliams bought these five cottages all were occupied by Evenlode folk so he bought the cottages with sitting tenants.

This sale and purchase gives a picture of the accommodation in all the Evenlode cottages.

The downstairs room of both sizes of cottage

Inside the downstairs "living" room of both sizes of cottage there was a range (fire and oven). Cooking was over the fire and in the oven. The furniture in such cottages was a large wooden table used for every purpose (food preparation, dress-making, ironing and eating) with wooden benches or chairs. Shelves held cooking utensils, plates and cups. There would have been a cupboard and perhaps a chest for storage. Outside on the wall hanging on a nail would be the family tin bath

The smaller cottages

These three smaller cottages had the one "living" room described above. There was a pantry that was probably a cupboard under the stairs. There was a back door leading outside where (perhaps just a few feet away) there were a coal shed and a closet. These were each about the same size and comprised one structure. There was a small garden.

Each of the smaller cottages had two rooms on the first floor but as these occupied some of the roof space there was no usable attic.

The description reads:
1 Living Room
1 Pantry
2 bedrooms
Garden with brick-built coal shed and closet.

In 1919, the tenants each paid a quarterly rent of £5/-/-d. The landlord paid the rates.

The larger cottages

In these larger cottages there was also only one "living" room downstairs and a pantry as in the smaller cottages. But in these cottages the back door opened into a scullery or washhouse. This probably had a stone sink and a "copper." A further door then led to a small yard. Here there was a similar structure of coal shed and closet, but there was a larger garden and additionally a pigsty.

The larger cottages also had two rooms on the first floor but as the roof space began at their ceiling height, there was in addition a relatively large attic. A ladder would have given access to the attic. The attic provided sleeping space for older children and lodgers.

The description reads:
1 Living Room
1 Pantry
2 bedrooms
1 Attic
Washhouse adjoining
Capital garden with brick-built coal shed, closet and pigsties

The tenants each paid a quarterly rent of £6/4/-d. The landlord paid the rates.

In addition the five properties shared "a capital well of water". This is significant for later it was realised that many of the "wells" in Evenlode were not fed from clean springs but were simply collection points for drained rainwater and were unfit for human use.

In 1901 a Census was taken of the whole country. Unlike earlier censuses, this included some indication of where people lived. The Census Officer who made the Evenlode Census walked a route that can be identified because he names those properties that bore a name.

This section recreates that Census Officer's walk visiting each home. He began with Evenlode Grounds Farm.

Evenlode Grounds Farm

In 1901 (as noted above) the farmer was *Walter Harvey Woolliams.* He was 29, born in Icomb and his wife Elizabeth, aged 30, in Shipton-under-Wychwood. They had two small children, Elizabeth and Frank. They had a housemaid, *Elizabeth Cook* from Bledington. At the time of the Census there was an unoccupied cottage on the farm.

Bell Inn

On that day in 1901, the Census Officer walked down from Evenlode Grounds Farm to the Broadwell turn and came to the Bell Inn.

Frank Elliott was the landlord of the Bell. He was 47 and came from Tenterden in Kent. His wife *Winifred* was 22 and came from Rudgwick in Sussex. *Flower's* then owned the Bell.

Springside Cottage and further cottages

Thomas Carey occupied the next cottage (Springside Cottage). He was 35 and was a Foreman platelayer on the railway. He came from Bledington. His wife was *Caroline* aged 31 who came from Stow-on-the-Wold. They had gone to live at Smethwick in the Black Country when they married and their first child Thomas was born there. Then they came to live at Oddington where Norah was born. Florence and Leonard were born in Evenlode.

Collection Five of the Evenlode Papers states that Thomas Napping (who farmed Church Farm) owned Springside cottage and the other properties. In 1914 Thomas Napping died whilst he was at the "George and Dragon" at Evesham. The cottages passed to his widow who died many years later in Springside cottage. She married a second time. Mrs Tooley (as she had become) left the properties to her daughter by Thomas Napping, Mrs Ruth Whittington who was married to Charles William Whittington. These were (presumably) relatives of the other Whittingtons. One Whittington family farmed Stockbridge Farm, another Woodbine cottage.

Returning to 1901, the Census Officer turned the corner and prior to walking up Horn Lane passed four dwellings on the right (though it is not evident whether these were the four dwellings owned by Thomas Nappping or other dwellings such as those that now exist).

The first dwelling was unoccupied.

Oliver Fletcher lived alone in the next dwelling. He came from Little Compton. He was 46 and was very deaf. He lived on the produce from his allotment.

George Jacques lived in the next house. He was 32 and was an agricultural labourer. His wife Mary was 22. They were both born in Evenlode.

Henry Cairns lived in the final house before Horn Lane. He was 39 and was Stockman for the Rector on his glebe. He came from Wyck Rissington but had been working in Kitebrook. His wife *Joyce* was born in Evenlode and was 29. They had four children by this time, Ellen, William, Harold (the late Henry Cairns' father) and Eva.

Grange farm

The Census Officer walked up Horn Lane towards Horn Farm. On the journey he passed on his right *John Badger's* and Mr *George Lovesay's* dwellings. These are likely to have been the Old Forge and Grange Farm.

Grange Farm had passed after the death in 1861 of Thomas Horne (the Moreton-in-Marsh grocer, farmer, entrepreneur and supporter of the Congregational Chapel) into the ownership of his two sons Henry and Frederick Horne.

In 1901, the farmer of Grange Farm was *George Lovesay* (spelt this way in the Census). He was 66 and his wife *Mary* was 64. He came from Temple Guiting and she came from Wolford. Their daughter *Sarah, aged* 42, lived with them and an 18 years old boy from Badsey, *James Willoughby*, helped in the house and on the farm.

Also at this point, the Census Officer notes the Badger family.

John Badger describes himself as a milkman and was employed by Charles Yells of Heath End Farm. He was 40 and came from Marston in Oxfordshire. *Mercy* his wife was 46 and came from Buckingham. They had five children. Mercy's father, *John Knapp*, was living with them. He was 83 and came from Goring Heath in Oxfordshire. John Badger later moved to Anchor Farm.

Horn Farm

He continued his walk to Horn Farm. The farm had passed from the Haines family who had farmed it since the fifteenth century. In 1841 it had been farmed by Richard Kibble and then had been owned by Mary Ann Clemans but was sold by auction in accordance with her Will that was proved on 7 December 1860.

The Census officer recorded that in 1901 *William Bryan* was the farm bailiff for Horn Farm. He was 60 and was native of Evenlode. His family name is found in the 1841 census (see earlier). His wife *Annie* was 58 and a laundress. She came from Broadwell. They had a son at home who was platelayer on the railway.

In Collection Three of the Evenlode Papers a copy of an article by Stanley Harris relates that he came with his parents to live in Evenlode at the end of the First World War. They lived in a house facing the Green for a short period of time and then Mr Harris (Stanley's father) became tenant of Horn Farm in 1919.

After William Bryan had been bailiff, Stanley Harris states that it had become a stud farm for Mr Byass of Wyck Hill, Stow-on-the-Wold but he sold it for £900 to George Freeman of Sherbourne near Northleach in 1918. George Freeman rented it to Stanley's father. He paid £2 rent an acre. Horn Farm was its traditional size of 35 or 36 acres. Stanley remembers that Mr and Mrs Freeman came twice a year in their pony and trap to collect the rent and usually stayed for lunch.

He recalls that Horn Lane (which was then a gated road) carried horse pulled vehicular traffic all the way to Chastleton. There was the sharp turn up into Conygree Lane then, as now, but in those days, despite the steepness of the slope, horses and carts frequently used it.

Fletchers Farm

The Census Officer walked back down Horn Lane and came to Fletcher's Farm. Fletchers Farm was still farmed by the Fletcher family in 1901. *Thomas Fletcher* was the farmer. This Thomas Fletcher was a single man aged 44. He had two older sisters living with him Jane who was 49 and Miriam who was 47. The Fletchers had spread all over the area and these three were born in Little Compton (as was Oliver Fletcher above who was therefore probably a brother of theirs).

Thomas Fletcher and his brother Charles Fletcher had been farming Fletchers Farm together. From documents in Collection Eight and further documents in Collection Two of the Evenlode Papers it appears that the brothers had borrowed £500 in 1888 by mortgaging the farm. Charles Fletcher had died leaving Thomas Fletcher with the mortgage unpaid. A decision must have been made to sell the farm to pay back the mortgage. It was bought in 1897 by George Groves of Oddington. It was apparently sub-let to Thomas Fletcher for life. This must have been a condition of the sale.

George Groves sold Fletchers to Mrs Mary Ann Lovesey (spelt this way) who was farming Grange Farm after the death of her husband George Lovesey, on condition she paid George Groves and his wife Mary a pension of £55 per year until both died. It was sold to Mrs Lovesey with Thomas Fletcher remaining the tenant. Mrs Mary Ann Lovesey died in 1915 and by her Will, Fletchers Farm came into the ownership of her daughter Miss Sarah Ann Lovesey. By this time Thomas Fletcher was no longer occupying the farm for whatever reason. George Groves had died in 1911 but Miss Sarah Ann Lovesey continued to pay the pension to his widow until she died in 1919.

Sarah was 42 years of age and living with her parents at Grange Farm at the time of the Census. She was aged 57 when she took over Fletchers Farm. She farmed it until 1941. She was then 82 years old.

Back in 1901 on his perambulation around the village, the Census Officer walked out from Horn Lane and turned north along Green Lane.

Evenlode House

There are no available records of who owned Evenlode House since the Bricknells though the land attached to it seems to have been sold, little by little. At the time of the census it had no residents but two servants *Fanny Jacques* the cook from Evenlode, aged 26, and *Laura Illes,* aged 19, the housemaid. She came from Broadwell.

The School

The School was passed next by the Census Officer. The schoolmaster was *John Trollope* from Horningsham in Wiltshire. He was 55. His wife, *Maria* was the schoolmistress. She was 47 and came from Shirley in Hampshire.

Bank cottages

These are the occupants presumably in order of occupation from south to north:

William Harwood, aged 80, and his son *Alfred Harwood,* aged 48, both agricultural labourers from Weston on Avon

George Jacques, aged 64, the village roadman and *Sarah* his wife, aged 54, both from Evenlode and their youngest daughter Florence, aged 15

William Gregory, aged 70, an agricultural labourer from Evenlode and his wife *Caroline,* aged 75, from Stonehouse

The next cottage was unoccupied

James Archer, aged 60, an agricultural labourer from Chipping Norton

The next cottage was unoccupied

Charles Bryan, aged 69, an agricultural labourer from Evenlode and his wife *Sarah,* aged 60, from Aston Magna. Their sons *James Bryan,* aged 27, an agricultural labourer and *William Bryan,* aged 22, a gardener, both born in Chastleton

Next came the separate <u>Bank Cottage</u>. This was occupied by:

Thomas Hope, aged 53, from Chastleton, an agricultural labourer, and his German wife *Catherine,* aged 46, and their two sons Alfred and Charles both born in Broadwell

Then two further cottages occupied by:

Joseph Gregory, aged 80, an agricultural labourer from Evenlode and his wife, aged 63, from Stow-on-the-Wold and their two sons *Frank Gregory,* aged 26, and *Thomas Gregory,* aged 21, both platelayers on the railway.

William Riley, aged 40, an agricultural labourer who was born on Four Shire Stone Farm, and *Martha* his wife, aged 40, from Fackley in Oxfordshire their elder son Robert, aged 18, a carter and horseman, and their other three children, Amelia, William and Mary.

<u>Hambidge's Farm</u>

This had been Davis's Farm. *Samuel Hambidge* was 41 in 1901 at the time of the Census and like Henry Cairns Senior had moved from Wyck Rissington. His wife *Anne* was 40 and came from Charlbury. They had four girls and one boy. An 80 years old aunt, *Susannah Hambidge,* lived with them, who insisted that the census officer record that she "was living on her own means"!

Stanley Harris's tale about the Hambidges' astute horse (in Collection Three of the Evenlode Papers) is worth inserting at this point:

(Mr Hambidge) always had several young horses and when they started to be always getting out on the road at one time it was somewhat of a mystery especially as the field gate was always open. In those days nobody would think of leaving a gate open so how did it happen? Well, one day someone saw one of the horses, a nice chestnut named Rusty, opening the catch on the gate with his teeth. In spite of trying all sorts of fastenings Rusty who was something of an equine Houdini always managed to get them undone. So a lock and chain it had to be.

The farm was owned however by George John Sandys. As explained earlier after the bankruptcy of Farmer Davis, the father of Miss Mary Christina Sandys bought it at auction. She married the Rector, Charles James and the farm was a wedding present and put in his name, although she is remembered as the farmer after his death. She outlived her husband by 26 years and it seems that after her death George John Sandys bought it (or inherited it) in 1899. This is recorded in Collection Seven of the Evenlode Papers.

Heath Farm

The Census Officer then turned up the track to Heath Farm (Stubbles) where *Joseph Griffin* farmed. Joseph Griffin was 33 and came from Turkdean. His wife *Caroline* was 23 and came from Longborough. They had three babies, Georgina aged 3, Eva aged 2, and John aged 1. *Emily Gillett* was their servant. She was 21 and came from Moreton-in-Marsh. Joseph Griffin was still farming in 1935. Heath Farm is in Evenlode but some of the land was in Chastleton and the farm then belonged to the Whitmore-Jones Estate.

The Census Officer then came back to the Moreton Road and walked to the Four Shire Stone Road. Before he reached there, there were two brick cottages beyond Choseley Brook.

Chosely Brook

The first cottage was unoccupied.

The next occupied cottage housed *Joseph Haynes,* aged 45, from Bampton in Oxfordshire and his wife *Sarah* aged 42, from Bledington. Joseph was a cattleman on an unspecified farm.

Woodbine Cottage

He came next to Woodbine Cottage where *Arthur T Whittington* lived. He was 62 and came from Somerset. He was a cattleman. His wife was Welsh and was called *Mary.* She was 56. They had a son at home who was called *Arthur P Whittington* who was 28. He worked with his father. There was a son called Sidney too who was only 13.

Far Heath Farm

The officer does not mention Far Heath Farm.

Lower Brookend Farm

Lower Brookend Farm was part of Brookend Manor though the farmhouse stood in Evenlode. The Census Officer does not mention Lower Brookend Farm.

Four Shire Stone Farm

The occupant at Four Shire Stone Farm was *Frederick Webb*. He did not own or work the land so the owners probably rented this out. He worked from the farmhouse as a carter. He was 37 and came from Moreton-in-Marsh. His wife was *Mary,* aged 40, who came from Bampton in Oxfordshire. His cousin helped in the carting work and lodged with them. He was *John Kent*, who also came from Moreton-in-Marsh.

Coldicote Heath Farm

The officer turned back and called in at the farm to the north of Four Shire Stone Road. This was then called Coldicote Heath Farm. *Henry Hunt* was the farmer. He was 47 and came from Little Wolford. He was married to *Agnes* who was 46.

Milne Barnsley owned the farm. As noted above, influenced by the Arts and Crafts Movement, he employed Guy Dawber to re-build the farmhouse and he called it Coldicote House.

Heath End Farm

Charles Yells occupied Heath End Farm. He was 46 and came from Winson. His wife was 36. *Emily* came from Ampney St Mary. They had three children Hilda aged 6, Charles aged 5, and Iris aged 4. *Maria Timms,* aged 20, lived with them. She came from Moreton-in-Marsh and describes herself as the "help". 14 years old *Elizabeth Pike* from Chastleton was a domestic servant.

Charles Yells farmed not only Heath End Farm but also Northfields. He had the milk round in Moreton-in-Marsh. His milkman was John Badger who later lived at Anchor Farm.

Northfields Farm

George Hawkins from Paxford, aged 32, lived there. He was the shepherd. His wife was *Alice,* aged 34, from Hereford. They had five sons, Harry aged 8, Albert, aged 7, William, aged 5, Charles, aged 2, and Ernest, aged 8 months.

Home Farm

The Census Officer walked back into the village and turned into Church Lane.

Charles Collins, aged 31, was the farmer at Home Farm. He came from Shrivenham in Berkshire. He had a housekeeper *Martha Hands,* aged 48.

Then came an unoccupied cottage (possibly on the bridle way at the back of the house) and so the officer came to Church Farm.

Church Farm

Thomas Napping, aged 53, farmed Church Farm. He came from Boarshall. He had two servants *Emily Whittington,* aged 31, from Broadway and *George Childs,* aged 48, from Little Compton, who also worked as an agricultural labourer.

The Census Officer then walked past the church to Manor Farm

Manor Farm

Manor Farm was farmed in 1901 by *William Hands* aged 48 from Ilmington. His wife *Mary* came from Yorkshire. She was 57. They had one daughter living at home called Sarah. She was aged 18. There was a servant *Sarah Wyatt,* aged 30, from Hanbury in Worcestershire.

In the cottage (Two Stones) lived *Edward Harrison,* aged 50. He was a farm bailiff but the census return does not say at which farm. His wife was *Jane,* aged 52, from Moreton-in-Marsh. They had a daughter *Pressie,* aged 20, living at home.

The Rectory

The Census Officer then crossed the road and came to the Rectory.

The Reverend Henry James Kelsall lived at the Rectory. He was 39 and came from Stafford. His wife came from Tutbury and was called *Isabella.* She was aged 30. They had no children recorded. There were two housemaids *Elizabeth Harris,* aged 19, from Evenlode and *Caroline Massey,* aged 30, from Honeybourne.

Anchor Farm

There is no mention of Anchor Farm.

Portland House and Terrace

James Newman occupied the next house listed. This seems to have been Portland House. He was a builder and contractor. Aged 58, he was born in Evenlode. His wife *Harriett* was 60 and she came from

Oxford. They had a daughter living at home called *Annie*. She was 16 years of age.

Portland Terrace should follow in the Census List. However, after the First World War a Mrs Mumford opened a shop in this Terrace but on this reckoning of the Census Officer's route a Mrs Mumford lived in Vine Terrace. This may therefore be inaccurate. However the next group of residents listed were:

William Claridge, aged 28, a platelayer on the railway who came from Finstock and *Henrietta,* aged 31, his wife who came from Charlbury. They had five children. Clarence, aged 8, Ethel aged 6, William aged 4, Florence aged 2, and Frank aged 1.

Herbert Dyer, aged 20, a bricklayer's labourer came from Barton-on-Heath and *Margaret* his wife, aged 19, from Kilcot. They had a baby Gladys, aged 9 months.

William Davis, aged 35, a carpenter and joiner from Harvington and *Rhoda* his wife, aged 32, from Evenlode. They had five children. Albert, aged 8, Rosalind, aged 6, Arthur, aged 3, Sidney, aged 2, and baby Laura, aged 6 months.

Reuben Gregory, aged 31, a gardener came from Daylesford and *Annie* his wife, aged 25, from Honeybourne. They had two babies Leonard, aged 2, and Marjorie, aged 9 months.

The next house in sequence seems to be what is now Lavender Cottage. *Eliza Harris* aged 70 lived here. She was a seamstress. Her granddaughter Elise, aged 9, lived with her.

Vine Terrace

This appears to be the next group (from east to west):

Henry Mumford, aged 44, a stonemason came from Cogges and his wife *Mary,* aged 49, from Evenlode. They had one daughter at home, Mary, aged 8.

The next dwelling was unoccupied.

Richard Harris, aged 62, a brick maker came from Northlea in Oxfordshire.

James Jacques, aged 57, a labourer was from Evenlode as was his wife *Julietta,* aged 54.

The Fox Inn

Sarah Gardner from Little Compton was the landlord. She was 66. *Bessie Mace,* aged 13, also from Long Compton was her servant. *Charles Stanley* from Blockley, aged 40, boarded at the Fox. He was a stonemason's labourer.

After the Fox Inn, the Census Officer visited four dwellings down the lane, before coming to Green Farm. These four residences were occupied by:

William Jacques, aged 59, a platelayer on the railway who came from Evenlode and *Selina,* aged 52, his wife from Broadwell. They had two sons at home. William was 18, and there was a younger son aged 14, both worked as cattlemen.

William Harris, aged 64, was an agricultural labourer who came from Evenlode. His wife was *Louisa,* aged 54, from Little Compton. They had twin sons at home, Frederick and Thomas, aged 14, both were agricultural labourers, and 13 years old Kate.

Charles Jacques, aged 49, was an agricultural labourer from Evenlode. He had a lodger who was also an agricultural labourer called *Henry Douet,* aged 45, from Windrush.

Sophia Timms, aged 81, from Broadwell lived alone.

Green Farm

Henry Hutt from Oxfordshire was farmer at this time. He was 39. His wife *Isabella* came from Tower Hill in London. She was 60. They had a lodger *Elizabeth Turner,* aged 85, and a servant *Edith Miles,* aged 15, from Ashton-Under-Hill.

The Census Officer then walked to Stockbridge Farm and the north side of this final road.

Stockbridge Farm

John Whittington, aged 34, from Broadway was the farmer. His wife was *Connie* from Rissington. They had living with them her son Edward Welby, aged 9, from her previous marriage. In a cottage lived *Ellen Hill,* aged 74, with her son *John Hill,* aged 36. He was an agricultural labourer.

The Cottages

Several of the cottages on the north side of the lane were unoccupied. *Eliza Fletcher,* aged 74, from Stow-on-the-Wold and her daughter *Anne Fletcher,* aged 40, from Evenlode occupied one. *Henry Hooper,* aged 45, a painter who came from Moreton-in-Marsh lived in another. His wife was *Elizabeth,* aged 44, from Longborough. They had five children living at home. Ernest was 17 and was a carter and horseman. There were four little ones, Hilda aged 9, Walter aged 7, Albert aged 3, and Esther aged 1.

Rose Terrace

The following four seem to have occupied Rose Terrace:

Ann Jacques, aged 68, who came from Northamptonshire and her daughter *Ellen Jacques,* aged 26, who was a nurse and domestic help, and Alfred Jacques, aged 8, Ellen's son.

George Reynolds, aged 30, who was a cattleman from Clifford Chambers and his wife *Alice,* aged 24, from Shropshire and their two babies, George aged 2, and Arthur aged 1.

Esther Payne, aged 78, lived with her servant *Mary Hooper,* aged 14.

Elizabeth Bryan, aged 52, who was a dressmaker and came from Evenlode lived with a servant *Florence Morgan,* aged 13, from Evenlode.

Thus the Census Officer had returned to where he started from in his tour of the village.

Evenlode School "before the War"

Miss Etheridge became Headmistress of Evenlode School in 1908 after Mr and Mrs Trollope, but it is only from 1912 that a logbook has been preserved. It is kept in the Gloucestershire Archive. The immediately noticeable theme is the weekly visits of the Rector, Henry Kelsall and the Managers' Correspondent, Mr Harvey Woolliams, who acted as Attendance Officer. Mr Woolliams checked the registers each week to see which children were at school and which not.

School holidays tended to vary with the needs of the harvest and in 1912 school resumed after the summer holidays, on 6 August. Miss Etheridge does not write in this year's log (unlike most later years) that the older boys had failed to turn up for school. She usually did. This was their last year in school and they were desperate to leave. However she does record in the logbook that at the Managers' wish the children were reprimanded for "ill manners" out of school.

There was considerable naughtiness among the children. On a serious note Joseph Griffin lost the sight of one eye (temporarily) from a stone thrown at him. Nellie Griffin and Leonard Ellis did not go to school one day but spent the whole day at Stow Fair. The older boys were regularly chastised for following the Hunt after it had met on the village green. The Heythrop's monthly meeting on Evenlode Green was looked forward to. Morning playtime was extended for the children to see the hounds and horses canter away, but with them went the older boys, laughing and larking as boys do.

A later entry reads:
Tom Gregory has been absent today. He is not improving in any way. During the play time two little boys went to see him and he spent his mother's change on jelly and ginger beer and they had it between them. (!)

A lot of illness is recorded among the children. The Headmistress records absence because of croup, bad coughs, feeling "unwell", "not looking well", inflamed eyes, bad colds. She closed the school for outbreaks of whooping cough. Absence was also recorded for having a "gathered finger", a "slight fit", being "kicked by a cow", "bit by a ferret" and (alarmingly) "hand cut in the chaff cutter".

George Hancock was hit in the eye by a cricket ball. Miss Etheridge records how she sent for Dr Denny who tested his sight and sent him to the Eye Hospital in Oxford. Later she writes without comment "George Hancock has glasses and is working well".

Miss Etheridge taught all the children all the subjects, though Miss Cayless her assistant taught the infants. The children were taught to read, write and do sums. They were taught bible stories and had to learn the Prayer Book Catechism (which includes the Ten Commandments) by heart. They did drawing and drill (outside if it was fine). The girls did sewing and knitting.

The children also were given a "home lesson". This often consisted of writing about a subject. Nellie Griffin (the same who had stolen off to Stow Fair for the day) had been given the subject "The horse". She sent her composition to a magazine and received a prize. This clearly pleased Miss Etheridge who makes special note of this great achievement in the logbook. No doubt Miss Etheridge's close friendship with Nellie's farming parents had nothing to do with this!

Games girls played during playtime are recorded in a paper of the Moreton-in-Marsh Local History Society. They skipped and jumped. They played hopscotch. They played with whip and top and with hoops. They threw a ball against the wall to catch it. No doubt they role-played the dramas they saw around them: "teachers", "nurses" and "mothers and fathers".

There is no record of what boys played at Evenlode. Boys generally played ball games, against the walls, with bats, and of course football. Popular boys' playground games included the chasing game

"Tally Ho" (from hunting). Also included were various tackling games and scrummaging games (from, or the origin of, rugby football). Buffalo Bill's Wild West show introduced all boys to "Cowboys and Indians".

The school was inspected regularly. There were two Inspectors. The Education Authority sent an Inspector and the Diocese another.

The Education Authority Inspector reported:

The children are in very good order; they attend regularly and are carefully taught and on the whole their progress is commendable. Oral composition needs increased attention. The children should learn to speak distinctly and in complete sentences; and they might read less monotonously. In Standards 2 and 4 there is no weakness in spelling. The sums set in the lower standards should be in concrete form, and for practical work in Arithmetic some apparatus is wanted. The children's drawings and written work should all be dated. The Head Teacher's terminal reports on the children's progress should relate to each subject of the syllabus.

A new copy of the Regulations contained in section 7 of the Elementary Education Act 1870, is needed.

The infants' long desks are too high and have the seats too far back; these should be replaced by dual desks. A proper desk for the Head Mistress has still to be provided. The hat pegs in the cloakroom should be in more than two tiers. The ventilation in the cloakroom would be improved if one of the windows in it were made to open.

The Diocesan Inspector visited within days of the Education Inspector. He reports:

The infants answered the questions very well and gave evidence of careful teaching.

The knowledge in the Upper Division was very fair. The repetition of scripture was good. The written work in the middle division was good with a few exceptions in spelling. The Prayer Book was good with some qualifications. The portion of the Catechism learned was very well known. Much good work done.

The Reports were handwritten and sent to Miss Etheridge. She wrote in the logbook on 26 February 1913 that the Rector had called to read them. In her remarks she expressed her opinion that "both (reports) were very good". So she gave the School a day off.

Intimations of War

On Empire Day, 23 May 1913, the flags were flown at the school and the National Anthem was sung. The year continued its normal routine at school. The summer holiday started on 31 July and the school re-assembled on 31 August.

On 7 September 1914 Miss Etheridge wrote in the logbook, "The girls are doing needlework and knitting to help supply the war needs". Later she notes that all the children have started saving to buy War Saving Certificates.

The winter of 1916 was dreadful in Evenlode. The school was closed for the last week of February for the snow was deep and the roads impassable. The school was also closed in the last week of March because of the depth of snow. It must have made all think of the Evenlode men in the trenches.

Four Evenlode families received telegrams that year. Three of the fatalities had been boys at the village school. These four fatalities were all in the trenches in France. Two Evenlode men James Nash and Alfred Jacques, former pupils at the school, were in the same regiment, the London Regiment. Victor Hooper the other former pupil at the school was in the Royal Warwickshire Regiment. The other Evenlode man who died with them was F Hutt of the Oxford and Buckinghamshire Light Infantry.

J E Sadler of the Worcestershire Regiment was another Evenlode man to die. He died a year later in Mesopotamia, fighting against the Turks of the Ottoman Empire.

After the War a carved wooden panel was placed in the school. It is now in the Church beside the village War Memorial. The panel reads:

Evenlode Council School
Former scholars who gave their lives
In the Great War 1914-1918
William Baldwin
Arthur John Brakespeare

Victor Hooper
Alfred Jacques
James Nash
At the going down of the sun
And in the morning
We will remember them

William Baldwin and Arthur Brakespeare though pupils at the school were not living in Evenlode so do not feature on the Village Memorial.

The Rector Henry Kelsall visited the bereaved families during the Great War. A brass War Memorial to the dead who had lived in Evenlode parish was erected. It reads:

"To the Glory of God and in Honoured Memory of the
following soldiers who gave their lives
for their King and Country
during the Great War of 1914-1918
A V Hooper Royal Warwick Rgt. 1916 France
F Hutt Oxford & Bucks L I. 1916 France
J C Nash London Rgt. 1916 France
A W Jacques London Rgt. 1916 France
J E Sadler Wor Rgt. 1917 Mesopotamia

"Proudly you gathered rank on rank to war,
as who had heard God's message from afar
all you had hoped for, all you had you gave
to save Mankind – yourselves you could not save"
"Splendid you passed, the great surrender made,
into the light that nevermore shall fade,
deep your contentment in that blest abode,
who wait the last clear trumpet call of God."

"In glorious hope their proud and sorrowing Land
commit her children, to Thy gracious hand"
"Their name liveth for evermore"

This tablet is erected by the parishioners

Photo: The Evenlode Collection

The Fox Inn

Photo: The Evenlode Collection

The Post Office

Chapter 16

In England's green and pleasant land (1918–39)

After the First World War, Evenlode began to change. Glimpses of this changing Evenlode can be seen in the writings of Stanley Harris. Stanley Harris came to live in Evenlode as a child just after the Great War. There was talk of him becoming a lawyer but his heart was in the countryside and it remained there all his life. His ambition as a boy was to be a sporting farmer. The Moreton and District Local History Society published two sets of his memoirs. Peter Drinkwater also recorded further memoirs in his book *Cotswold Memories*. Extracts are among the documents of Collection Three of the Evenlode Papers.

TheRevd Henry Kelsall
Rector 1895 –1922

Stanley Harris gives us a good picture of a rector as a farmer. Henry James Kelsall was inducted into the benefice of Saint Edward's Evenlode in September 1895. Evenlode Grounds Farm was part of his Glebe, this he rented out but later sold. He had other glebe land and unusually for that time, he farmed it himself with the help of a farm foreman, Henry Cairns (father of Harold and grandfather of the late Henry Cairns).

As a dairy farmer, Henry Kelsall worked with other dairy farmers to set up the "Direct Delivery Company" for the distribution and sale of milk. He was a shareholder in it.

As Rector, Henry Kelsall had overseen the re-hanging of the Church Bells for Queen Victoria's Jubilee in 1897. Whether the result of enthusiastic ringing or not, the tower had to be repaired in 1905–6, and the opportunity was taken to clean and paint all the gutters.

Perhaps as a result of this, it was decided to have a collection taken every Sunday instead of once a fortnight. This also enabled the Parish Clerk's salary to be increased to £3/10/0d per year.

In 1910 it was decided to insure the Church. The building was insured for a value of £750. The fittings, bells, organ and vestments were insured for a value of £250, and the church plate for a value of £20.

The clock was installed for the coronation of King George V, in 1911.

Henry Kelsall has earned the affectionate anecdotes that still circulate about him. He drove a four in hand it seems, and is supposed to have put harness on the font and practised his whipping from the pulpit. So it is said! He was a keen follower of racing, but as the Rector he felt unable to attend racing at Moreton-in-Marsh, so he followed the races from the top of the church tower with binoculars. So it is said!

What is true is both his commitment to farming and to the church. Stanley Harris tells how the summer of 1920 had been bad and November was approaching and still there was hay to cut, but every Sunday was fine. In those days farmers faithfully observed the Sunday rest but eventually, at their request, Henry Kelsall sought the Bishop's advice. He gave the judgement, that under the circumstances the farmers could farm on Sundays except during the time of worship.

The Revd Henry Kelsall was the last Rector to farm his glebe. Times were changing. He died in October 1922. He was only 60 years old. Not only was he the last farming Rector, he was also the last Rector to come as a young man intending to give his life to the parish until he died.

Sketches of Evenlode folk

What were Evenlode folk like in those days? Stanley Harris as a boy knew old Henry Cairns and his wife and also Harold his son. He gives wonderful verbal pictures that may also reveal much about the sort of people living in Evenlode in that period:

(Old) Henry Cairns who worked for the Revd Kelsall and was, in fact, his farm foreman, was a typical countryman;

230

gentle of nature, quietly spoken and always unhurried as he went about his work. His wife was the village nurse and for many years gave devoted service to the village community. Old Henry was an experienced stockman, a highly skilled rick builder, thatcher and hedger and could turn his hand to any job on the farm. Whatever he did was meticulously done. He was the local pig killer, cut hair, mended shoes and kept bees.

When he retired, his son Harold took over the job of local pig killer and he, like his father, was an exceptionally skilled all-round craftsman. At thatching ricks he was especially outstanding, an artist to the highest degree. Indeed, it was a shame to start using the hay for feeding the stock, or a corn rick, when it had to be threshed.

Harold Cairns later became landlord of the Fox Inn and his widow Mrs Annie Cairns lived there until her death in 1988 at the grand age of 95.

The village shops between the wars

Mrs Mumford ran the village shop in Portland Terrace. This is probably the same Mrs Mumford of the 1901 census who may have then lived in Vine Terrace. When Mrs Mumford gave up, Miss Hodgetts (who was a retired nurse) ran the shop from her home on School Bank. The late Henry Cairns remembered this well. The shop was in the cottage next to the school. He remembered that during the Second World War, the newspapers for the village were delivered to the shop on the milk lorry. It was a well-stocked shop. In those days, when few had cars, and with buses only twice a week on Tuesdays and Fridays, it must have been essential.

There were many travelling tradesmen with their vans or carts, grocers, bakers, butchers, greengrocers, clothiers, a general dealer, the rag and bone man and the occasional visit by the scissors grinder. No doubt these were welcome visitors providing an opportunity to bargain and to pick up the local news.

This also shows that the villagers were no longer self- sufficient but were looking beyond Evenlode to supply their needs

The village school between the wars

When Henry Cairns Junior started school in 1931, Mrs Harris was the Headmistress. She was the wife of John Harris of Green Farm. He was fully occupied with beekeeping, having a very considerable number of hives in many parts of Evenlode. Henry (who grew up next door at the Fox Inn) recalls he was "accident-prone". Once he turned his pony and trap over. Apparently, on another occasion, he performed the classic error of sawing a branch off a tree whilst sitting on the part that fell to the ground. Stanley Harris recalls that John Harris's father, William Harris, lived in Portland House. He owned this and Portland Terrace. (They were not relatives of Stanley's.) Mr William Harris was a gentleman and a naturalist who was always willing to share his knowledge with the children.

Mrs John Harris became Headmistress at a time of change. In 1931 the school ceased to be "All Age" and the older children were transferred to secondary schools. Evenlode School was re-designated as a Primary School. There were 23 children in the School after this re-designation. By 1939, the number of pupils had dropped to 19.

It was possible (but not mandatory) to sit the Entrance Examination for Chipping Campden Grammar School. Those children whose parents wished them to do so, had to sit the examination in the village school. This meant the rest had the day off. Henry Cairns recalled how in one year nobody was planning to take the examination so there would be no day off. This disaster was averted by one of the boys taking the examination with no intention of passing (and he did not) in order that the day off could be awarded for the rest. Henry refused to be drawn into naming who this was!

During the war the school had the addition of evacuee children. Henry Cairns recalled that Mrs Dee became Headmistress. She remained at the school until after the war when it was closed.

The Rectors of Evenlode and the Church between the wars

After the death of Henry Kelsall it became clear that the Rectory was very expensive to maintain. Once many clergy had been third sons of wealthy families and used to living in fine residences. They relished the big old Rectories and their family supported them. Increasingly this was not the case for many clergy. The fact that Henry Kelsall sold Evenlode Grounds Farm just before the First World War may indicate that even then there was a shortfall in the cash necessary for maintenance work. (In those days, this was the Rector's responsibility).

The Bishops regularly thought of fine residences like Evenlode Rectory as a "reward" for the final years of an elderly clergyman after a hard life in an industrial place. This was attractive if one had private means.

The *Revd Charles C Pratt* was Rector from May 1923 to January 1927. He mortgaged the Rectory to carry out repairs.

The *Revd Clarence R Gorman* was Rector from October 1927 to December 1933. The late Henry Cairns remembered that he had the telephone installed in 1931.

The *Revd Charles M Alford* was Rector from January 1935 to June 1936.

The *Revd Stanley J Hersee* was Rector from August 1937 to September 1939. During his incumbency Church Farm was sold. The purchasers were the trustees of The Foundation of The Schools of King Edward VI in Birmingham. Groups of boys came from these schools both in term time and during school holidays (even during the Christmas holidays) between spring 1938 and summer 1939. They got on well with Stanley Hersee who loaned books and magazines. They attended Evenlode Church on Sundays. This must have been a welcome addition to the congregation and a delight for the Rector. In the school magazine they thanked him for "kindnesses too numerous to count".

The village Chapel between the wars

One of Farmer Hambidge's daughters played the harmonium at the services in the Congregational Chapel. Local preachers always took the services. Chief of these was Mr Wren from Long Compton. He walked the ten miles round trip from Long Compton to Evenlode and back to take the service on a Sunday. After his retirement, his daughter (Miss Wren) took on the task. Inevitably said Henry Cairns, the children nicknamed her "Jenny" Wren. He recalls that between the wars the chapel was well attended. In the summer, services were sometimes held on the village green. During the war, the chapel was closed and designated as an emergency mortuary. It was never re-opened.

The village pubs between the wars

In Stanley Harris's time the Fox Inn's landlord was a Scotsman, a former whipper-in with the Heythrop, called Donald Miller. Donald also cut hair so it was customary to have a pint whilst your hair was cut. Stanley tells how Edward Harrison, ("Old Neddy Harrison"), who lived at Two Stones Cottage, sometimes needed a stick to walk with. On one occasion, the young men in the village called for him and wheeled him to the Fox in a wheelbarrow for a pint and a haircut.

Donald Miller died of a burst appendix and his wife died shortly after him with TB. Henry Cairns and his parents moved to the Fox Inn on 5 January 1931 when Henry was five years old. There was no electricity. In the public room there was a central table with an oil lamp overhead. The "regulars" each had their own seat and woe betide anyone sitting in someone else's place. Harold Cairns served beer, cider and stout. The latter was termed porter. There was no bar. The drink was in barrels in the cellar, so Harold would climb down the stairs into the cellar, with the tankard, to get whatever had been ordered.

The Fox Inn was closed when Mitchell and Butler's decided it was no longer viable. Earlier the Bell Inn closed too, when Flower's made the same decision.

The lure of the Playhouse Cinema

A complete change for the villagers was the cinema. Each Wednesday evening the Playhouse Cinema bus called at Evenlode and those wanting to go to the "pictures" bought their cinema ticket on the bus and were taken to Moreton. Andrew S Jackson wrote in his article entitled "The Playhouse Cinema – The Final Years", in the papers of the Moreton-in-Marsh and District Local History Society, that, "After a hard day's work it was nice to walk on a soft, thick carpet and be shown to your seat by an usherette. You felt you really were somebody". The cinema was opened in 1921. The founder was George Samuel Thomas. He died in 1959 and The Playhouse closed in 1961. Many in Moreton-in- Marsh and the villages missed it.

Pigs, Water and the Telephone

Henry Cairns recalled that between the wars keeping pigs in the cottages' pigsties gradually died out, but the custom was resurrected during the Second World War. The Fox Inn had two pigs.

He also recalled that, whereas the Fox Inn had a forty feet deep well and this water was fine, most of the other wells were really just soakaways and the water was not good for humans though satisfactory for the animals. The consequence was that everyone collected water from the spring outside Portland House.

However the supply of water in the village proved to be erratic and a bore well was dug in one of the fields of Home Farm. A windmill was erected next to it that drove a pump and the water was pumped to a reservoir above Poplars Farm. From there it flowed through pipes into troughs at various places. If there was no wind it was possible to disconnect the pump from the windmill and connect it to a petrol engine which then operated the pump for a couple of hours to bring up the water level in the reservoir. Mains water had to wait until after the Second World War.

The telephone arrived in the village in 1931 when the Rector had it installed. By 1935 Robert Woolliams had it installed at Evenlode Grounds Farm. The number was Moreton 82. Edward Weaver who farmed both Home and Heath Farms quickly followed. His number was Moreton 88.

Local Government re-organisation

Evenlode had always been an island of Worcestershire floating in the lake of Gloucestershire, and a detached parish of the diocese of Worcester, having once, long since, been in the Hundred of

Oswaldslaw, with the Prior and Bishop of Worcester as overlord. That was a long time ago.

Since the nineteenth century, the Parish had increasingly had links with Stow-on-the-Wold. It made sense to tidy up the county boundaries. In fact, the Church of England took the lead and the ecclesiastical parish of Evenlode was transferred from the diocese of Worcester to the diocese of Gloucester, the Archdeaconry of Cheltenham and the Rural Deanery of Stow-on-the-Wold in 1919.

The Worcestershire to Gloucestershire Transfer Order of 1931 (which took effect on 1 April 1931) transferred Evenlode civil parish from the County of Worcestershire to the County of Gloucestershire and to the Rural District, Petty Sessional Division and County Court District of Stow-on-the-Wold.

Birmingham pupils at Church Farm

An interesting experiment took place in Evenlode towards the end of the 1930s. The story is contained in Collection Ten of the Evenlode Papers.

The experiment was an initiative of The Foundation of the Schools of King Edward VI in Birmingham. The Foundation is a charity that now manages two independent schools in Birmingham and five voluntary aided schools. The endowments of this charity arose from the suppression of a Chantry in New Street in Birmingham at the time of the Reformation by the 1545 Act of King Henry VIII. After a little difficulty, King Edward VI released the proceeds and property of the Chantry in 1548 for educational purposes in Birmingham.

The charity now owns extensive landholdings in central Birmingham. In 2004-2005, the charity's investments produced an income of £14 million.

The two Independent Schools are:
King Edward's School (boys)
King Edward VI High School for Girls at Edgbaston;
The five Voluntary Aided Schools are:
King Edward VI Aston (boys)
King Edward VI Handsworth (girls);
King Edward VI Camp Hill (boys)
King Edward VI Camp Hill (girls) since 1956 at King's Heath;

King Edward VI Five Ways (co-educational) since 1957 at Bartley Green.

In 1938 the Foundation Governors purchased Church Farm, Evenlode. With it came about two acres of paddock and kitchen garden. They described it as "an eighteenth century stone farmhouse" although the house is likely to be sixteenth century in origin, as are the other older houses in the village.

The purpose in buying the property is stated in the school magazine for summer, 1938:

The purpose is to provide healthy, physical and mental activities in one of the most naturally blessed parts of England, for boys of the Grammar Schools of the Foundation. Nature can be studied at first hand. Sun, wind, rain can work their natural miracles upon the body. Opportunities for study and thought are to live side by side with this physical activity. In time it is hoped that experience at Evenlode will become an integral part of every boy's school life."

It was to be called the Edwardian Country School, Evenlode.

In the process of purchasing they quickly made arrangements with Mr Edward Weaver of Home Farm and Heath Farm to allow the boys access to his land to get to know the animals. They also bought a five acres field for games.

Getting to Evenlode from Birmingham was not easy. Transport was difficult. The boys travelled by train from Birmingham Snow Hill Railway Station. They had to change twice and sometimes three times to get to Moreton-in-Marsh Railway Station. They seemed to have walked from there, for there was much joy on one occasion when there was a bus for them to use. One boy records how he cycled from Birmingham. It seems he was not the only one.

The first boys came in May 1938. From then on groups came in turn. They thoroughly enjoyed what was to be a very short time as War broke out in 1939. The Schools were evacuated to Monmouth where land was bought to turn into a farm, building on the brief experience of Evenlode.

Collection Ten of the Evenlode Papers includes photocopies of a number of articles in the school magazines that make reference to the time at Evenlode. These also give us glimpses of Evenlode on the eve of the Second World War. One such glimpse is of an Evenlode cricket team with the village green as its ground. This must have been an interesting ground to play on for Stanley Harris says that ponies roamed on it and round the village as they do today in the New Forest. The school magazine says,

Many evenings were spent in cricket matches with the village team on the village green, or in playing in the paddock. Indoor, the boys' sitting room was a very happy place. Books and magazines have been provided by kindly friends (particularly the Rector), and a gramophone brought music as relaxation. No wireless set will be installed at the Farm, as part of the purpose of Evenlode is to give a little rest from the continual impact of the troubles of the outside world.

There are some very interesting glimpses of the Evenlode Annual Flower Show and Fete.

The villagers were not perturbed when, at the Annual Flower Show and Fete, W. Hardaker carried off the joint of meat which was the first prize for clock golf. It was however a little different with the live pig (in the crate under the walnut tree in the Rectory garden), which was to be the prize for the highest score at skittles. For several hours this bid fair to become the property of the Headmaster, and boys gazed eagerly within the crate at the attractive physiognomy of the pig. The village then felt itself on its mettle, and in the last hour some magnificent bowling took place, and much money was coined by the keeper of the stall. Finally the pig was won by our farmer friend opposite (Edward Weaver), but there were sad hearts at Church Farm. If only the Headmaster had won the pig.

Perhaps the Fete organisers today do not offer live pigs and joints of meat as prizes, but the tradition continues with the raffle for a "Chicken Dinner!"

There is a glimpse too of an Evenlode farmer's indulgence. He was the same Edward Weaver who farmed and lived at Home Farm and also farmed Heath Farm. A boy writes:

The afternoon is spent following various pursuits. Some disappear on cycle-back, others embark on a rambling excursion, and the rest inspect the farm of our obliging neighbour, Mr Weaver. He grants permission to ride his ponies, and Kirk announces that he intends to demonstrate the finer art of pony trick-riding. He does so, and after he has been picked up, and the worst of the Cotswold clay removed from his person, he declares that he knows everything about riding ponies but that this one was the wrong sort of pony.

There is also a glimpse of a peaceful Mattins on a fine summer's morning when the only sound to compete with the Rector's measured voice is the sound of the birds singing in the trees.

We went to church in the morning. 21 clean faces and 42 clean knees. The sun streamed through the windows of the little stone church whilst the nodding trees and the clamour of the birds never ceased to remind us that we were far from the smoke of our own city.

The boys enjoyed the opportunity to live in the countryside as this parody of John Masefield's poem, composed by "W.R.S.," indicates:

I must go down to the farm again, to the cloud-swept
country sky,
And all I ask is an ancient bike and a map to steer it by,
And a clear road and a wind behind, and a cheery farmer's
greeting,
And a brief farewell to smoke and noise and trams and
central heating

I must go down to the farm again, to the clinging Cotswold
mud,
To the cow's byre and the pig's lair and the land of the
homely spud,
And all I ask when the day is done and the campfire's dead
Is a last song and swift sleep and no beetles in the bed.

I must come back from the farm again through the blinding
rain and the sleet,
While the gale shrieks, and the ice cracks on my aching
hands and feet,
And all I ask when I get back home and the steak and chips
are frying,
Is a hot bath and a bright fire while my underclothes are
drying.

W.R.S. must have been one of the boys who cycled from
Birmingham to Evenlode and obviously cycled back in the teeth of an
icy gale!

The boys had fun but they also had lessons that included talks on
animal husbandry by one or two of the farmers. There was in addition,
the physical labour of renovating the building. They tamped down
concrete on the barn floor to create a refectory. They laid floorboards
in one of the upstairs rooms. They dug the kitchen garden and planted
vegetables. They also took turns to clean and cook.

The school was evacuated to Monmouth when war started and
there they used their school method to get rid of rats. Although this
extract refers to Monmouth, they may have used the same method at
Evenlode. It shows the initiative of the English schoolboy and his
sense of fun. Many of them might have had to use such initiative as the
war called them up, class by class.

Mr Davies linked up about fifty feet of hosepipe to the
exhaust pipe of his car, put the other end down the rat holes
and switched on the engine. About a dozen of us stood over
the remaining holes and as they came out, hit them with a
hammer. After an exciting morning…

With the outbreak of war, school equipment was put into store and Church Farm was requisitioned for evacuees.

The concept of bringing boys from cities into the countryside was one common to many organisations such as the Boy Scouts, the Boys Brigade and the Church Lads Brigade. A number of churches organised camps in the countryside for boys from the slums. It was probably less common then for schools to do this, but after the war Local Education Authorities created Outdoor Centres in many places.

After the war, Church Farm was dilapidated and much money would have been needed to renovate it. Travel after the war remained difficult and those who had the vision of the 1930s had passed away. However, the Edwardian Country School, Evenlode, remained in the hearts of a small number of Birmingham boys who valued the experience in their education.

Evenlode people on the eve of the Second World War

A description of Evenlode on the eve of the Second World War in 1939 can be gleaned from population statistics and Kelly's Directory. The number of people living in Evenlode was slowly declining. The population in 1931 had been 215. By 1961 it had fallen to 202 though the number of dwellings remained the same. Evenlode School, now a primary school, only had 19 pupils. The farms were still flourishing. The farmers in 1939 were:

Mrs Lucy Baughen,
William Coombes Champney, Grange Farm
Ernest Dix, Horn Farm
Herbert Austin Lane, Far Heath Farm
Norman Lawrence, Anchor Farm
Mrs Winifred Jane Lawrence, Manor Farm
Miss Sarah Ann Lovesey, Fletchers Farm
Albert Preedy, Four Shire Stone Farm
Charles Sivyour, Lower Brookend Farm
Mrs Lucy Taylor, Church Farm
Edward Weaver, Heath Farm and Home Farm
John Edward Hopkins, Poplars Farm
Arthur Whittington, Stockbridge Farm

Robert Woolliams, Evenlode Grounds Farm
O Weaver, Heath End Farm *(this incorporated Northfields)*
Sidney Whittington, Woodbine Cottage Farm

The Ministry of Agriculture was soon to instruct the farmers about what was required from them. Land was ploughed up that had never known a plough. Crops were planted as instructed. Double British Summer Time meant that the land could be worked till very late at night.

Henry Cairns related that during the war villagers had allotments just outside the village along the Moreton Road. The Council bought the land in 1939 from Poplars Farm. The details of the purchase are in Collection Seven of the Evenlode Papers. Each allotment holder planted "one chain" with vegetables and each "two chains" with barley for pig food. The barley was harvested communally and threshed communally. The grain was then shared out for the pigs. Frank Gregory and Harry Jacques, being railwaymen, had allotments on the railway embankment at Stockbridge.

Bill Cairns cycled to RAF Moreton-in-Marsh where he and others worked. He also cared deeply for the garden and continued to do so until his death many years later. In so doing he continued the food growing tradition of Evenlode gardeners into a time when most gardens had become predominantly floral and leisure gardens.

Trains ran on the GWR track beside Evenlode 24 hours a day moving goods and soldiers round the country. Although after the war the railway track and railway stock were worn out, vital work to keep the trains running during the war, meant jobs for people.

Advantages came too. Henry Cairns recalled that during 1944 an electricity line was being laid across Evenlode and his father argued successfully that if permission was needed to cross his land he should be given electricity in return, and surprisingly this happened. So in 1944 electricity arrived marking the beginning of the end of the oil lamp.

There was also the dramatic side to life. Kerry Johnson has put into print in a paper of the Moreton and District Local History Society this wartime story which brings alive some of the people of those times. He writes:

From my mother, an Evenlode girl, I learned long ago of the night in May 1942 when a German bomber dropped its string of bombs both sides of the farm (*Lower Brookend Farm*). A pond still exists alongside the Moreton Road southwest of Brookend, which was formed by one of the craters. From Mr Edgar Whittington, who until his death in 1993 farmed and lived nearby at Woodbine Cottage Farm, I later learned more of that night. Edgar told me how everyone had been woken by the bombing. Old Charles Sivyour (*who farmed Lower Brookend Farm*) soon came rushing across the fields, in a state of shock, Tilley lamp in hand, lamenting the death of one of his dairy cows killed in the blast. Edgar also reminisced how the following morning the baker, who I believe lived at Chastleton, turned up in his delivery van full of the bombing, and telling of another casualty discovered earlier that morning. He then held up a dead field mouse which he had plucked from the tall thorn hedge next to the pond crater.

After the war farming gradually changed. As farmers retired the farm did not necessarily continue. Land was bought or rented by neighbours and farmhouses became private residences. A new Evenlode began to emerge.

Photo: Jenny Hill Exhibition

The Village Hall

Chapter 17

A time of change

Sturdy farmhouses into delightful private residences

One by one after the Second World War, many of the farmhouses of Evenlode did indeed become private residences. Some farms have continued as working farms, and much of the land of the other farms has been rented or sold to the remaining farmers, or to farmers from outside the parish. In some instances new owners of former farms manage the land or have changed land usage. Sometimes part of the land has been added to the property's garden and sometimes land has been put to use as paddocks.

The story of the farmhouses that have become private residences follows. The detail of a property's change of use is given if it is available but for obvious reasons the present owners are not identified. It should be noted that despite comments in the text referring to earlier modernisation most of the present owners have engaged in further considerable programmes of extension, adaption and modernisation and have wonderful homes. A feature of these residences is the beautiful gardens that have been created and are lovingly maintained.

Horn Farm

Horn Farm became separate from the Manor some time before 1451 when John Petyt, Lord of the Manor, granted it to William Heynes. The Haynes family held it until 1765. In 1939, Ernest Dix was farming Horn. George Dix (his son) followed Ernest Dix. Ernest's widow continued to live with her son George and daughter-in-law Miriam. The old lady died in 1958 but left the farm in her last Will and Testament to George's brother Bill. Bill's daughter sold it and it became a private residence. The Dix family held land elsewhere but the original Horn acres remain attached to the house. Further details are in Collection Nine of the Evenlode Papers. The present occupants have extensively developed and expanded the farmhouse into a fine mansion.

Grange Farm

After the Seond World War Mr Champney continued farming Grange Farm. The original core of Grange farmhouse can be dated to the seventeenth century when it seems to have been linked to Horn Farm. It came into separate existence during the ownership of Thomas Horne. When Mr Champney ceased farming, the farmhouse, farm and two cottages became the property of Major Charles Stairs Duffus. Eventually the property came into the present occupant's family. Additional land was acquired from Fletchers Farm and the Ridgeway fields and Further Cart Gap were also bought. Historically these were part of Heath Farm. The details are in Collection Eight of the Evenlode Papers. The garden is an oustanding feature that is from time to time open to the public.

Fletchers Farm

The unique record of the Lord of the Manor of Evenlode granting tenancy of this farm and its newly built small mansion began a detailed story of the evolution of this farm under the Fletcher family. It has been told in stages. Towards the end of the nineteenth century it passed from the Fletcher brothers and for many years was farmed by Miss Lovesey. After her death, Fletchers was sold in 1941 to Maurice Henry Brown who also bought some land to the west of Horn Farm. In 1960 after the death of Mr Brown, Colonel Ivor Leith Reeves of Adlestrop House bought Fletchers Farm, modernised it and extended it, though he never lived in it. The details are in Collection Two of the Evenlode Papers.

Eventually, Fletchers became the home of Lady Rosie Northampton. She was the third wife of "Dougy" Spencer Compton the Seventh Marquis of Northampton. She was probably unaware that a sixteenth century Compton (Henry Compton, Lord of the Manor of Evenlode) built her home. Ironically, Henry Compton's son became the 1st Earl of Northampton.

Fletchers Farmhouse was described in the *Victoria County History* as a "fine small mansion". It has been extensively modernised and improved and is now known as Evencourt.

Evenlode House

Like the other "small mansions" of Evenlode the core of Evenlode House is sixteenth century. It may have had links with recusants and Chastleton House, and posseses what may be a priest hole. It became the summer residence of Edward Poer and his wife in the seventeenth century. It then passed, in mid-eighteenth century, to the Bricknells. In 1935 Richard Abercromby King lived in Evenlode House. He kept poultry on his land. Later, part of the land was sold to the Council in order to build houses. Evenlode House is currently being renovated, restored and modernised prior to occupation.

Poplars Farm

The first references recorded, reveal that by the early nineteenth century, it was known as Davis's Farm. It came into the ownership of the Sandys family after Farmer Davis became bankrupt. It was farmed later by Samuel Hambidge and was known as Hambidge's farm. The story is taken up in Collection Seven of the Evenlode Papers.

In 1913, Samuel Hambidge sold it to William West Wyatt. This sale was an investment purchase as he was a businessman in Oxford where he owned an ironmonger's business. After his death his widow, Mrs Edith Wyatt, instructed that it be sold by auction at the White Hart Royal Hotel in Moreton-in-Marsh.

The purchaser was Samuel Weaver. He farmed it himself and changed the name to Poplars Farm. He farmed Poplars until 1937 when he moved to a bungalow that he called "The Oaks", from which he farmed 52 acres. He later retired to the bungalow called "Little Orchard". It is believed he had this built. John Edward Hopkins continued to farm Poplars after him.

John David Marsh bought Poplars in 1970. In 1971 he sold part of the property (including land) to Mr and Mrs Nuttall. In 1975 Mr and Mrs Nuttall's property was formally divided from Poplars farm and became known as Martlett House. In 1977 Martlett House was sold to Mr and Mrs Jerrams, who then sold it to the present occupants. They have engaged in considerable improvements.

Independently, the barn was sold. The details of this initial sale are in Collection Seven of the Evenlode Papers. Poplars Barn is now a distinct and distinctive private residence.

Parts of the orginal farmhouse (still known as Poplars Farm) date back to the sixteenth century. It was sold as a private residence.

Lower Brookend Farm

The place of Brookend Manor in the transmission of the lordship of the manor of Evenlode is related above. Lower Brookend Farm was a late separation from Brookend Manor, the farmhouse being in Evenlode parish. The owner in 1920 had been the Hon. Ellen Joyce. She put it up for auction in that year. The farm had 129 acres and was advertised as a dairy and sporting farm. Milne Barnsley of Coldicott

House (later Wells Folly) bought it. He re-sold a portion of it to Mr Whittington at Woodbine Cottage Farm. (This is related in a paper on the Moreton and District Local History Society). In 1935 Charles Sivyour was farming Lower Brookend but at some stage the house was allowed to become derelict and was later dismantled.

Four Shire Stone Farm

The later story of Four Shire Stone Farm is drawn from Collection Six of the Evenlode Papers. There are glimpses of it at the Saxon "Gild" or "Ild" barrow where King Edmund Ironside engaged King Canute in battle and where Odo of Bayeux met truculent young knights, but there are only a few further glimpses. In the twentieth century it had become part of the estate of Charles William Rolph who died in 1940. The farm was then sold. The purchaser of the farm was Herbert John Preedy (who seems to have been known as Albert). He farmed the land himself. He bought a neighbouring field (in Moreton-in-Marsh) from Harry Emms and this has become part of the farm. Mr Preedy sold the farm in 1964. One field was subsequently sold to Wells Folly Farm. Four Shire Stone Farm has now been re-structured into a comfortable and satisfying private residence.

Heath End Farm

The story of Heath End Farm appears at various points in the book particularly in its description as an "old inclosure". It was farmed in the early twentieth century by Mr Yells and latterly by one of the Weaver family. The farmhouse is now a private residence

Northfields Farm

Northfields Farm, originally created at the division of Manor Farm at the end of the seventeenth century, became part of the Fothergill Estate and featured in the transmission of the lordship of the manor to the Jones family of Chastleton. The buildings are now private residences.

Home Farm

Edward Weaver farmed Home Farm jointly with Heath Farm until after the Second World War. By 1971 he had retired and was living in Kingham. Eventually, Home Farm came into the ownership of Robin and Rachel Montgomerie Charrington. It has now been sold, and is undergoing considerable extension and modernisation, prior to occupation.

Church Farm

Though late sixteenth century in origin, few records remain for Church Farm. Thomas Napping farmed it at the beginning of the twentieth century and before the beginning of the Second World War, The Foundation of the Schools of King Edward VI in Birmingham bought it. Mrs Lucy Taylor was farming it in 1939 though the farmhouse was requisitioned for evacuees during the Second World War. It was not de-requisitioned until 1950. It was in a dilapidated state. It was then sold to the present occupant's father.

Anchor Farm

Anchor Farm seems to have begun a separate existence in the early decades of the nineteenth century when Richard Anchor gave the farm his name. Norman Lawrence farmed Anchor Farm latterly. The farm buildings and yard have been converted into a spacious private residence.

Green Farm

The origin of Green Farm is unrecorded. Mr Hutt farmed it at the beginning of the twentieth century. It became the home of Mr Harris the beekeeper and his wife. Mrs Harris was the schoolmistress. The house continues as a private family residence.

Stockbridge Farm

Dolly Whittington is remembered for her numerous cats. She is also remembered standing and gossiping whilst her cows munched the verges and ambled their leisurely way, of their own accord, from the pasture to the milking parlour at Stockbridge Farm. Stockbridge Farm is no longer a working farm. The buildings have been re-structured and a modern "small mansion" built to complement the properties of the village.

Other private residences

The Rectory ceased to be used as such after the Second World War. It has long been a private residence and is now named Evenlode Place.

The school also is now a private residence.

Larger cottages such as The Old Forge, Bank Cottage, Pump Green House and Lavender Cottage must have long histories but little is recorded of it. Two Stones and Springside cottages have interesting pasts. These are recorded earlier. They are both charming single residences.

The Bell Inn and the Fox Inn are private residences. Harold Cairns farmed land from just before the Second World War from the Fox Inn, and the Bell Inn until recently was a Pottery.

Most of the terraced cottages, from being the homes of agricultural workers, shopkeepers, tradesman and seamstresses, have now become private residences.

Portland Terrace has remained as four distinct cottages adjoining Portland House, but it is the only Terrace to do so. The cottages in Vine Terrace are eighteenth century and now are converted into three private residences. Two of the Rose Terrace cottages have been merged into a private residence and the others are private residences. The cottage opposite Rose terrace (once divided into four dwellings) no longer exists.

The first recorded building of Bank Terrace was in 1751. It was re-built at some time before 1841. Later, some cottages were replaced by council property. This property passed into private hands. Recently an interesting and individual substantial stone house with five bedrooms has replaced this. School Bank House complements the ancient small mansions in the village and in combination with its neighbours creates an interesting roofscape.

Private businesses in private homes

The unusual but attractive feature of School Bank House is that the residents uniquely use it to test and show the products of their business enterprise. This involves interior design, decoration and furnishing. Their workshop is based locally. Their home features regularly in country living magazines. A recent article describes it:

> Square-fronted and compact, with a door in the middle and windows on either side like a dolls' house, this is both their testing ground for new designs and a showcase for publicity photos, so the furnishings change constantly as they repaper walls, hang different curtains and try out new fabrics as covers for old junk-shop chairs.

Other businesses exist in Evenlode. There are of course the farms and in addition, horses have created a demand for a number of equestrian related businesses. There is an agricultural engineering business on Four Shire Stone lane.

Modern communications enable businesses to be conducted from home, so a number of residents engage in business via the Internet, email and telephone.

Last days of the village school

All these changes in house occupancy had consequences. The village school did not survive the changing pattern of residential life. In 1962 there were 15 pupils. When it closed there were 12. However the villagers valued it. An article contained in Collection Four of the Evenlode Papers recalls it as it was in 1964.

The School was still open (in 1964) and our elder daughter Lisi became one of the thirteen pupils in the one-teacher school who were fortunate enough in having almost individual attention and going on to Chipping Campden School, well versed in the three Rs. Our son James later swelled the numbers and he and a girl, Libby, from a family at Wells Folly were the last pupils to be enrolled, at Christmas 1965, as the school closed in 1966 when Mrs Dee retired.

The standard of education was indeed good. A measure of its effectiveness is that in 1960 four Evenlode school children gained entrance to Chipping Campden Grammar School. But, with falling numbers and given the climate of educational thinking in those days it was inevitable that Evenlode School would be closed. It was closed in the summer of 1966. The remaining pupils were transferred to Saint David's School in Moreton-in-Marsh.

Last days of the village shop

The shop did not survive. In Collection Four of the Evenlode Papers the last days of the village shop are recorded:

Nine o'clock in the morning and four o'clock in the afternoon were times of great social activity in front of the school mainly due to the fact that there was a shop conveniently next to the school. Jan and Mike Smith ran it together when we first came but, as more people had cars, custom dropped and Mike took a job as a long distance lorry driver. Jan soldiered on, but they finally could not make a go of it and emigrated to America.

The Post Office existed in 1964. In Collection Four there are recollections of it. Mrs Williams ran the Post Office from her home, now called Lavender Cottage. Her husband was a chimney sweep and sold ice cream in the summer. Mrs Simpson then took it over. She used her own home as the venue.

The last Rector of Evenlode

The *Revd Thomas Smith* became the Rector in 1940, and he remained Rector until 1947. He was the last clergyman to hold the Rectory of Evenlode as a sole benefice and the last clerical occupant of the Rectory. During his time, he and Mr Dee (husband of the headmistress of the school) erected the glass screen to divide the tower from the nave. From photocopies of the Stow Deanery Magazine contained in Collection Three of the Evenlode Papers it is noted that Evenlode then became a vacant benefice.

Regret for the passing of the old Evenlode

I visited Evenlode in June 1971. The village is changing. There is no longer a resident rector, nor a village inn. The only shop and the village school have closed their doors for the last time. As farms and houses come on to the market they are increasingly bought for retirement so it is an ageing community. Farmer (Edward) Weaver, now over 80, left Home Farm in 1960 and lives alone in retirement at Kingham. His brother (Samuel Weaver) is now 89; he has sold Poplars at the end of the street. Mrs Cowling who once cooked for us still lives in the village.

This was the opinion of a teacher knew the Edwardian Country School, Evenlode, in 1938–9. It is recorded in Collection Ten of the Evenlode Papers. The words were apparently written in sadness and he recorded the situation accurately. As is noted above, farmhouses were beginning to be changed into private residences. The school and the shop had closed, as had the Fox Inn. There was indeed no resident rector. He regretted that the old farming village he remembered was fast disappearing.

New residents

The changes brought new people into Evenlode. Although the new residents of the second half of the twentieth century came from different backgrounds than those of earlier generations, this arrival of newcomers was the continuation of a long tradition in Evenlode.

The census of 1901 revealed what had become obvious. Evenlode had a few surnames like Gregory, Bartlett and Bryan, that had been passed down through the ages but the population was surprisingly mobile. The Census shows that more than half of those who were living in Evenlode in 1901 had not been born there. Farmers moved from elsewhere to take farm tenancies often bringing servants and men with them. Agricultural labourers moved from farm to farm all over the North Cotswolds as the Hirings led them. The consequence of this movement is that the same surnames are found in all the North Cotswold parishes and it sometimes seems as if everybody is related to everybody else.

The difference with the newcomers of the second half of the twentieth century was that they were only exceptionally young married couples with children, intending to farm. The newcomers were usually professional people. Some were indeed young but working in the city or elsewhere whilst living in the country. Others came to spend their "Third Age" in the country amongst other new arrivals with whom they had much in common. To keep a balance, the Council built new houses for rent in 1949. As recorded above, these were built on land bought from Evenlode House. The architect was Thomas Rayson. This kept some of the younger families in the village, and provided bungalows for some elderly people.

The new residents recognised the need to create and maintain a community when the traditional bonds of the old Evenlode (shared farming concerns, the school, the shop and the pub) had gone.

The Village Hall

The villagers decided that the village needed a centre for the community. After the Congregational Chapel was released from its wartime role as a temporary mortuary (never having been used as such) it was decided not to re-open the building for worship. Collection Four of the Evenlode Papers discloses that Bosely and Harper offered it for sale on 2 December 1949. The description was as follows:

1 building 22 feet by 17 feet
1 small outbuilding
1 walled in garden 34 feet by 26 feet
1 harmonium
3 desks
1 pulpit
3 oil lamps

The villagers were aware of the impending sale and had already raised enough to purchase it for a village hall. They paid £160. After working on it, it was opened for use in April 1950. It became a place, other than the school or the Fox Inn, for meetings.

From 1955 talk began about enlarging it, but by 1958 most agreed that it was more sensible to pull it down and build a purpose built village hall. Funds were raised for this purpose and the new Evenlode Village Hall was opened in January 1964.

The opening of the hall enabled community events to take place. In Collection Four of the Evenlode Papers it is related that in 1950 the Women's Club was formed. It first met on 22 November 1950 and still thrives today. Early meetings were about new-fangled things such as washing machines and pressure cookers. Latterly topics have included modern issues such as crime prevention, and new activities such as line dancing. Since its foundation, the Women's Club has been a constant force for cohesion in the village

Other new ventures

Other ventures emerged revealing the willingness of villagers to respond to modern needs. In the 1960s a nursery school was established. This ran successfully for forty years. There was the opening of a day centre in 1977 in the hall. This was intended to provide a meeting place for elderly people from the district. They were brought for coffee each Wednesday morning and played cards or dominoes and engaged in handcrafts. Lunch was served. After lunch there was entertainment.

Two private enterprises emerged. A Toy Museum opened in the former school. The owner lived in part of the school and her museum was housed in another. There were children's books and toys and card games. Also on display was her personal collection of beautiful and sometimes historical dolls.

The Bell Pottery was opened in the 1960s. The artist potter produced sgraffitto-decorated ware at first but later he moved into classic Old English earthenware. He has three pieces on display in the University of Warwick Art Collection. Retirement has brought about the closure of the Pottery.

In 1993 Evenlode was a TV location for a production of Joanna Trollope's "The Rector's Wife". The exterior of Lavender Cottage was used as background, one of the cottages in Portland Terrace was turned into a Post Office, and part of Portland House was used for interior scenes.

Of course some long established things continued through the time of change. The Annual Fete and Flower Show are held each summer and involve many in the village. The Heythrop Hunt continues too in the colder months and regularly thunders along in the chase, a sight that never palls for the spectator. A report in the *Cotswold Journal* for 1 March 1973 gives the flavour of the spectacle:

The mixed pack met in a big field in front of Mr and Mrs John Aird's house at Evenlode, and showed a most enjoyable day's sport. They found first at the Mains and went away to the railway as far as Oddington Fishponds, whence they turned up hill through Baywell to the edge of Adlestrop Hill, turned down through Daylesford and were defeated above Cornwell, after a good hunt of 70 minutes and a four-mile point. They were soon running down again over Chastelton Hill, to drop down the vale of Little Compton, left over Durhams Farm to Harcombe, whence they made a ring down by Brookend. In the evening they killed a fox which had done good work at Yelds Osiers, and ran sharply from the Four Shire Stone round by Woodbine Farm, past the Mains to the Moreton Sewerage, where they were again rewarded.

The Church faces change

Though there had been no Rector of Evenlode since 1947 Saint Edward's Church still existed and was in use. However the financial situation and the drop in numbers of clergy in the Church of England created a need for huge changes.

Glimpses into the story of the church are in Collection Three of the Evenlode Papers. From January 1948 to February 1951 the *Revd Canon F M Christian Hare* Rector of Stow-on-the-Wold was priest in charge. His telephone number was the mystical number Stow-on-the-Wold 7. Interesting things were done. In 1950 electricity was brought to the Church. The congregation organised an outing to the Festival of Britain. Two coaches went. Canon Hare remarked that all appeared to enjoy the visit but it seems he did not join them.

From the registers it is evident that the curate of Stow was the one who usually took the services. He normally lived at Broadwell and took the Broadwell services too. These are noted in Collection One of the Evenlode Papers.

The Revd Hugh Potts Rector of Stow-on-the-Wold from 1952 to 1961 tackled this unsatisfactory arrangement. He remarked that in the previous six years Broadwell had had a succession of four curates. This was not good enough either for Broadwell or for Evenlode. He became priest in charge of Evenlode, additionally, in 1959, in order to address this.

In Crockford's it is recorded that Mr Potts was born in 1907. He graduated from Lincoln College, Oxford and prepared for ordination at St Stephen's House, Oxford in the Anglican Catholic tradition. He was ordained deacon in 1937 and priest in 1938. His first curacy was at Cirencester parish church. He left in 1944 to become Vicar of Chepstow and left there in 1949 to become Rector of Eastington and

Frocester. He became Rector of Stow-on-the-Wold in 1952, Rural Dean of Stow Deanery in 1959 and also priest in charge of Evenlode.

He proposed that Broadwell be separated from Stow-on-the-Wold and be united to Evenlode creating a new benefice of "Broadwell and Evenlode". He announced that the current curate of Broadwell had decided to decline invitations to move and was prepared to become the first Rector of the new parish.

Rectors of Broadwell and Evenlode

The Order in Council establishing the new parish was presented to the Queen who signed it in June 1960. *The Revd D V Kennedy* became the first Rector of Broadwell and Evenlode and lived in the house provided at Broadwell.

In order to accommodate Mr Kennedy, Broadwell and Evenlode agreed to have the 11am service alternately in each Church.

Mr Kennedy was Rector of Broadwell and Evenlode until 1965. At some stage he changed the title to "Broadwell and Donington and Evenlode". During his time as curate of Broadwell, and then Rector of Broadwell and Donnington and Evenlode, the children's corner in Evenlode Church was created, and a robed choir re-introduced.

The Revd W F Paddock became Rector of Broadwell and Evenlode in December 1966 and remained so until February 1970. *The Revd Colin McCarter* became Rector of Broadwell and Evenlode in July 1971 and remained so until November 1978.

In 1975, a further clergy shortage meant that the benefice of Broadwell and Evenlode was united with the Benefice of Oddington and Aldestrop. This became one parish. The merging was clearly unpopular and in 1978 the united parish was split into three distinct parishes, though still sharing one Rector. The three were Broadwell and Donnington, Evenlode, Oddington with Adlestrop.

The Revd Ron Lowrie became Rector of the three parishes in July 1979. He was of the liberal tradition in that he prepared for ordination at Ripon Hall, Oxford. He had been a curate at Knowle in Birmingham diocese and then at Bourton-on-the-Water. He left in November 1978 to become a Team Vicar at Trowbridge in Salisbury diocese.

The Revd John Morris became Rector of the three parishes in October 1982. He was born in 1920. He graduated from Keble College, Oxford and prepared for ordination at Wycliffe Hall, a college of the evangelical tradition. He was ordained deacon in 1944 and priest in 1945. He served a curacy in the city of Liverpool and then was incumbent of several parishes in Liverpool diocese. He remained Rector of Broadwell, Evenlode, Oddington and Adlestrop until 1988 when he retired to Bourton-on-the-Water.

In 1988, the benefice was put into suspension prior to further pastoral reorganisation.

The future of the Church

In 1989, *the Revd Ralph Mann* was appointed priest in charge. He was ordained deacon in 1982 and priest in 1983 at the age of 56. For three years he was a non-stipendiary curate at Kingham where he wrote a history of the Kingham Rectors. He possibly planned to do the same for Evenlode as various writings of his and items he copied are contained within Collection One of the Evenlode Papers.

He remained priest in charge of Broadwell, Evenlode, Oddington and Adlestrop until 1997 when he became priest in charge of Upton St Leonards. He did much to weld people together by his personality and enthusiasm.

The Revd Colin Wilson came after Ralph Mann. Colin was born in 1963. He prepared for ordination at Cuddesdon College, Oxford in the liberal Catholic tradition. He was ordained deacon in 1994 and priest in 1995. He served as a curate at High Wycombe until 1998. In 1998 he was made priest in charge of Broadwell, Evenlode, Oddington and Adlestrop. The difference between his duties and those of Ralph Mann were that additionally, he was made priest in charge of Westcote with Icomb and Bledington.

After the departure of Colin Wilson, the seven villages and the eight churches remained as traditionally separate parishes but were united in a single benefice.

The Revd Richard J Rendall became Rector of the united benefice of Broadwell, Evenlode, Oddington and Adlestrop and Westcote with Icomb and Bledington in 2004.

Postscript

The village of Evenlode lies adjacent to the Cotswolds Area of Outstanding Natural Beauty. Although just outside this designated Area, Evenlode is within the wider geographical area that is commonly called the "Cotswolds". Thus the report by the Cotswolds Conservation Board for the Area of Outstanding Natural Beauty on "Landscape Sensitivity in the Evenlode valley" is relevant not only for that part of the valley within the Area, but also for Evenlode itself. The following is a paraphrase of this report:

The setting

The Evenlode valley is described as an intimate, small scale, settled and relatively busy landscape contrasted with the more remote neighbouring areas of high wold. It is noted that the river corridor provides main transport routes through the valley. These introduce movement and noise to an otherwise quiet, rural landscape.

The buildings

The historic character of the villages is evident in their distinctive layout, building styles and use of oolitic limestone. Linear settlements are often located at ancient bridging and fording points established in the Saxon or medieval period. Prolific archaeological remains are likely to be hidden by fluvial and human activity.

The valley

The broad valley is well defined with open flat floodplains, river terraces and gentle convex slopes. The river floodplain has features such as meanders, water meadows, ponds, old river channels and islands. This provides visual interest and variety to the floodplain landscape, as well as being of nature conservation interest. Floodplain and riverside trees, including pollarded willows, are a distinctive element of the landscape. Land use within the valley floor and floodplain is dominated by pasture, although some extensive areas of arable land also occur on areas less prone to flooding. This offers contrast and seasonal variations in colour and texture. The river channel habitats, including standing water habitats, are important to a diverse range of flora and fauna.

The slopes

The valley sides are cloaked in improved pasture and arable land, thus forming a backdrop to the valley floor landscapes and settlements. Wooded bluffs, and areas of species-rich grassland on areas of steep landform, form habitats of considerable nature conservation value in an otherwise agricultural lanscape. Hedgerows and some stonewalls define the fields, although this robust framework is eroded in places by hedgerow loss and the use of post and wire fences.

This paraphrase explains why the Evenlode valley has been designated as part of an Area of Oustanding Natural Beauty. This means that its natural beauty is to be conserved and enhanced as part of English heritage, whilst bearing in mind the needs of residents, local businesses and the desire for public access.

These aspirations are likely to shape modern political thinking about the future of Evenlode too, because it lies adjacent to the designated Area.

In 1992 Cotswold District Council created a Plan. It recognised the beauty of the place:

Evenlode has a generally open character with the paddocks, surrounding open countryside, trees and hedges all contributing to its very pleasant setting. The gaps between buildings, which often allow for views out of the developed area, are as important as the buildings themselves.

However, the Council was more concerned with development. The villagers responded to the Plan and the search for development. The Council officers summed up the villagers' views in this way:

It was felt that some infill development may be acceptable, but most residents would only support some form of low cost housing. Open areas of importance were highlighted on the approach to Evenlode, adjacent to Anchor farm and

260

along Church Lane. Although there is support for local employment, there seem to be no suitable sites, even for existing businesses. There is no desire to see tourism increased in the area. In common with many villages, there were perceived problems with parking and speeding traffic on the narrow lanes. The general feeling was that little change should occur within the village.

Here is an indicator of a battle that may come Evenlode's way. It is the struggle in today's society between forces for change urging development, and defenders of heritage urging conservation.

Whatever the future is for Evenlode, today's community is committed to maintaining its loveliness and historic environment. As one generation passes, another generation must take on the responsibility. Evenlode, nestling in the English countryside that is our heritage, is worthy of such support.

Bibliography

I realise my indebtedness to the primary sources I have used in writing this book. These have all been willingly loaned to me and I reiterate my thanks to those whom I acknowledged at the beginning. There is much more information available about individuals and the lands they have owned (and sold) in centuries gone by. This lies in many bundles of documents (marked "of historic interest only") presented by several local solicitors to the Gloucestershire Archive. Many of these remain unsorted.

General
I have obtained a vast amount of secondary information from the Internet and I acknowledge my indebtedness.
I have used these books following, but many more books (now forgotten) have shaped my thinking over the years. I thank authors remembered and forgotten.
John Moorman *History of the Church of England*
D M Spence-Jones *The Church of England*
John Campbell-Kease *A companion to local history research*
David Verey and Alan Brooks *The Buildings of England*
A H Smith *The place names of Gloucestershire*
Jeremy Gould *Stow Deanery Churches*
Victoria County History
Records of the local and county historical societies
Dictionary of national biography
Alumni Oxford University

Particular subjects
Jones and Mattingly *An Atlas of Roman Britain*
Bede *Ecclesiastical History*
The Anglo-Saxon Chronicle
Isabella Strachan *Emma*
Thomas of Marlborough *The History of the Abbey of Evesham*
Eamon Duffy *The Stripping of theAltars*
Philip Hughes *TheReformation*
Antonia Fraser *Mary Queen of Scots*

J Adair *By the sword divided*
A Thompson *The Battle of Hopton Heath*
Ralph Mann *The Rectors of Kingham*
J Arthur Gibbs *A Cotswold Village*
Livinia Jenkinson *The diary of a foxhunting lady*
Peter Drinkwater *Epitaphs*

Variations in the spelling of Evenlode

Eowlangelade (AD 500)
Euulangelade (AD 772)
Eunelade (AD 777)
Eowenilade (AD 779)
Eowengelad (AD784)
Eowniglade (AD957)
Eownelad (AD964)
Eunilade (1086)
Evenlade (1185)
Ewenelod (1284)
Ewenelode (1291)
Evenlod (1369)
Emlade (1378)
Emlode/Evenload
Evenlode

Rectors of Evenlode

There are no records of clergy of Saxon times

1270 William de Saltmarsh
before 1330 Thomas Deyville
1333 William Reynall
1335 Richard Deyville
1384 William Marssh
1389 William Frankelyn
before 1560 William Farr

1610 William Holme
1636 Gervaise Kecke (deprived 1646)
Puritan Minister
1647 Ralph Neville
Rectors
1662 Ralph Neville
1696 Charles Neville
1717 Ralph Neville
1727 George Pye
1735 Robert Dagge
1737 Charles Leader
1767 Edward Phillips
1786 William Horton
1805 William James
1825 William Jones
1830 Charles James
1857 Henry Worsley
1858 Windsor Hambrough
1867 James Meaburn Stainland
1869 Thomas Everard Buckworth
1875 Thomas Holford Buckworth
1877 Charles Peach
1895 Henry James Kelsall
1923 Charles Chesterfield Pratt
1927 Clarence Randolph Gorman
1934 Charles Millet Alford
1937 Stanley J Hersee
1940 Thomas Smith
Priests in charge
1948 Canon F M Christian Hare, *Rector of Stow*
1952 Hugh Potts, *Rector of Stow*
Rectors of Broadwell and Evenlode
1960 D V Kennedy
1966 W F Paddock
1971 Colin McCarter
Rectors of Broadwell, Evenlode, Oddington with Adlestrop
1979 Ron Lowrie
1982 John Morris
Priest in charge of Broadwell, Evenlode, Oddington with Adlestrop

1989 Ralph Mann
Priest in charge of Broadwell, Evenlode, Oddington and Adlestrop
And Westcote with Icomb
And Bledington
1998 Colin Wilson
Rector of Broadwell, Evenlode, Oddington and Adlestrop
And Westcote with Icomb
And Bledington
2004 Richard John Rendall

Lords of the Manor of Evenlode

775 Ridda
969 Ealhstan
Athelstan
Before 1158 Hugh Poer
Before 1182 Matthew Deyville
Nicholas of Evenlode
About 1288 Richard Deyville of Evenlode
Before 1327 William Deyville
1348 Piers (Peter) Deyville
1398 Philippa Deyville=John Petyt
1415 Amice Deyville (Peter's widow)=William Lisle
1421 Amice Lisle (Peter's and William's widow)=Richard Eton
1431 Philippa Deyville and John Petyt (resumption)
1455 Thomas Petyt
1473 William Petyt *(deprived by the King)*

Date? Lawrence Albrighton and William Leicester
1528 Sir William Compton
before 1541 Lady Compton (Sir William's widow)=Sir Philip Hoby
Peter Compton
1546 Henry Compton (Baron)
1589 William Compton (Ist Earl of Northampton)

By sale
1601 John Croker
1603 John Croker junior

By sale
1605 Edward Freeman
before 1631 Coningsby Freeman
1639 Edward (Thomas) Freeman

through one of his three sisters and their families
Milcah ? =Thomas Greenwood
Ellen Greenwood=Thomas Griffith Biggs
Ellen Biggs=Thomas Fothergill

By sale
1786 John Jones of Chastelton

By inheritance to the Whitmore family
1827 John Henry Whitmore-Jones
1853 Arthur Whitmore-Jones
1872 Miss Mary Elizabeth Whitmore-Jones

By inheritance to the Harris family
1900 Thomas Whitmore-Jones (formerly Harris)
1917 Mrs Irene Whitmore-Jones

By inheritance to the Cluttock-Brown family
1955 Alan Cluttock-Brown
1976 Barbara Cluttock-Brown

Select Evenlode Index

Rose Tce *221*
Saint Edward *37f*
School *152, 161, 185f, 215,*
222f, 232, 249, 251
School Bank House *250*
Shops, *231, 251*
Smithy *see Old Forge*
Springside Cottage *162, 175,*
212, 250
Stockbridge Farm *221, 241,*
249
Stubbles *see Heath Farm*
Sunday Schools *202f*
Tithes *58, 109, 131f, 171*
Two Stones Cottage *57, 74,*
127, 218, 234, 250
Vestry Meeting *148f, 157, 185,*
200
Village Hall *254*
Vine Tce *162, 220, 250*
Wells Folly *34, 172, 205, 218*
Westwold *210*
Woodbine Cottage *217, 242*
Workhouse (Poor Law Union)
153, 160, 188